AMAZONIA

Center Books in Natural History

Shannon Davies, *Consulting Editor*

George F. Thompson, *Series Founder and Director*

Published by the Johns Hopkins University Press in cooperation
with the Center for American Places, Santa Fe, New Mexico,
and Harrisonburg, Virginia

AMAZONIA

Territorial Struggles on Perennial Frontiers

Paul E. Little

THE JOHNS HOPKINS UNIVERSITY PRESS
Baltimore and London

© 2001 The Johns Hopkins University Press
All rights reserved. Published 2001
Printed in the United States of America on acid-free paper
9 8 7 6 5 4 3 2 1

The Johns Hopkins University Press
2715 North Charles Street
Baltimore, Maryland 21218-4363
www.press.jhu.edu

Library of Congress Cataloging-in-Publication Data
Little, Paul E., 1953–
   Amazonia : territorial struggles on perennial frontiers / Paul E. Little.
     p. cm. — (Center books in natural history)
Includes bibliographical references and index.
   ISBN 0-8018-6661-8 (hardcover : alk. paper)
   1. Human ecology—Amazon River Valley—History.   2. Amazon River Valley—
Economic conditions.   3. Human ecology—Brazil—Jari River Valley (Amapá and
Pará).   4. Human ecology—Ecuador—Aguarico River Valley.   5. Jari River Valley
(Amapá and Pará, Brazil)—Economic conditions.   6. Aguarico River Valley
(Ecuador)—Economic conditions.   I. Title.   II. Series.
GF532.A4 L57   2001
304.2′098′1—dc21   00-011507

A catalog record for this book is available from the British Library.

To the memory of the Tetete people,
who did not survive the onslaught of development,
and in loving memory of my father, Frank L. Little

Contents

Preface and Acknowledgments

Amazonia has long functioned as a unique geographical entity in the social imagery of humankind. It has been characterized as a "land of cinnamon and gold" by early Spanish explorers, as an "earthly paradise" by seventeenth-century European romantics, as both a "green cathedral" and a "green hell" by early twentieth-century novelists, as both the "last chapter of Genesis" and a "counterfeit paradise" by scientific researchers, as "empty lands" by national military leaders, as "virgin rain-forest landscapes" by the tourist industry, as the "lungs of the earth" by some environmentalists, and as a potential "red desert" by others.[1] Recently, Amazonia's extraordinary biophysical characteristics have received a great deal of attention: it holds 20 percent of the earth's fresh water; it has world record rates of faunal and vegetal genetic diversity; and it houses the largest block of tropical rain forest left standing in the world (Rojas and Castaño 1991, 19–31).

These highly diverse and contradictory visions often obscure our understanding of this vast tropical biome by oversimplifying it. Even the straightforward term *tropical rain forest* can hide the fact that Amazonia contains a wide variety of ecosystems that include savannas, marshlands, flood plains, black-water ecosystems, upland forests, and flooded forests (Moran 1990). On the other hand, by focusing almost exclusively on Amazonia's natural attributes, these visions tend to downplay the social dimensions of millennial human occupation (Nugent 1993). Still another problem is that many of these visions stereotype local peoples. Centuries-old notions of a romanticized and naturalized Amazonian Indian continue today through the construction of either a "hyperreal Indian," which fits the needs of indigenist activism (Ramos 1994), or an "ecologically noble savage," which undergirds environmental discourse (Redford 1990). There are no generic Indians in Amazonia; rather, there are hundreds of distinct indigenous societies that have enormous sociocultural and adaptive diversity. Furthermore, indigenous peoples make up less than 5 percent of the more than 22 million people who live in the Amazonian watershed (BID 1991). The other 95 percent comprise farmers, cattle ranchers, loggers, gold miners, riverside fishing communities, rural black communities, and a significant and growing urban population (see Browder and Godfrey 1997).

When one approaches the topic of territorial disputes in Amazonia, this minefield of hyperbolic traditions of writing about this biome must be traversed, and one is made acutely aware of the need for offering new knowledge about this highly studied biome. The selection of Amazonian frontiers as an object of analysis was made according to academic and political criteria. Academically, they are a privileged site from which to analyze human territoriality because of the visibility of territorial claims whereby social groups are involved in the contentious and often chaotic process of establishing distinct territories in these jungle landscapes. Politically, the need to resolve contemporary territorial disputes in Amazonia involving indigenous peoples, *caboclos, quilombolas,* colonists, gold miners, developmentalists, environmentalists, and numerous other groups makes social scientific understanding of these situations an urgent endeavor. By imbuing an academic problem with social urgency, we establish new links between the academy and social problems and develop a critical approach toward working in the present.

Narratively, the researcher must confront the problem of voice. Recent reflexivist anthropology has shown that, even within small, supposedly homogeneous groups, there are many voices available to the ethnographer. The problem of voice is intensified by expansion of the scope of study to include distinct social groups, each with its own set of internal multiple voices. The researcher confronts a plethora of voices from which to choose, voices to hear, transcribe, and subsequently inscribe in the text. These voices often represent specific territorial claims that are opposed to claims of other groups, making the problem both discursive and political.

Just as each social actor has a voice that is backed by interests and power, so does the researcher. In such a situation, neither the notion of scientific objectivity nor that of partisan struggle offers adequate approaches for the ethnographic and historical task. As the author of the final text, I have the responsibility of ordering this cacophony of voices and these contentious disputes into a written document using a specific set of theoretical and methodological tools. Thus, I maintain firm narrative control over the organization and description of events. This is my voice speaking, my quota of power exercising itself in the frontier situation.

Fieldwork for this study was carried out intermittently from 1991 to 2000. Four trips to the Aguarico Region in Ecuador were made in 1991–92, with follow-up visits in early 1995 and early 2000. Research in the Jari Region in Brazil began in 1992 and was followed by five trips from 1994 to 1997. In addition to the responsibilities of ethnographic research, I was also involved in diverse professional activities which, in most cases, complemented my research. In Ecuador, I headed a four-person investigative team in the study of development complexes in the Cuyabeno portion of the Aguarico Region and was responsible for the research and writing of the anthropological section of the second management plan for the Cuyabeno Wildlife Production Reserve (Little 1992; MAG 1993). In Brazil, I was jointly responsible for writing and researching a socioeconomic study of the Maracá Settlement Projects and was involved in the elaboration of the Maracá Settlement Projects Utilization Plan (Little and Filocreão 1994; IEA and INCRA 1995). I also served as a consultant for the Amapá state government, researching and writing on an ecotourism project for Amapá (GEA 1995), and conducted an analysis of the social effects of the Champion Paper Corporation's eucalyptus plantation. All of these varied activities constitute an important part of my presence and involvement in the two regions of study.

I express my heartfelt thanks to the many people and institutions who helped me while I conducted my research. The fact that each and every one of them cannot be listed here in no way diminishes the importance of their help nor the fullness of my gratitude. I offer special thanks to Gustavo Lins Ribeiro, my academic advisor, professor, and friend; my professors at the University of Brasilia and FLACSO; the members of my doctoral examination board; my colleagues in anthropology and sociology; CAPES and CNPq for financial assistance during four years of study; the ANPOCS Program of Research Stipends, with funding from the Ford Foundation, and the III ABA-Ford Scholarship Awards: Society, Culture, and Environment for essential financial assistance in fieldwork; IBAMA and its staff for its excellent technical assistance in cartography; the libraries and their staffs of the University of Brasilia, ISPN, IBAMA, Senado Federal, NAEA, Museu Goeldi, Purdue University, Indiana University, and the University of Florida; IEA and the many people who worked there over these years; Transturi Inc. and Petramaz for their logistical support in Ecuador; Analuce, Rosa, Paulo, Danilo, Pedro, Cristina, and Mariza for their constant assistance; the many people of the Aguarico and Jari Regions who have helped and befriended me in innumerable ways; my parents and siblings who have accompanied me from afar; and my loving Claudia.

Acronyms

ACOINCO	Associación de Comunidades Indígenas de la Nacionalidad Cofán
AMCEL	Amapá Celulose Ltda.
ASPLAN	Assessoria de Planejamento e Coordenação Geral
BID	Banco Interamericano de Desarrollo
BNDES	Banco Nacional de Desenvolvimento
CAEMI	Companhia Auxiliar de Empresas de Mineração
CAPES	Coordenação do Aperfeiçoamento de Pessoal de Nível Superior
CEDI	Centro Ecumênico de Documentação e Informação
CEEIBH	Comitê Especial de Estudos Integrados de Bacias Hidrográficas
CEPCO	City Ecuatoriana Production Company
CEPE	Corporación Estatal Petrolera Ecuatoriana
CNPq	Conselho Nacional de Desenvolvimento Cientifico e Tecnológico
CNPT	Centro Nacional de Desenvolvimento Sustentado das Populações Tradicionais
CNS	Conselho Nacional de Seringueiros
COICA	Coordinadora de Organizaciones Indígenas de la Cuenca Amazónica
CONAIE	Confederación de Nacionalidades Indígenas del Ecuador
CONFENIAE	Confederación de Nacionalidades Indígenas de la Amazonía Ecuatoriana
DINAF	Dirección Nacional Forestal

EIS	Environmental Impact Study
FAO	Food and Agriculture Organization
FECODES	Fundación Ecuatoriana para la Conservación y el Desarrollo Sustentable
FEPP	Fondo Ecuatoriano Populorum Progressio
FLACSO	Faculdade Latino-Americana de Ciências Sociais
FUNAI	Fundação Nacional do Índio
GATT	General Agreement on Tariffs and Trade
GEA	Governo do Estado do Amapá
GEBAM	Grupo Executivo de Terras do Baixo Amazonas
GTZ	Deutsche Gesselschaft für Technische Zusamenarbeit
IBAMA	Instituto Brasileiro de Recursos Naturais Renováveis e do Meio Ambiente
IBDF	Instituto Brasileiro de Desenvolvimento Florestal
IBGE	Instituto Brasileiro de Geografia e Estadística
ICOMI	Indústria de Comércio e Minérios S.A.
IEA	Instituto de Estudos Amazônicos e Ambientais
IERAC	Instituto Ecuatoriano de Reforma Agraria y Colonización
ILDIS	Instituto Latinoamericano de Investigaciones Sociales
INCRA	Instituto Nacional de Colonização e Reforma Agrária
INEFAN	Instituto Ecuatoriano Forestal y de Áreas Naturales
ISPN	Instituto Sociedade, População e Natureza
ITERPA	Instituto de Terras do Pará
IUCN	International Union for the Conservation of Nature
MAG	Ministerio de Agricultura y Ganadería
MICI	Ministerio de Comercio y Industria
NAEA	Núcleo de Altos Estudos Amazônicos
NGO	nongovernmental organization
OISSE	Organización Indígena Siona-Secoya del Ecuador
OPEC	Organization of Petroleum Exporting Countries

PICOP	Paper Industry Corporation of the Phillipines
PIN	Programa de Integração Nacional
PNMA	Programa Nacional do Meio Ambiente
PROFORS	Programa Forestal-Sucumbíos
REBRAF	Red Agroflorestal
RESEX	Reserva Extrativista
SEMA	Secretaria Especial de Meio Ambiente
SESP	Serviço Especial de Saúde Pública
SIL	Summer Institute of Linguistics
SIVAM	Sistema de Vigilância da Amazônia
SPI	Serviço de Proteção aos Índios
SUDAM	Superintendência de Desenvolvimento da Amazônia
SUFOREN	Subsecretaría Forestal e de Recursos Naturales Renovables
TERRAP	Instituto de Terras do Amapá
UNCED	United Nations Conference on Environment and Development
UNDP	United Nations Development Programme
UNEP	United Nations Environment Programme
WWF	World Wildlife Fund
ZEE	Zoneamento Ecológico-Econômico

AMAZONIA

Approaching Amazonian Frontiers

This book chronicles, from the perspective of environmental anthropology, centuries of territorial disputes among a wide variety of social groups in Amazonia. Natural and social factors in Amazonia are so inexorably intertwined that writing a social history of the region requires the recounting of some natural history, and vice versa. The growing fields of environmental history and political ecology will serve as guideposts for this study (see Little 1999). The notion of frontiers will be the organizing motif for the environmental history, whereas a political ecology approach will be applied to territorial disputes. Before entering directly into the history of these disputes in chapter 1, some brief theoretical and methodological considerations are in order.

Amazonian Frontiers in Time and Space

Frontiers are commonly defined as sparsely populated geographical areas peripheral to political and economic centers of power that experience accelerated rates of demographic, agricultural, or technological change. In analyzing frontiers within a framework of environmental history, we must give special attention to the multiple ongoing interrelationships between humans and nature over time, as well as to the often conflictive relations among different human groups.[1] In the literature on the frontier, the diverse relationships among geographical space, the forces of modernity, and the expansion of the nation-state are crucial.

Frontiers have been characterized as "the first wave of modernity to break onto the shores of an uncharted heartland" (Watts 1992, 116). Amazonia, however, does not fit well into this mold. Modernity has broken onto its shores for centuries, and Amazonian peoples have responded in so many ways that Amazonian social history is a fragmented quilt of time frames.[2] Frontier expansion in Amazonia is clearly tied to the forces of colonialism, imperialism, and mercantile capitalism; the arrival of new social groups from diverse parts of the planet over many centuries has generated a unique, long-term globalization process (Wolf 1982). While these processes have long been worldwide in scope, each region of the world "globalizes" according to the specific mix of forces that enter the region, the moment and rate at which they enter, and the way they are locally absorbed or resisted (Mintz 1998).

Latin American writers have been keenly sensitive to the meanderings and weavings of historical time on this subcontinent and offer an excellent guide to deciphering the temporal dimension of Latin America. In his short story "The Garden of Forking Paths," Jorge Luis Borges evokes an "infinite series of times, in a dizzily growing, ever spreading network of divergent, convergent, and parallel times" (1962, 100), while Alejo Carpentier's novel *The Lost Steps* (1967) likewise conjures up the plurality of times that exist side by side throughout Latin America. The social sciences are finally beginning to incorporate these insights into their analyses. Rowe and Schelling, in their study of the popular culture of Latin America, affirm that "old, new and hybrid forms coexist, thus invalidating those approaches which assume that there has been an evolution in which the old is superseded by the new. Latin America is characterized by the co-existence of different histories" (1991, 18).[3]

The study of frontiers is often approached as a variant of Frederick Jackson Turner's famous thesis (1920). While Turner's notion of the U.S. western frontier as a specific historical process that served as a foundation for nation building is important, Latin American frontiers, and especially Amazonian ones, offer so many historical, cultural, and geographical particularities that they must be understood in their own right and not as yet another variation on the Turner theme. Long before the Amazonian biome was divided up among nation-states, social groups struggled to establish human territories in this vast rain forest in accordance with their own ways of appropriating geographical space. When nation-building efforts did emerge in the nineteenth and twentieth centuries, Amazonia was assaulted by seven different nation-states, each with its own national policies and interests.

In Amazonia there was not a single "tidal" frontier as in the U.S. West but, rather, a plethora of frontiers spanning centuries and coming in surges or waves, many tied to "cyclical booms in different commodities" (Hennessy 1978, 12). Each wave was based in the new desires, knowledge systems, technologies, and forms of social organization brought by social actors into Amazonia and was marked by the resources they extracted, the markets where they traded, and the biophysical effects they produced. These social groups interacted with groups already there, provoking changes in both, and continue to participate in ongoing historical changes at local, regional, national, and world levels, thereby generating a new frontier dynamic.

Each social group establishes its own demographic and spatial momentum, the force of which is greatly responsible for the degree of political power achieved and the magnitude of environmental effects produced in the region. The notion of momentum implies floods and ebbs in flow, a phenomenon common on Amazonian frontiers (Sawyer 1984). On these frontiers social groups wax and wane: some groups simply disappear (e.g., indigenous societies pushed into extinction); other groups reach high peaks of power only to disappear as a social force later (e.g., the Jesuit missions, the rubber barons); still other groups experience violent transformations yet retain elements of their core character (e.g., *caboclo* and maroon societies); finally, some groups are able to maintain a certain constancy over time (e.g., small, isolated indigenous societies).

Thus, in Amazonia, frontiers have not only been opened and closed but reopened and reclosed again and again. The existence of frontiers in the region is not a one-time occurrence, a definitive arrival of modernity, but rather a perennial phenomenon spurred by the constant arrival of ever-new social groups seeking ever-new resources and their subsequent reterritorialization based upon differential ways of appropriating geographical space. This phenomenon has been going on for centuries, and in recent decades it seems to be accelerating.

Spatially, the arrival of new groups in Amazonia has occurred in a highly fragmented manner because of the vast size of this biome, the widely dispersed locations of its multiple resources, and the limited communication and transportation technologies used by many social groups. Frontiers have often been established in distinct watersheds of Amazonia where they have little direct contact with each other. Thus, I do not speak of *the* Amazon frontier (cf. Hemming 1978) but rather of *regional* Amazonian frontiers to signal the different locales and interrelations generated by each frontier site. While regional frontier interactions form partially structured systems, their volatile dynamic is constantly modifying, and sometimes destroying, these established systems, causing regional boundaries to oscillate over time.

Regional analysis offers an alternative way of dividing up geographical space that does not use preestablished political boundaries, such as the nation-state, as its primary universe of analysis (cf. Smith 1976). Given the enormous size and complexity of Amazonia, regional analysis also allows smaller units of analysis to be delimited, thus facilitating the task of approaching the issue of human territoriality from an ethnographic standpoint. Two distinct watersheds—the Aguarico River basin in Ecuador and the Jari River basin in Brazil, located along the equator at two extremes of the Amazon Basin—provide the basis for delimiting the two regional universes of analysis in this study. Rivers have long been the principal means of transport for social groups living in Amazonia, directly influencing their settlement patterns, providing access to resources, controlling the radius of their intergroup contacts, and orienting their trade patterns, leading to the establishment of distinct social regions with foundations in watershed topography.

By encompassing the dynamic, historical, two-way interactions between and among social and natural factors, these watersheds can be understood as "socionatural regions" (Bennett 1969).[4] In this usage, regions—and, more specifically, regional frontiers—are more than just a biophysical backdrop for human action; they are conceived as spatial spheres of interaction between and among social actors and biophysical elements that are partially structured and have a unique history. The rate and intensity of frontier formation thus can vary from region to region, depending upon the specific biophysical characteristics and social histories of distinct watersheds.

A Political Ecology of Amazonian Territorial Disputes

In analyzing territorial disputes on Amazonian frontiers, a framework of political ecology is useful, since it focuses upon the occupation of and struggle over geographical space as well as the definition of, rights to, and use of the resources contained by this space and the biophysical effects of that use.[5] Human territoriality is one of the most powerful and ubiquitous of human behaviors. It exists in distinct domains of daily life, has many motivations, and is contingent upon different sets of circumstances (Casimir 1992; Malmberg 1980).[6] For the purpose of this study, *human territoriality* is defined as the collective effort of a social group to identify with, occupy, use, and establish control over the specific parcel of their biophysical environment that serves as their homeland or territory.[7]

The history of Amazonia is filled with examples of people in movement: nomadism, group migrations, long distance trade, explorations, forced dislocation, colonization, labor migration. Many of these movements have existed among indigenous societies for millennia, long before the arrival of Europeans to this region, and form a constitutive part of Amazonian social history. Nonetheless, the arrival of Europeans to Amazonia and their multiple encounters with native peoples greatly disrupted existing interethnic dynamics because of the magnitude of their destructive power and the "depth of distance" between European and American peoples both culturally and biotically (Paine 1996, 6). From a territorial perspective, these multiple migrations (i.e., human deterritorialization) have invariably been followed by processes of reterritorialization. People who are uprooted or who uproot themselves seek to reroot themselves in their new locale.

I use the concept of cosmography to describe ethnographically the process of establishing human territories. In 1887, Franz Boas made a call for founding a science of cosmography that would encompass the study of the "mutual influence of the earth and its inhabitants upon each other" (1940, 646). This concept, revived and adapted, can serve as a guide for analyzing territorial disputes on Amazonian frontiers. *Cosmography* is defined here as the collective, historically contingent identities, ideologies, and environmental knowledge systems developed by a social group to establish and maintain human territory. Cosmographies encompass the symbolic and affective relationship a group maintains with its biophysical environment, which creates bonds of identity between a social group and a geographical area in what Bachelard calls *topophilia*: "the human value given to occupied spaces, to spaces defended from adverse forces, to loved spaces" (Bachelard 1989, 19; see also Tuan 1974).

Cosmographies are applied to biophysical environments through the "material and social appropriation of nature" (Godelier 1986), which in turn is part of the broader process of the "production of space" (Lefebvre 1991). This process includes the demographic presence of a social group in an area, the transportation and communication infrastructure they install there, and the technologies and adaptive practices they employ. At the same time, the social structures of the group doing the appropriating provide for different types of access to the environment oriented by kinship relations, gender roles, internal social hierarchies, and notions of property rights.

By linking cosmographies to specific social groups, historical and

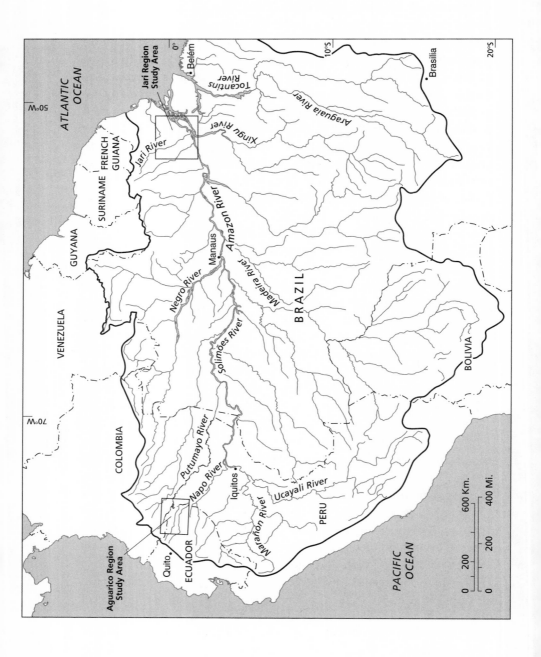

ethnographic analysis is facilitated and human agency is placed in the foreground of human territorial behavior. Through the differential appropriation of the biophysical environment, each social group makes its own mark on it, gives it a unique social and natural history, and begins to establish this parcel of geographical space as a group's own territory.[8] In Amazonia, where the diversity, harshness, and power of natural environments have generated highly specialized knowledge and specific adaptive technologies, territoriality has played a forceful role in consolidating the identity of social groups. Thus, territorial social groups, rather than ethnic, religious, or linguistic ones, are the central unit of social analysis used here.[9]

The spatial and temporal superimposition of cosmographies is a common outcome of frontier situations and produces situations of direct conflict, as would be expected from the direct overlap of territorialities, but is not limited to them. Simultaneous situations of mutual influence, unilateral accommodation, and interpenetration are also engendered in this process, resulting in the continual transformation of cosmographies and territories.[10] In such situations, an ethnographic approach to territoriality makes the territorial claims put forth by each group a principal object of analysis.

Territorial claims surface in situations of dispute: if no one disputes a group's territory, then the claims lie dormant. Hence, claims are imminently political and involve a host of territorial behaviors—social organizing, legal appeals, the select use of violence, public denouncements, and negotiations—which occur in a specific "field of power" (Bourdieu 1998).[11] In frontier fields of power, many social groups are engaged in the process of constituting (or reconstituting) themselves within a biophysical environment little known to them. Hence, the arrival of each new group involves the establishment of new territories where other people already have territories and actively defend them.[12]

Territorial disputes within Amazonian frontier fields of power revolve around the play for hegemony between competing cosmographies with distinct ideological, social, and material bases and are generally founded in highly asymmetrical power relations between the different social groups involved. The constant flows of people and resources into and out of the frontier region also generate an unstable dynamic, making the

The Amazon River Watershed: Aguarico and Jari River Region Study Areas *(opposite)*

frontier field of power unpredictable and even chaotic.[13] The frontier, thus, can be defined as a highly unstructured field of power (i.e., a contested space) where the rules of interaction are not clearly established and which "has the capacity to engender new realities and has a high political potential" (Becker 1988, 66).

These multiple and diffuse conflicts are rarely played out within a single space of negotiation. As people move physically through space more rapidly because of new means of transportation and as they move virtually across space almost instantaneously with new communication technologies, a major restructuring of human agency occurs. Local scenarios become partially shaped by social actors who do not live there but exercise agency within them by their ability to coordinate actions across time and space in a phenomenon that Giddens calls "time-space distanciation" (1990). This has major implications for ethnography because any description of a local society must now include the many social actors physically absent but phantasmogorically present and actively influencing it.

Due to these new time-space dynamics, local territories are often multisited, meaning that each social group is part of different social networks that function at distinct levels of social articulation (Marcus 1995). Understanding these connections becomes a key element in defining the particular play of power and hegemony within a specific frontier field of power. In an effort to grasp this phenomenon ethnographically, I introduce the concept of fractal scaling, originally developed in the field of mathematics.[14] Fractal scaling offers a way of showing how, at different scalar representations of a particular entity, self-similarity (the "repetition of detail at descending scales") appears (Briggs and Peat 1989, 96). This self-similarity is not the same as social reproduction (in the neo-Marxist sense) because of the importance of irregularity, unpredictability, and randomness in the reconstitution of the entity at a different scale. Human territories can be considered as fractal to the degree that they are dispersed across scales in often irregular and unpredictable ways, yet retain conditions of self-similarity that allow them to be classified as part of a common, fragmented territory. Another scalar dimension of fractal territories is the way the connections between them can jump across levels, such that local territories will not have direct connections with the next higher level but will connect with other even higher ones.

Fractal territories can be identified early in Amazonian frontier history. Seventeenth- and eighteenth-century Jesuit villages were directly articulated to a global Jesuit order while bypassing the colonial administrative structures of America. The rubber estates of the late nineteenth and early twentieth centuries linked local rubber barons to London markets through direct trade in a process that generally bypassed national control. Many of the mining and plantation enclaves installed in Amazonia, both in the past and today, have a clear fractal dimension, since they have limited relations with the territory into which they are encrusted while maintaining extensive relationships with higher levels. In the contemporary world economy, the illegal cocaine trade has produced yet another set of fractal territories in Amazonia that connect fields of coca leaf production in Bolivia and Peru with processing and packaging plants in Colombia and then with distribution regions and consumption sites in major cities of the north, all occurring outside the legal channels of state control.

The connections across levels are imbued with power, since social groups and actors at one level of social articulation use the connections they have with people holding similar interests located at other levels to promote their specific local interests. This further complicates the play for hegemony mentioned above; the differential power of social actors who reside outside the local level, yet who have direct influence in another level of social articulation due to fractal connections, must be taken into account, thereby requiring an analysis that incorporates each social actor's extraregional articulations and shows how they are strategically employed in the frontier field of power.

What makes these cross-level political struggles on frontiers into ecological struggles is how access to natural resources and control over technologies used to exploit them become a central source of power for the social group in its efforts to establish and maintain territories. This source of social power is often counterbalanced by the power that emanates from the functioning of biophysical forces, which do not passively receive human interventions but respond to interventions in their own specific ways. Thus, such events as floods, fires, plagues, and resource depletion can be understood as a type of "natural agency" that needs to be factored into the frontier power dynamic (Serres 1995). The natural environment also is structured according to different scales of organization, and the connections between these biophysical scales also affect social action (Allen and Hoekstra 1992). The flows of bacteria, viruses, plants, animals, minerals, and other natural resources and commodities from one locale to another can generate new, often unpredictable consequences at the new locale as well as provoking devastating effects in the region from where they were removed (cf. Crosby 1986).

All of these forces enter into the political ecology of Amazonian territorial disputes. Because of the long time frame and dual regional scope of this study, I do not present detailed descriptions of individual social actors, as is common in more tightly circumscribed ethnographic studies, but emphasize instead major changes in settlement patterns, techniques of resource use, knowledge systems, language, and social organization of social groups.

Comparison and Cartography

In this comparative analysis we seek to understand convergent and divergent tendencies in the historical flows of people into, within, and out of the two regions and the human territories that emerged from them. The selection of the Jari and Aguarico Regions as the basic universes of comparative analysis was predicated on a set of minimum requirements: (1) their geographical separation from each other, which minimizes the effects of direct mutual influence; (2) their location in two different nation-states, which brings the differential effects of state policies and ideologies in territorial disputes into the comparative purview; and (3) the presence of perennial frontiers in both regions, which provides an ideal site for the ethnographic study of human territoriality because of the explicit presence of territorial disputes.

The comparison between just two regions provides for "a type of detailed confrontation that is difficult to achieve when the analysis includes many cases" (Dogan and Pelassey 1984, 40). By delving into two cases, the empirical scope of the comparison is limited, particularly given the large number of regions in Amazonia as a whole, but the advantages of examining these two cases in depth compensate for these empirical limitations.

The diachronic dimension of the comparison seeks to demonstrate how social groups within these two regions have responded to powerful external forces within specific historical epochs. Each chapter's approximate time frame historicizes the comparison between regional territorialities. In the comparative effort here, we seek elucidation of the way, on the one hand, similar historical actors emerge during similar world epochs under the aegis of similar ideological hegemonies and produce similar types of human territories. These similarities provide the basis for postulating the existence of convergent pan-Amazonian tendencies. On the other hand, the comparison demonstrates the highly divergent paths that social groups and regional dynamics have taken over the past several centuries in these two regions.[15] Finally, a controlled, multiple juxtaposition spans the length of the study; within each chapter the types of territories that are generated within specific historical epochs are analyzed for both regions.

The main narrative is supplemented by *field entries* interspersed throughout the succeeding chapters. These selected rewritings of my original field notes describe revealing personal experiences and are presented here not only for the color that they may provide, but also to offer a narrative voice that contrasts with the impersonality of the analytical narrative.

The maps presented here are cartographic readings of differing claims to territory by distinct social groups in each of the regions under study. Mapping a claim is a difficult endeavor, since it is never quite clear if one is mapping an existing geographical reality or merely the aspirations of a social group. By giving cartographic representation to the claims to territory of a social group, the map becomes a source of power (Wood 1992). The play of power also stems from whose claims are being mapped. Those groups that have been left out of the official planning and mapping scheme of Amazonia have never had a cartographic voice, since it has been muffled by other maps. So, to the degree that a group's claims are mapped, they begin to regain this voice and increase the legitimacy of their claims.[16]

By using a regional cartographic scale that is larger than a specific social group's immediate territory yet smaller than that of the nation-state, the homogeneity of territorial control is placed into question, indicating that territoriality can be seen from vantage points other than those of either one social group or the nation-state. This serves to counteract the territorial hegemony of political maps that show each nation-state with clearly defined borders and its own color, presenting a picture of the "discrete spatial partitioning of territory" (Malkki 1992, 26). In such a view, human territoriality is little more than a giant jigsaw puzzle in which every piece has one, and only one, place. As Lewis asserts, "Humankind is simply not divisible into one-dimensional social entities that fit neatly into geographical space" (1991, 606). By mapping the claims of all the principal social groups within the two regions of study and giving them equal visual weight, we can demonstrate superimposed cosmographies spatially and provide a heuristic complement to the narrative text.

Chapter 1 presents a historical reading of frontier dynamics up to 1950 in the Upper and Lower Amazon Basins. Within these two *mesoregional* contexts, I present the frontier histories of the more tightly circumscribed Aguarico and Jari *microregions,* in which the transformation of indigenous cosmographies through the processes of ethnocide and ethnogenesis provides a common historical thread. Chapter 2 (1945–95) chronicles the reopening of the frontiers in these two microregions through large-scale development projects and massive colonization guided by development cosmographies. Chapter 3 (1970–99) narrates the process of establishing protected areas in both regions that were created from increasingly powerful environmental cosmographies. Some of these protected areas were subsequently transformed into sustainable use territories by local social groups. The analysis of contemporary territorial disputes in both regions in chapter 4 (the 1990s) is derived from direct participant observation and adopts an event-oriented analysis. Finally, the conclusion provides a brief comparative summary of territoriality in the two regions and discusses some wider pan-Amazonian insights and policy implications.

CHAPTER ONE

Invading Indigenous Homelands
Historical Frontiers in Amazonia to 1950

The Lower Amazon River Basin
Hydrography and Early History

After the Amazon River receives the waters from its two largest tribu-taries, the Negro River to the north and the Madeira River to the south, it forms a wide, deep channel often referred to as the Lower Amazon River. These waters then flow into and fertilize the Amazon Delta, where they are fragmented by a labyrinth of islands, anchored at the western end by the large Gurupá Island and at the eastern end by the even larger Marajó Island. The mouth of the Amazon River, at its confluence with the Atlan-tic Ocean, is roughly 300 kilometers wide and stretches from Cape Ma-guari along the southern shore of Marajó Bay to Cape North in Amapá to the northwest. The interplay of waters between the Amazon River and the Atlantic Ocean creates highly volatile currents that make navigation treacherous throughout the delta's numerous channels, canals, bays, and rivers. Incoming Atlantic tides block downflowing river waters, creating freshwater tides and causing rivers to flow upstream, and during outgoing tides Amazonian fresh water is ejected out into the heart of the ocean for over 200 kilometers.

The Lower Amazon River and the Amazon Delta, along with upland areas that are part of this drainage area, form the Lower Amazon Basin. Two of the most important Lower Amazon Basin ecosystems are the *várzea,* annually flooded riverside lands that receive rich alluvial deposits of silt and sediment from upstream areas, and the *campos alagados,* ex-tensive marshlands and palm groves that occupy flat inland and island areas. The extremely rich aquatic life of these ecosystems has been im-portant for the numerous peoples who have inhabited this area over the centuries. Further inland, in what is referred to as *terra firme,* the Lower Amazon Basin houses dense upland tropical forests dominated by tower-ing Brazil nut trees.

The peopling of the Amazon Delta is a topic of heated archeological debate. Meggers and Evans's pioneering archeological work at the mouth of the Amazon arrived at the hypothesis of "a slow filtration of the Tropical Forest Pattern of culture from west to east down the tributaries and along the main course of the Amazon River" (1957, 598). More recent archeological studies postulate the early presence on Marajó Island of large, sedentary societies that later formed complex, military-capable chiefdoms along the main course of the Amazon River. These, in turn, functioned as territorial focal points from which indigenous groups expanded, contracted, and entered into conflict (Roosevelt 1991). This theory suggests that these groups subsequently "dispersed up the major tributaries to the ecological edge zones of the uplands of *tierra firme*" (Wilbert 1994, xxxv).[1]

While we know little of the pre-Columbian territorial dynamics of the Amazon Delta, the ethnohistorical work of Wilbert among the Warao of the Orinoco Delta can provide some possible clues (1979). He describes how this group "carefully inventoried the different micro-environments of their world, placed themselves squarely in its center, and made their cultural-ecological wisdom a lasting part of their tribal lore" (135). He goes on to show how their origin myth serves as "an ethnoecological blueprint of residence, subsistence, and territoriality patterns" (145). Here territoriality unites use patterns with cosmological principles to found a cosmographical framework for human occupation. What is clear from the archeological record is that the Lower Amazon Basin was a major crossroads of peoples for at least three thousand years, though probably much more (Prous 1991).

The intricate web of waterways within this basin formed the hydrographic network through which indigenous peoples moved, migrated, settled, and traded. These territorial societies maintained fluid interrelations marked by intergroup cooperation and conflict. Cooperation was maintained through extensive inter- and intra-Amazonian trade networks that often encompassed thousands of kilometers and moved forest and river products from varied ecosystems between widely dispersed groups (Roth 1974; Whitehead 1993). These trade networks offer further evidence of the importance of river transport to the early occupants and underscore the frequency with which migrations have been made in this area over the centuries. Conflict developed as groups moved into new areas and conquered the groups already occupying these areas, pushed them out, or merged with them. The formation of sedentary chiefdoms along the Amazon River and its major tributaries allowed these societies to dominate the territorial dynamic of the riverside areas because of their military organization and demographic power (Roosevelt 1987). Meanwhile, the smaller nomadic and seminomadic groups located in upland areas or in areas distant from the major rivers of the Amazon River Basin continued to control their own territories and often simultaneously maintained cooperative and conflictive relationships with neighboring groups.

Cosmographies of Conquest

The Spanish explorer Vicente Yáñez Pinzón, who is generally given credit for being the first European to find the Amazon River in January 1500,[2] named this great river Santa María de la Mar Dulce (Saint Mary of the Sweetwater Sea), battled with one Amazonian indigenous group, and entered into peaceful relations with another, although he breached this friendship by taking thirty-six Indians captive (Hemming 1978, 183). A month later, in February 1500, Diego de Lepe, another Spanish explorer, led an expedition into the mouth of the Amazon, where he, too, entered into war with an indigenous group. Although this cost him the lives of eleven of his men, he took some natives captive and brought them back to Spain (569).

In spite of this flurry of early exploratory activity,[3] the sixteenth century was relatively calm with respect to European intrusions into the Lower Amazon Basin. A Spanish attempt to colonize the river in 1531 ended in the shipwreck of one of the two colonizing vessels, leaving the survivors stranded along the Amazon without any support. Four years later, an even larger Portuguese colonization effort consisting of twelve ships and fifteen hundred people faced similar obstacles and abandoned their attempt. These were followed by the pan-Amazonian expeditions of Orellana (1541–42) and Ursua/Lope de Aguirre (1560–61). On the basis of these experiences, Amazonia "had earned a bad reputation, with its difficult navigation, fierce inhabitants, and lack of obvious riches" (Hemming 1978, 184). The general lack of activity by Spain and Portugal in the Amazon River Basin during the remainder of the sixteenth century can be explained partially by the Spanish Crown's primordial interest in consolidating its dazzling conquests in Mexico and the Andes and by the desire of the Portuguese to expand their lucrative trade networks in Asia.

Starting around 1590, the Dutch, English, Irish, and French began entering into the Lower Amazon Basin, where they established friendly trading relations with local indigenous groups and attempted colonization efforts. The French established friendly relations with the Tupinambá and consolidated their presence by building the fort of Saint Louis on the island of Maranhão along the Atlantic coast in 1613. English and Irish entries into the mouth of the Amazon came from the north in what is now the Brazilian state of Amapá. Dutch efforts to expand were centered farther upriver, where they established forts in Gurupá in 1626 and along the northern Atlantic coast between the Mayacaré and Cassiporé Rivers (Di Paolo 1990, 74; Hemming 1978, 583).

The successful Portuguese effort to expel these European powers from the area and establish unchallenged control over the Lower Amazon Basin began in 1615 with the fall of the French fort of Saint Louis and the building of a new Portuguese fort there. A year later, the Portuguese, under the leadership of Bento Maciel Parente, established the fort of Presépio at the mouth of the Guamá River in what was to become the city of Belém, the first permanent Portuguese settlement in the entire Amazon River Basin. A three-year war between the Portuguese and the Tupinambá resulted in annihilation of the indigenous forces and subsequent subjugation of the Tupinambá by the Portuguese. Over the next two decades, the Portuguese systematically expelled the Dutch, English, and Irish who had made settlements and established forts in various parts of the Amazon Delta. Di Paolo calculated that indigenous troops made up at least 70 percent of the fighting forces in the various battles between Europeans and stated that, "without the participation of Indians, the Portuguese conquest and control of the Amazon would not have been possible" (1990, 74).

The entrance of the Portuguese into the Amazon Delta initiated the brutal process of capturing and trading Indian slaves. The Portuguese settlers refused to undertake almost any kind of manual labor and needed Indian labor for agricultural activities; hunting; fishing; the building and paddling of canoes; the construction of houses, churches, and public buildings; the digging of wells; the blazing of trails; and domestic chores such as hauling water, cooking, cleaning, and gardening.

Slaving expeditions—armed raids on indigenous villages during which Indians were captured and often branded to indicate ownership—began shortly after the arrival of the Portuguese into the Amazon River Basin, since the existing practice of gaining slaves in trade with other Indian groups quickly proved inadequate as demand far exceeded the indigenous groups' ability to supply new slaves. These raids gained an official character with the formation of so-called rescue expeditions (*resgates*), whose stated objective was to free those Indians held hostage by other indigenous groups (only to place them under new bondage). The large indigenous populations along the rich *várzea* lands of the Lower Amazon Basin provided ample "raw material" for slave raids and acted as an incentive for private raids. With the destruction of many of the indigenous villages within easy reach of Belém, the slave raids pushed farther and farther up the Amazon River, with resultant disruption of indigenous life. As more settlers arrived in the area, the need for labor increased, creating a constant demand for Indian labor that would fuel the struggle for control of the indigenous peoples over the next two centuries.

The culmination of the Portuguese conquest of the lower and middle portions of the Amazon River Basin came with the expedition of Pedro Teixeira, a veteran of the previous two decades of conquests, wars, and slaving expeditions. The Teixeira expedition set out from Belém in October 1637 with forty-seven canoes, all manually powered by a force of hundreds of Indians.[4] After eight months of traveling, the expedition reached the Upper Amazon Basin where, under secret orders from the governor of Maranhão, Teixeira claimed possession of the land in the name of the king of Portugal. This audacious act pushed the Portuguese border some 2,000 kilometers to the west of the land ceded to the Portuguese in the Treaty of Tordesillas of 1494 and anticipated the split of the Portuguese crown from Spanish dominance in 1640. Teixeira and part of his crew continued on to Quito and in 1639 began the much easier return trip down the Amazon (Hemming 1987, 230–35).

Settler and Mission Cosmographies

The increasing presence of Portuguese settlers in the Lower Amazon Basin after 1640 played an important role in the Portuguese Crown's claim to this region as part of its colonial domain. The settlers operated from two sites: the cities of the area (of which Belém was the most important) and the small towns (*vilas*) scattered along the riverside areas. Initial attempts to create a large-scale agricultural economy in Portuguese Amazonia, modeled on the sugar plantations that had been successfully established in the northeastern part of colonial Brazil, failed because of poor soils and other unfavorable biophysical conditions, as well as a lack of equipment and basic infrastructure.

By the mid-seventeenth century, demand for products harvested in the wild from the Amazon forest—particularly cocoa and wild clove—had spawned an expanding, extractivist export economy. These products required much less capital to exploit than did agricultural ones and rapidly became the principal economic activity of the settlers. Since extractive forest products were dispersed throughout the jungle, small, decentralized settler towns from which to exploit these resources were established along major rivers to facilitate trade and export. To extract these products, however, the settlers needed even more Indian labor, since indigenous peoples had intimate knowledge of the jungle ecosystem and were most adept at finding and harvesting forest products. For these reasons, the Amazonian extractive economy imposed a specific settlement pattern on the settlers and maintained a high demand for Indian slaves among them.

The political power of the Portuguese-speaking Amazonian population in the area was aided by the important processes of colonial territorial consolidation taking place at a continental scale. The Treaty of Madrid of 1750 established new boundaries between the colonial claims of Spain and Portugal and reflected the effective control of their colonists over the inner portions of the South American continent. The Portuguese diplomats who participated in the negotiations proved highly effective in carving out a major part of the interior of the continent for their Crown. The modern limits of Brazil can be clearly seen in this treaty, and the boundaries underwent only minor changes (most of them expansions) in the ensuing 150 years. Shortly after the Treaty of Madrid, with the rise of the Pombal era, new policies concerning colonial government relations with indigenous peoples were introduced.

The Portuguese slave raids met with vociferous protests from the Franciscan missionaries working in the area, who saw the slave trade as antithetical to their desire to Christianize the Indians. These protests were not tolerated by the settlers, whose demand for slave labor fueled the entire colonization process, and they led a crusade against the Franciscans which, in one case, led to the lynching of a Franciscan friar in his chapel by an angry mob. By the 1630s the Franciscans had withdrawn from the public debate and the slave raids intensified (Sweet 1974, 47–49). The arrival of the Company of Jesus in Portuguese Amazonia in

1652 changed this dynamic as the Jesuits, under the inspired leadership of Father Antonio Vieira, strongly opposed the slaving raids and gained support for their efforts from a royal decree of 1655, which gave them control over Amazonian Indians. During the next few years, the Jesuits would establish more than fifty mission villages throughout Portuguese Amazonia. In 1661, the settlers revolted, desperate for direct access to Indian labor, and the "rescue expeditions" were resumed under the control of the settlers' town councils (*câmaras*), although they required Jesuit accompaniment to guarantee that the Indians were taken in "just wars" (Sweet 1974, 126–27).

The issue of the Indian slave trade, or, more precisely, the control of Indian labor, would put the Jesuits and the settlers at loggerheads over the next century. This conflict was structured by the duplicitous peace *and* war policy of the Portuguese Crown, which alternately favored one side and then the other. After a twenty-year interlude of nominal control of the slave trade by the settlers, the Jesuits regained the forefront with the promulgation in 1686 of a royal *regimento* that "granted full spiritual, political and temporal authority [over Indians] to resident Jesuit and Franciscan missionaries" (Sweet 1974, 136). By this time the Jesuits had also gained exemption from the paying of all customs on products exported in and out of the colony, thereby further strengthening their economic power and autonomy.

Indian manpower for the Jesuit system came from the practice of *descimentos* (literally "descents"), whereby Indians were enticed with gifts or forced to move into Jesuit villages (*aldeias*) located along the Amazon River and its main tributaries (hence the need for the Indians to "descend" to them). These villages were highly structured political entities in which "control over the village Indians by the Jesuits was absolute" (Parker 1985b, 11). Rigid work schedules were established for these so-called free Indians, who lived and worked in the mission villages so that they "would not fall into anti-civilizatory laziness and would provide for their own sustenance" (Leite 1938, 93). However, since the "priests had a monopoly over all operations of production, transport and sale of commercial goods" (Moreira Neto 1988, 24), the work of the Indians helped enrich the Company of Jesus and turn it into the wealthiest group in Amazonia.

Although the economic systems of the Jesuits and settlers were based on two different social systems for exploiting Indian labor and two distinct forms of exploiting the tropical Amazonian ecosystem, when seen from an indigenous perspective, the differences between the economic systems were not great, since both depended on forced Indian labor. As the historian Azevedo put it, "The tyranny of the missionaries in the mission villages was probably no less than the tyranny of the secular colonists on the ranches" (quoted in Moreira Neto 1988, 22–23). Both systems established sedentary settlements in riverside areas that were tied to the commercial demands of distant markets; in fact, Jesuits and settlers often made their settlements close to each other where they formed a symbiotic relationship. Neither system respected the specific ethnic heritage nor the particular lifeways of indigenous peoples. This provoked the breakdown of internal social structures through which indigenous societies had previously reproduced themselves as a people. Indeed, as stated by the historian Nash, in the battle "between the Brazilian slave-hunters who wanted the Indian's body, and the Jesuits who wanted his soul . . . the aboriginal American was destined to lose both" (1926, 106).

The new associations and interactions among the Indians that had been "descended" and the Europeans were conducted in the *língua geral* (literally "general language"), an indigenous creole tongue derived from the Tupi language family, one of the principal linguistic stocks of the entire Brazilian portion of South America. This *língua geral,* however, was not the language of any single indigenous group; though it stemmed from Tupi, it was "so profoundly grammatically and phonetically modified, that it was transformed into a type of patois with a large number of grafts taken from Portuguese" (Ribeiro 1970, 30). The Jesuits played a key role in the establishment of the *língua geral* as the lingua franca of the Middle and Lower Amazon Basins, since their missionary work with the Indians was conducted in this language. The use of a single indigenous-based language greatly facilitated the mixing of disparate ethnic groups within the mission villages and also served as the language of commerce along the river.[5]

The Portuguese Directorate and the Emergence of the Tapuios

By the mid-eighteenth century, Jesuit economic and political (not to mention spiritual) power had grown so strong and had such a high degree of autonomy that European monarchs became alarmed that the so-called mission territories had "become a type of 'State within a State' under the guise of religion" that seemed beyond their effective control (Haubert 1990, 291–92). The attitude of the Portuguese Crown toward the Jesuits experienced a sea change, and this change was promptly implemented by Sebastião José de Carvalho e Melo, the Marquis of Pombal, who rose to power in 1750 as chief minister under King José I and single-handedly ruled the Portuguese empire until his fall from power in 1777. In 1751, Pombal appointed his brother, Francisco Xavier de Mendonça Furtado, to the governorship of the State of Maranhão and Pará, with the goal of expelling the Jesuits from the area. Mendonça Furtado commissioned an investigation of the Jesuits, which produced a scathing critique of their activities, claiming that they had failed in their principal goal of civilizing and Christianizing the Indians. In 1759, the Jesuits were expelled from the Portuguese territories, an example that was followed by the French in 1764 and the Spanish in 1767. The Company of Jesus was extinguished by Pope Clement XIV in 1773 (Di Paolo 1990, 84).

The centerpiece of the Pombal reforms for Portuguese Amazonia was the Directorate (*Diretório dos Índios*), a document promulgated by Governor Mendonça Furtado in 1757 containing ninety-five clauses stipulating how Indians were to be managed (Almeida 1997). The immediate aim of the Directorate was to take indigenous affairs out of the hands of the Jesuits and place them directly under secular, colonial government control. This legislation was designed to eliminate the Indian slave system through incorporation of the Christianized Indian population into the colonial structure by making them direct subjects of the Crown. Toward these ends, the speaking of the *língua geral* was prohibited and the compulsory teaching of Portuguese as the official language of the Amazon Valley was decreed.

The Directorate also explicitly encouraged miscegenation among the various Amazonian populations as part of a strategy to build a local population that pledged allegiance to the Portuguese Crown. The "freedom" granted the Indians, however, was illusory, since the implementation of the Directorate was placed in the hands of locally appointed village directors who continued to abuse and exploit Indian labor according to the norms of slavery. By 1798, when the Directorate was repealed, it seemed to have failed in most of its efforts: the *língua geral* was still the most widely spoken language in Portuguese Amazonia, indigenous peoples exercised almost none of their rights as equal citizens of the Portuguese colony, and the Amazonian economy was in deep crisis. From a long-range perspective, however, the expulsion of the Jesuits and the implementation of the Directorate had set in motion a series of changes that would show their final effects only a century later.

Meanwhile, the indigenous peoples of the area had suffered from cataclysmic external forces that over two centuries had disrupted their lifestyle, invaded their homelands, and provoked dramatic demographic declines. The period of the most telling depopulation of the region was between 1620, marking the start of the slave raids in Amazonia, and 1759, marking the end of the struggle between the Jesuits and the settlers over Indian labor (though not the end of Indian slavery). Rapid depopulation led to breakup of the internal social structures of the indigenous groups and destruction of ethnic groupings and their respective territories, processes that coincided with forced restructuring of territorial claims through the settlers' *resgates* and the Jesuits' *descimentos*.

There were three main causes of massive dying among the Indians: warfare, the slave system, and disease. Warfare produced high mortality rates through direct clashes between the European invaders (and their indigenous allies) and indigenous societies. The slave system killed large numbers of indigenous peoples in a relatively short time because "the high density settlements found within the Amazon River floodplain were particularly easy prey for the slavers and these populations quickly succumbed" (Parker 1985b, 8). Indigenous lives were lost in the brutal process of capture; through slave labor itself because of abuse, overwork, brutal punishments, and subhuman living conditions; and through the hasty, forced migrations of indigenous individuals, groups, or entire societies seeking to escape the plight of slavery.

Among diseases, smallpox was the number one killer, but other introduced diseases such as measles, influenza, and tuberculosis also proved deadly. Smallpox first arrived into the Amazon Delta in 1621 on a boat coming from Pernambuco; there were documented epidemics in 1644, 1662, the 1690s, and 1724. Measles epidemics were registered in 1662 and 1749 (Sweet 1974, 78–83; Hemming 1987, 58). The high population density of the sedentary, indigenous societies allowed large numbers of people to be exposed to new diseases and served to accelerate the rate of contact; by 1750 large areas of the Lower Amazon Basin were devoid of indigenous inhabitants. Estimates made at the time mention that 500,000 to as many as 2 million Indians died (Leite 1943, 137).

Among those indigenous peoples who were able to survive the demo-graphic holocaust that had beset them, two distinct types emerged. The first type, commonly referred to in the literature as tribal Indians, were those who maintained a relatively autonomous social structure, continued to speak their own language, and controlled a distinct territory. These groups often were isolated from the main river thoroughfares or had successfully fled European invasions, and they are the ancestors of the contemporary indigenous population of Brazilian Amazonia. The second type were those who were captured, descended, enticed, tricked, or simply enslaved by the European invaders, be they Jesuits or settlers, and who entered into a new, ethnically confused life in the villages and towns. These indigenous peoples were called *tapuios,* who Moreira Neto described as "detribalized and deculturated Indians" characterized by "the loss of their ethnic identity which was substituted by a composite culture, a type of *contact culture* produced by the missions, which could not be referred to by the name of any specific indigenous culture" (1988, 16, 46).

Both the destruction and the mixing of indigenous societies diluted these groups' territorial claims by breaking down their collective identities and disrupting their settlement and land use patterns. The creation of the *tapuios* was an important part of the process of alienating indigenous peoples from their homelands and advancing colonial claims to and control over the lands formerly controlled by distinct indigenous societies. Although the depopulation of Portuguese Amazonia was great, the density of the original population allowed a sizable population of *tapuios* to emerge from this process, in a clear example of Amazonian ethnogenesis resulting from previous processes of ethnocide. In fact, the *tapuios* formed the majority of the population of Portuguese Amazonia at mid-eighteenth century. They were crucial in the functioning of the colonial system, since they comprised the majority of the labor force in the entire Amazon Valley and, according to Reclus, were also "intermediaries of all local commerce and of the service of passenger transport" (quoted in Moreira Neto 1988, 101).

With the expulsion of the Jesuits, the segregation of the *tapuios* became less pronounced. The formation of colonial towns facilitated greater mixing between the *tapuios* and the settlers than had previously occurred. Even at this stage in the development of the area, however, there were already a significant number of racially mixed peoples, among which the *mamelucos,* those of mixed European and Indian ancestry, were the most prominent.

A Brazilian National Cosmography and Caboclo Ethnogenesis

By the beginning of the nineteenth century, the social and economic gap between those few who effectively controlled the economy and political power in the Province of Pará (created in 1815 by the Portuguese Crown) and the mass of people who lived at a subsistence level remained. This gap would be one of the underlying causes of the Cabanagem rebellion, which would explode in the 1830s. With the proclamation of Brazil's independence from the Portuguese Crown in 1822, the elite of Belém was split between those who favored Portuguese control and those who favored increasing control by locally born Brazilians under governance from the new empire's capital in Rio de Janeiro.

These tensions erupted into civil war with the assassination on 7 January 1835 of Bernardo Lobo de Souza, president of Pará, by rebel forces led by Felix Malcher. Malcher had garnered support among a conglomerate of poor people known as *Cabanos,* a term that referred to their residency in humble cabins and that provided the name of *Cabanagem* to the general rebellion. For the next eighteen months, Belém was nominally ruled by three separate Cabano presidents, during which time a series of clashes between the Cabanos and the supporters of the Brazilian imperial government destroyed the bulk of the infrastructure of Belém and killed a large part of its population (Cruz 1960, 163–206). Although the rebel Cabano government had the support of large parts of the population, it did not maintain effective control over the people. What started as a conflict among the ruling elite, in which oppressed groups were enlisted by one of the political parties involved, rapidly evolved into an uncontrollable rebellion by the masses against whoever happened to be in a position of leadership.

This rebellion spread rapidly up the Amazon River Valley and erupted into spontaneous revolts against local elites. After centuries of arbitrary oppression by a handful of colonial and settler leaders, *tapuio, mameluco,* black, and other marginal populations turned the initial Cabanagem rebellion in Belém into an open call for social justice *and* revenge as they attacked homes, killed families, destroyed towns, and sacked cities along the entire Amazon Valley from Belém to Manaus. The rebel Cabano government in Belém was finally crushed by the Brazilian government in June 1836, but in other parts of the Amazon Valley the revolts continued. The surrender of the last rebel Cabano group on the Maués River in the Middle Amazon Valley in 1840 was followed by the issuance of a general amnesty by the imperial government on August 22 of the same year (Di Paolo 1990, 354). The Cabanagem rebellion also produced another wave of depopulation in the Amazon in which an estimated thirty thousand people, one-quarter of the total population of the Province of Pará, were killed (Raiol 1970, V-806).

All of the different ethnic and racial populations participated in the revolt to some degree, with the bulk of the Cabanos coming from the ranks of the *tapuios*. A report made by General Francisco Soares d'Andréa, the president of Pará responsible for quelling the rebellion, includes a list of the Cabanos killed by imperial government forces during the final six months of 1837 and classifies them according to their "race." This report identified 40 percent of the slain Cabanos as *tapuios,* 16 percent as *mulatos* (black-white mix), 9 percent as *mamelucos* (Indian-white mix), 8 percent as *cafusos* (Indian-black mix), 7 percent as *brancos* (whites), 6 percent as *mestiços* (mixed bloods), 5.5 percent as *índios* (Indians), 4 percent as *pretos* (blacks), 4 percent as *pardos* (brown-skinned), and 0.5 percent as racially unidentifiable (cited in Moreira Neto 1988, 67). This list is revealing in several ways. First, it shows a predominance (though not a majority) of *tapuios* as participants in this phase of the rebellion, while clearly distinguishing them from Indians. Second, it reveals the variety of different groups that participated in the rebellion as well as the racial categories used at the time to classify them. Finally, the term *caboclo,* which in seventeenth-century Portuguese Amazonia was a pejorative synonym of *tapuio,* was not used, suggesting that its current usage for a rural, mixed-blooded Amazonian resident came into being only after the Cabanagem.

The emergence of the *tapuio* population, who were predominantly full-blooded, deculturated Indians, was the initial stage in the making of a *caboclo* population comprising far more racially and culturally mixed populations. This mixing process increased during the Directorate reforms and continued into the nineteenth century. By the time of the Cabanagem rebellion, however, clearly defined ethnic and racial categories were still in use. The survivors of the rebellion would continue with their poor, isolated existence under conditions that would slowly eliminate the existing distinctions between the different racial groups, giving way to the ascendancy of the term *caboclo*.

While the Cabanagem was "the decisive historic test that excluded the *tapuio* as a social category of Amazonian society" (Moreira Neto 1988, 48) and sounded the death knoll for the speaking of the *língua geral* in the Middle and Lower Amazon Basins, it was at the same time equally decisive in turning the *caboclo* into the principal rural inhabitant of Brazilian Amazonia. The ethnogenesis of the *tapuio* population, which had occurred over a three-century period as the result of the destruction of numerous indigenous societies who lived along the main stream of the Amazon River, would be aborted, only to give rise to yet another process of ethnogenesis with the emergence of the *caboclo* as a culturally distinct people made up of an eclectic mix of many different racial stocks. This process would coalesce during the rubber boom of the late nineteenth century, when Brazilian northeastern migrants adopted the lifeways of the existing *caboclo* population and slowly integrated themselves into it through intermarriage.

In spite of this emphasis on racial characteristics, the term *caboclo* "came to mean a culture—a way of life—and a position in the Amazon socio-economic hierarchy" (Wagley 1985, x). Wagley goes on to argue that, on a cultural level, Iberian elements would predominate, most notably in the gradual adoption of the Portuguese language (which, by the time of the rubber boom, was virtually complete) and of nominal Catholic beliefs (which derived directly from the 150 years of missionary work by Franciscans and Jesuits) (Wagley 1967). Galvão, however, has shown how the religious beliefs of the *caboclo* are a "fusion" of Amerindian and Iberian traditions that "did not result in a uniform or homogeneous religious system or ideology" but rather in "the integration of religious elements . . . produced in stages and in an unequal mode" (1976, 7). Moran has presented *caboclo* regional culture as an "adaptive system" that, over the centuries, has been uniquely tuned to the demands of Amazonian micro-ecosystems, where the *caboclo* earns a living from the simultaneous pursuit of several productive vocations (1974). Nugent, on the other hand, argues against both culturalist and ecological emphases in characterizing the *caboclo,* choosing instead to define the *caboclo* as "an historical Amazonian peasantry which has emerged amidst the abandoned colonial apparatus of empire and state" in which society was transformed "by virtue of particular kinds of social relations maintained between an enclave economy and remote structures" (1993, 26, 60). When reviewing the historical emergence of the *caboclo*, it seems clear that each of these factors—racial, cultural, ecological, economic— has played an important role and that all must be placed together within a multiplex social and historical analysis.

With the crushing of the Cabanagem rebellion, the Brazilian state had demonstrated that it was the principal administrative authority over Brazilian Amazonia. It began to implement a series of policies designed to integrate these lands into its political, legal, and administrative structures and in the process consolidated a Brazilian national cosmography into which the *caboclo* population was incorporated. The formation of the state of Amazonas from the western portion of Pará in 1850, with Manaus as its capital, was a major step in that direction. That same year, an important land law (no. 601) was promulgated, seeking to formalize the imperial government's control of its territory. This law allowed the legal recognition of *sesmarias* (colonial land grants) and existing squatters' rights to the land they occupied and tilled, while turning all other lands into *terras devolutas* (lands returned to the public domain), which could then be sold by the government (Silva 1996). This law was most applicable to the densely populated coastal regions of Brazil and had little effect on the land situation in Amazonia, where effective possession of the land continued to be the main means of appropriation used by individuals.

Brazil consolidated its control over its northern Amazonian borders toward the end of the nineteenth century. In 1895 Brazil and France fought a brief war for control of the area between the Araguari and Oiapoque Rivers. Swiss arbitration of the dispute was settled in Brazil's favor in 1900, establishing the current international border between Brazil and French Guiana (Meira 1989).

The Mercantile Cosmography of Rubber

While the extractive nature of the Amazonian economy had predominated since the seventeenth century, it was only with rubber that Amazonia became a key world actor in the global market economy. Rubber had been known and used for a wide variety of purposes by indigenous peoples in Amazonia for centuries. During the late eighteenth century, several experiments were made in Europe with this substance, and by

1803 the first rubber factory was established near Paris to make elastic suspenders and garters. Soon other products, such as industrial belts, gloves, tubes, fire hoses, shock absorbers for horse-drawn carts, caulking for boats and roofs, and lining for tarpaulins were being produced (Santos 1980, 45). With Goodyear's discovery of the vulcanization process in 1839, which made rubber impervious to the effects of temperature, its utility increased dramatically, demand grew, and exports began to rise. Brazil exported only 93 tons of the product in 1825, but this climbed to 418 tons by 1840 and to 2,531 tons by 1860 and soared to 9,133 tons by 1880 (Santos 1980, 52; Dean 1987, 169). New uses for rubber were constantly being invented and, with Michelin's use of rubber for inflatable tires, worldwide demand skyrocketed, particularly as a result of the bicycle craze that hit Europe in the 1890s (Hemming 1987, 273). Yet another dramatic increase in demand for rubber came with the emergence and growth of the automobile industry during the first quarter of the twentieth century.

While rubber was produced from a variety of trees located throughout the tropics (Central America, Central Africa, Southeast Asia), none of these trees produced as high a quality of rubber as did the *Hevea brasiliensis* (known in Brazil as the *seringueira*), the rubber tree found exclusively in the Amazon River Basin and, within this biome, almost entirely within the territorial limits of Brazil. This biophysical fact created a virtual monopoly on one of the most novel and highly sought after products of the world. During the first four decades of the nineteenth century, rubber was collected in the immediate area of Belém and the Amazon Delta islands by local *tapuio* and *caboclo* populations. As demand for the product began to grow, yet another Amazonian labor shortage was produced, and farmers and city dwellers of the area abandoned their activities to engage in rubber collecting throughout the Amazon Delta. The growing labor shortage coincided with a severe drought in the northeastern region of Brazil starting in 1877 and set in motion massive migrations into Brazilian Amazonia by poor people from Northeast Brazil, particularly the state of Ceará. During the next thirty years, an estimated 300,000 northeasterners migrated into Brazilian Amazonia (Santos 1980, 99–100).

The initial system, whereby isolated *tapuios* and *caboclos* sold their produce to small intermediaries, rapidly gave way to the *aviamento* system, whereby trade goods were supplied on credit within a nested hierarchy of commercial relations extending from the exporter, at the upper end, through various levels of *aviadores* (creditors or forwarders) all the way down to the *seringueiros* (rubber tappers). This system concentrated the rubber trade into the hands of a few export houses located in the thriving port cities of Manaus and Belém and was rife with exploitation of the rubber tappers. The *aviadores,* known locally as *patrões* or *seringalistas,* had direct control of a group of rubber tappers to whom they charged astronomical prices for goods lent out while paying low prices for rubber received, thus trapping the tappers in a vicious cycle of debt from which it was almost impossible to escape. Those *aviadores* who were able to control large tracts of land used for rubber collecting turned into extremely wealthy rubber barons, and the tracts of land they controlled were called *seringais* (rubber estates).

The creation of extensive *seringais* established a new territorial entity in Brazilian Amazonia that would dominate the entire area until the dawning of the developmentalist cycle after World War II. In most cases, the rubber barons did not have legal title to the *seringais* they controlled, but simply maintained exclusive rights to the rubber produced in these areas, rights that were supported by a tradition of loyalty to the rubber baron, by the economic ties of debt, and by the violence of hired henchmen. In most cases, the rubber barons did not even own the rubber collected from their *seringais,* for this belonged to the individual rubber tapper, who was obligated to sell his produce to the rubber baron by the cultural, economic, and political norms of the *aviamento* system. The claiming of large tracts of land by the rubber barons during the later part of the nineteenth century was possible only because of the previous three centuries of dispossession of these same lands from indigenous peoples, a process that had started with the settler *resgates* and the Jesuit *descimentos* and that was consummated with the emergence of a mixed-blood *caboclo* population directly tied to the needs of the national and international economy.

The Amazonian rubber boom came to an abrupt halt in 1913 as plantation-grown rubber from Asia, grown from *H. brasiliensis* stocks stolen from Brazilian Amazonia in 1876, entered the world market in massive quantities and greatly undercut the price of Amazonian rubber. Brazilian exports fell from a high of 31,133 tons in 1912 to 4,582 tons in 1932, a total roughly equivalent to exports in 1870 (Dean 1987, 169). The collapse of the Amazonian rubber boom ushered in an era of relative

The ruins of a *seringalista* trading post and warehouse, Jari River, 1995

economic decadence throughout the area and provoked an overall out-migration from Brazilian Amazonia to other parts of the country. The *caboclo* population that lived dispersed along riverside areas throughout the Amazon River Basin remained and passed once again into obscurity, while they continued with lifeways and adaptive strategies that had long provided for their sustenance.

In this phase of Brazilian Amazonian history, the territorial dynamics of the area once again began to change. While the larger rubber barons suffered economic decline, many local *aviadores,* who had functioned as intermediaries for the larger exporters, continued to dominate local *caboclo* populations through maintenance of the *aviamento* system. Other extractive products partially filled the gap left by the collapse of rubber, such as Brazil nuts, *copaíba* oil, and an assortment of resins. World War II offered a brief respite from the economic hardships of the previous thirty years as demand for Amazonian rubber increased because of occupation of the Malaysian rubber plantations by Japanese forces. Rubber produced a mini-boom during the years 1941–45, though production levels never reached the highs they had experienced during the first decade of the twentieth century (Dean 1987, 87–107).

By this time, a new mentality toward Amazonia among national political leaders, directly linked to notions of progress and development, was emerging, and it would become dominant in the postwar era. An early expression of this viewpoint can be found in a famous Amazon address given by Brazilian President Getúlio Vargas in 1940. He called for "the conquest and domination of great valleys of equatorial torrents, transforming their blind force and extraordinary fertility into disciplined energy. The Amazon, with the fecund impulse of our will and of our work, will cease to be a mere chapter in the history of the Earth, and . . . will become a chapter in the history of civilization" (Vargas 1943, 160). This new outlook was accompanied by a series of government-sponsored programs in the areas of public health, education, and infrastructural investment designed to lift the region out of its economic doldrums and provide for the minimal needs of its inhabitants. This enthusiasm was also expressed by Wagley, who studied in Amazonia during this time and who hailed the arrival of "DDT, the new wonder insecticide" and praised the "missionary spirit which the personnel of SESP [Special Public Health Service] seemed to share just after World War II" (Wagley 1964, 12, 305).

Yet the biggest push in the direction of a developmentalist ideology would come from the installation of large-scale development projects. A manganese mining center in the central part of the Federal Territory of Amapá, located to the northeast of the Jari Region, was the first industrial mining operation in Brazilian Amazonia and would serve as a model for many future development projects. Bethlehem Steel of the United States, in joint collaboration with the Brazilian firm of ICOMI, established an economic enclave in the middle of the jungle, where they built an entire town—Serra do Navio—to house workers and management and constructed a 194-kilometer rail line connecting the town and mine to the Amazon River port of Santana, which, in turn, was renovated to support the flow of mineral products (Ribeiro 1992).

The Jari River Region

This historical review of the social and territorial dynamics of the Lower Amazon Basin provides the necessary context from which to recount the history of the Jari River Region. The Jari Region is located at the junction of the eastern end of the Lower Amazon River and the western edge of the Amazon Delta and encompasses the area along the left bank (mainland) of the North Canal of the Amazon River, a deep channel that starts at the western tip of Gurupá Island and hugs the shores of the states of Pará and Amapá before flowing into the Atlantic Ocean. The North Canal is now the major route of entry into the river for ocean-going vessels. Starting with the Paru River to the west and continuing downriver, the North Canal receives waters from the Jari, Cajari, and Maracá Rivers, among others.[6]

The Jari Region receives its name from the 800-kilometer-long Jari River, a major northern tributary to the Amazon and an important fluvial crossroads located at the intersection of the Amazon Delta and the Lower Amazon River. Its headwaters form along the southern slopes of the low-ranging (300–700 meters above sea level) Tumucumaque Mountains, which separate Brazil from Suriname and French Guiana. The Cajari and Maracá Rivers, smaller tributaries of the North Canal, have their source in the Iratapuru Hills of central Amapá, which are covered with dense tropical rain forest and harbor extensive natural groves of Brazil nut trees (*Bertholletia excelsa*). In the middle portions of these two river basins, the upland tropical forest becomes interspersed with grassy upland savannas. The savannas, in turn, slowly give way in the lower stretches of the rivers to extensive marshlands and floodplain forests, which are the habitat for abundant groves of the assai palm tree (*Euterpe oleracea*), which produces hearts of palm and an edible purple berry. The Iratapuru River, a tributary to the Jari River, also has its source in the Iratapuru Hills and houses extensive Brazil nut groves.

At the beginning of the sixteenth century, when the Europeans first arrived, the Jari Region was home to the Tucujú peoples, an Arawak-speaking society and one of the most populous indigenous groups along the left bank of the North Canal of the Amazon River. The Tucujús maintained peaceful relations with their Aruã and Nheengaíba neighbors, who inhabited the Delta Island Region. Though no precise population figures are available for these groups, Jesuit estimates placed the combined Tucujús and Nheengaíba population at 100,000 (Leite 1943, 137), indicating the existence of densely populated villages. These groups would be left relatively undisturbed by the Europeans for most of the sixteenth century.

The arrival of Dutch, English, and Irish traders and settlers into the area beginning in 1590 was predicated on friendly trading relations with the local indigenous groups. In 1620, English and Irish colonists under the command of Captain Roger North made several settlements along the North Canal of the Amazon River and, shortly thereafter, established trading relations with the Tucujús of the mainland and the Aruãs and the Nheengaíba of the delta islands. These trading alliances quickly turned into military ones as the Portuguese initiated a series of wars over the next decade designed to expel all other European powers from the region.[7] The Tucujús suffered heavily from these wars, since their alliances with the English, Irish, and Dutch made them the target of brutal Portuguese attacks and provoked their flight inland, whereby they abandoned their fertile riverside and island homelands.

In 1637, with Portuguese control over the Jari Region complete, King Phillip IV granted control of the Capitania do Cabo do Norte, which included the entire north shore of the Amazon River between the Paru and Oiapoque Rivers, to Benito Maciel Parente. Maciel Parente had led the slaughter of the Maranhão Tupinambá, and his sons were notorious slavers. By receiving this grant, the family was given free reign to exploit the thousands of Indians living in the area that is today the Brazilian state of Amapá (Hemming 1978, 229–30). Maciel Parente's death in 1645 and his sons' lack of interest in the region, however, spared it some of the harshest of the slaving raids. In 1654, João de Bittencourt Muniz led an expedition up the Jari River, where he defeated the Anibá indigenous group and established an alliance with the Aroaqui peoples (Reis 1949, 24), now both extinct.

During the mid-seventeenth century, Jesuit missions began to be established in the Jari Region and the torturous process of *descimentos* unleashed "a new phase in the history of indigenous peoples, resulting in their rapid disintegration and the extinction of thousands of individuals" (Gallois 1981, 8). The small populations of the Amapa and Aracajú peoples, for example, located in the area of Almeirim at the time of the Jesuit missions, were greatly reduced, and survivors gradually integrated themselves into the regional population (Gallois 1986, 289–90). In 1688, the small town of Macapá was founded by Portuguese settlers along the left bank of the North Canal at its confluence with Atlantic Ocean waters, and it became an important site for new settlers to the area. By the mid-eighteenth century, wars, slave trading, missionizing, imported diseases, and settlement had provoked massive indigenous de-population. In 1749, an observer wrote of Macapá: "There used to be ample Indians in it, but successive epidemics of smallpox and measles have left it destitute of inhabitants of either sex or any age" (quoted in Hemming 1987, 5). By the beginning of the nineteenth century, the once numerous Tucujús had become extinct.

New groups moved into the region, once again changing its ethnic composition and territorial claims. The Waiãpi peoples began their long migration from the lower Xingu River during the mid-seventeenth century, and by the early eighteenth century had moved into the lower Jari River basin, where they intermixed with the remaining Tucujús. They finally settled in the uplands of what is now central Amapá, where they live today (Gallois 1994). Blacks also participated in the repopulation of the region. The left bank of the Amazon River was an important end-point for runaway slaves from Maranhão and Belém, who formed small, independent communities (*quilombos*), starting with one founded along the Anauerapucu (Vila Nova) River in 1749. With the founding of Mazagão in 1771 by Jewish Portuguese colonists and their slaves, who had been expelled from Morocco, yet another contingent of blacks began to be introduced into the area (Santos 1993, 41).

The building of the massive stone fortress of Macapá in 1764–82 would mobilize masses of black and indigenous labor and establish the town of Macapá as a strategic point for the entire north bank of the Amazon River (Reis 1949, 43–52). The Cabanagem rebellion would also sweep through this area, starting with the taking of the Amazonian riverside town of Almeirim by Cabanos in 1835. From Almeirim they moved up the North Canal to the port city of Santana, only to be thwarted in their attempt to capture Macapá. By 1836 all the revolts in this area had been defeated by imperial government forces.

The arrival of José Júlio de Andrade, a native of the Brazilian state of Ceará, to the Lower Amazon River in 1882 would radically alter the territorial dynamics of the Jari Region during the first half of the twentieth century. After some brief experiences with rubber and Brazil nut collecting and small commerce, in 1899 José Júlio (as he was generally known) began buying up land throughout the region, mostly land held by the state of Pará and the Almeirim municipality. He rapidly established himself as the most important *aviador* in the region. From his headquarters in the town of Arumanduba, located along the main chan-

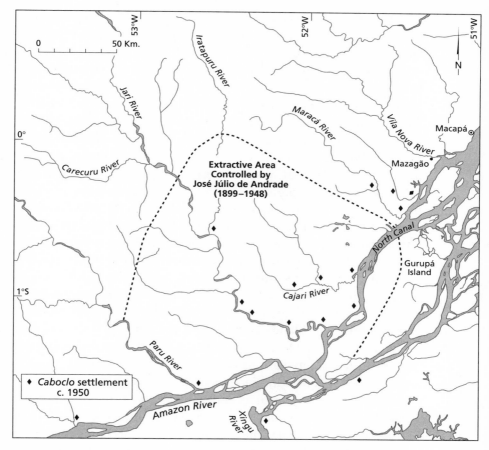

The Jari River Region: The Andrade Brazil Nut Estate and *Caboclo* Settlements

nel of the North Canal just west of the mouth of the Jari River, he began to build an immense Brazil nut estate. This estate included the lower basins of the Paru, Jari, Iratapuru, and Cajari Rivers and covered an area of approximately 3 million hectares, making José Júlio one of the largest of extractive *latifundiários* (estate bosses) in the entire Amazon River Basin (Lins 1991, 35–43).

The estate of José Júlio had a structure similar to the *seringais* of the rubber barons. The important distinction was that he ruled supreme over *castanhais* (Brazil nut groves) located in the Jari, Iratapuru, and Cajari river basins. His reliance on Brazil nuts rather than rubber as his principal extractive product would spare him economic demise from the rubber boom collapse and permitted him to continue his extractive operations until the mid-twentieth century.

Brazil nut trees, known in Brazil as the *castanheira,* reach heights of up to 50 meters, have diameters of up to 2 meters, and produce numerous hard, round shells (*ouriços*), each of which, when opened, contains 15 to 20 individual nuts (Porto 1917, 23–26). Brazil nut exports began in Pará in 1818 and, after a brief decline due to the Cabanagem rebellion, maintained an irregular rate of growth throughout the remainder of the nineteenth century. In 1901, just two years after José Júlio began to consolidate his estate, exports of Brazil nuts from Amazonia were 55,573 hectoliters. By 1919, this figure had skyrocketed to 557,249 hectoliters (Santos 1980, 183). The United States and England were the two largest importers of Brazil nuts, where they were used in chocolate bars and other sweets. José Júlio supplemented this extractive trade with the export of rubber and oils extracted from the *andiroba, balata,* and *copaíba* trees. He also raised thousands of head of beef cattle and in 1907 began introducing water buffalo into his ranching domain, since they were well adapted to grazing in the marshlands located along the Amazon River. José Júlio owned a fleet of over a dozen ships, which carried these varied products to markets in Belém, giving him vertical control of production from its source in the forest to its international export (Lins 1991, 65–71).

After a half-century reign as undisputed ruler of this region (1899–1948), José Júlio finally sold his company to a Portuguese firm in 1948. The new owners continued the existing extractive operations and made some infrastructural improvements, such as the installation of a Brazil nut processing plant in Jarilândia, on the left bank of the lower Jari River. They also greatly increased the extraction and sale of *balata,* which was primarily sold to the United States, where it was used to make golf balls and was mixed with rubber to make airplane tires (Lins 1991, 95–114). The Portuguese firm also bought from José Júlio a hodgepodge of vague and contradictory land titles. Though formal legal control over the land of the estate had always been clouded, it was not directly contested during José Júlio's lifetime nor under the control of the Portuguese owners.

Meanwhile, during the fifty years that José Júlio reigned over his estate, the thousands of *caboclos* who collected nuts, grazed cattle, operated the fleet of ships and, in general, were subservient to their boss as employees were also establishing themselves on the land and making their living from it. Some of these workers migrated each year to the

Brazil nut groves from the delta islands, but many of them began settling permanently along the rivers of the region. Here they developed an economic and adaptive system centered around the territorial unit of the *colocação*, a family-run productive unit on a small tract of land (20–100 hectares) that includes the *caboclo* family's house, manioc garden, fruit orchard, horticultural plantings, and *casa de farinha* (shed where manioc flour is made). The effective use area of the *caboclo* family is much larger than the *colocação*, since it includes areas of hunting and fishing informally shared by other *caboclos* living in the region. By establishing their *colocações* in the midst of José Júlio's Brazil nut empire, these *caboclos* created their own territorial presence and began turning this area into their new homeland.

Caboclo social structure is founded on a loosely knit, extended family unit that often includes adopted children, godparenting, and non-kin (Nugent 1993). This extensive network of family relationships is strategically used in exploiting the forest and by having family members living in nearby cities. The extended family is the basis of economic production of the *colocação*, since the labor force used in the garden, orchard, Brazil nut grove, and home is almost exclusively of family origin. Collective work sessions (*mutirões*) are a voluntary form of communal organization that serves to reinforce community ties. *Mutirões* are used for the construction of community works of benefit to all and as a reciprocal aid mechanism in which local families help each in major subsistence activities such as the clearing of a patch of jungle for the planting of a new garden.

The settlement pattern of isolated *colocações* precludes the grouping of *caboclos* into large, nucleated settlements. *Caboclo* communities are loosely organized assemblies of *colocações*, usually centered around a church, school, or community center and rarely with any formal political or administrative capacities. These *caboclos* claimed control of the area on the basis of the Brazilian tradition of *posse* (effective possession), whereby those who resided on and worked a parcel of land for years were considered to be its rightful owners. This set up a confrontation between private property claims based on land titles held by successive corporate owners of the estate and the effective use and possession claims of the *caboclos*, a dispute that would continue for the remainder of the twentieth century.

On a larger scale, other territorial changes were occurring in the area. In 1943 the Brazilian government created the Federal Territory of Amapá

A Catholic procession, Central do Maracá, 1992

out of the northernmost portion of the state of Pará, in a move designed
to encourage the development of this long-neglected area. The western
boundary of the Federal Territory of Amapá was the Jari River; thus, the
Jari Region was split into two political-administrative realms: the state of
Pará and the territory of Amapá. This division would have important
territorial consequences during the coming decades.

Looking at the map of the Jari Region in 1950, we find three principal
territorial actors: (1) the Portuguese firm that bought José Júlio's Brazil
nut estate and claimed the entire area for themselves, (2) small-scale

patrões who had established control over local *caboclo* groups and laid claim to *castanhais* and ranches, and (3) the *caboclos* who inhabited the area. These three territories were spatially superimposed. The indigenous population had been effectively removed from the area, though the Waiãpi had a significant presence to the north of the Jari Region in central Amapá and a small community of Aparai was situated along the middle Jari River, also to the north of the region.

The Upper Amazon River Basin
Hydrography and Early History

The Upper Amazon River Basin encompasses the eastern slope of the Andes mountain range and the tropical lowlands directly to its east between the latitudes of 2° north and 2° south. While the Upper Amazon Basin covers all of what is now Peruvian, Ecuadorian, and Colombian Amazonia, the mesoregion that will be analyzed here refers to the central portion of this greater region, an area that includes all of Ecuadorian Amazonia and that portion of Peruvian Amazonia north of the Marañón River. The eastern edge of this mesoregion is formed by the junction of the Putumayo River with the Amazon (Solimões) River,[8] a point commonly considered to be the dividing line between the Upper and Middle Amazon Basins.

The numerous rivers born in the Andes drop rapidly through mountain gorges and then flow through the lowlands, where they gradually converge into a single dominating river—the Amazon. The Andes mountain range functions as a shield that traps the movement of the clouds over the tropical lowlands, and the sharp temperature differences produced by varied elevations cause frequent rains, making this one of the wettest regions within the entire Amazon River Basin. The wide range of elevations, topographies, climate regimes, and micro-ecosystems of the Upper Amazon Basin has generated over millennia one of the earth's richest areas of floral and faunal diversity.

The settlement of the Upper Amazon Basin is a history of the demographic expansion and retraction of different indigenous societies over the past three or four thousand years (if not more). Little is known of the early peoples who lived and moved through this area. We lack archeological evidence, in part because of the extremely wet climate, and we lack

The Middle Cuyabeno River Basin, 2000

sustained indigenous oral histories because of the extinction of most of the indigenous groups that once inhabited these lands. Meggers's archeological excavations in the Napo River Basin revealed the existence of a "Yasuni" ceramic-making culture (200 B.C. to A.D. 50), followed by a "Tivacundo" culture (A.D. 400–900) and distinct "Napo" and "Cotacocha" Phases during the second millennium A.D., and led her to conclude that the pattern of settlement on the Napo River has two major characteristics: "1) it is intermittent, and 2) each complex is of independent origin" (Meggers 1967, 151). She also postulates that the Upper Amazon lowlands were a possible destination of early migrations from the Andean highlands (Meggers 1979).

Lathrap proposed that the original settlement of the Upper Amazon Basin was by groups moving upriver from the Middle Amazon Basin (1970). He documents the expansion of the Omaguas-Yeté, a branch of the large, sedentary chiefdoms of the Omagua, who moved upriver to the Napo and Aguarico Rivers during the first half of the second millennium A.D. During this same epoch, chiefdoms comprising "small, class-structured village federations, politically organized under territorial chiefs," in the Colombian Sub-Andean area showed a "marked capacity to develop the natural resources of their respective territories far beyond mere biophysical needs and beyond what these groups considered to be their cultural subsistence level" (Reichel-Dolmatoff 1973, 28–29). Among the demographic movements of these peoples, one of the most notable was the "great territorial extension of the Chibcha peoples" onto the Amazonian lowlands, which was "a passive spread, not a military conquest" (35).

Numerous small, seminomadic groups that practiced typical tropical forest cultural adaptations were sandwiched between, and influenced by, these large indigenous societies. The intergroup relations in the Upper Amazon Basin were multiple and, as was the case in the Lower Amazon, based on a complex mix of conflict and cooperation. From a territorial viewpoint, the Upper Amazon Basin was the home of relatively autarkic indigenous societies.

Ethnographies of contemporary indigenous groups seem to indicate that rivers have long been essential elements of the various indigenous cosmographies that have operated, and continue to operate, throughout this area. In his study of the Campa of Peruvian Amazonia, Weiss notes that "it is the main river system flowing through Campa territory that gives orientation to Campa notions of geography" (1969, 74). Within the framework of these river systems, indigenous territories are often proscribed by kinship and descent systems, as Descola describes for the Achuar groups in Ecuadorian Amazonia (1994). Among the Makuna of Colombian Amazonia, Århem notes that "each sib and phratric segment is associated with a particular river or river section and is said to be the owner (*uhu*) of the river or tract of land drained by it. Descent units are conceived of as territorial units" (1981, 113–14). Furthermore, an indigenous group's territory is often "related to a cultural history. This history, often placed within a mythic-religious language, orients and defines the spatial movements of settlements from their current location to a new one" (Ramos 1986, 19). Thus, the practice of collective access to the land coupled with specific cosmologies form the foundation of indigenous cosmographies in the Upper Amazon Basin.

Shortly after the Spanish conquest of the Inca empire and its various Andean highland indigenous groups, the Spaniards turned their sights on the Amazonian lowlands, which were known from indigenous references as the Land of Cinnamon (*El País de la Canela*) but were believed by the Spaniards to house a Land of Gold (*El Dorado*). The major entry point for Spaniards into the Upper Amazon Basin was from Quito in the northern Andes. By traveling due east from Quito, passing over the eastern range of the Andes, and descending into the jungle, one gains direct access to the Napo River Basin. It was from this entry point that Gonzalo Díaz de Pineda launched one of the first expeditions into the Upper Amazon Basin in 1538. This was followed by two more expeditions, both launched from Quito in 1541, one led by Pedro de Vergara and the other by Gonzalo Pizarro.[9] This last expedition is especially noteworthy. Pizarro, who was camped on the Coca River, a tributary to the Napo River, sent Francisco de Orellana downriver to look for food. Orellana and his men never returned. Instead, they sailed down the Napo River to its mouth into the Amazon and, from there, continued the remaining length of the Amazon River, arriving at its mouth into the Atlantic Ocean in 1542.

The first towns established by Spaniards in the Upper Amazon Basin were along the Quito route at the base of the Andes in the area of the upper Coca and Napo Rivers. Between 1559 and 1562, the towns of Baeza, Avila, Archidona, and San Juan de los Dos Ríos de Tena were founded by Spaniards who sought to establish land grants (*encomiendas*) similar to those given out by the Spanish Crown in the Andean highlands (Muratorio 1991, 2). These land grants faced numerous difficulties, not the least of which were the indigenous uprisings of 1562 and 1578–79, which rejected this foreign presence in their homelands. This last uprising, organized by various indigenous groups, destroyed the towns of Avila and Archidona, only to be repulsed by a forewarned population in Baeza (Irvine 1987, 25–33). These small towns survived for two decades from the mini–gold boom based on alluvial deposits. Upon the depletion of these deposits in the 1580s, many of the Spaniards left the area; others attempted an only partially successful transition to the harvesting of cotton by native labor (Taylor 1994, 22–25). This labor force was increasingly difficult to secure, not only because of open resistance, but also because the deadly cycle of epidemics, which decimated the native population of this area, had begun. Indeed, because of these and

numerous other problems, the land grant system was gradually abandoned in the Upper Amazon Basin after a century and a half of attempts
to install and maintain it (Muratorio 1991, 41).

Mission Cosmographies and Quichua Ethnogenesis

One of the major sources of indigenous upheavals during the colonial
period was the expanding work of the Catholic missionaries, particularly
the Jesuits.[10] The initial Jesuit presence in the Upper Amazon Basin dates
from 1595 and lasted until their expulsion from Spanish America in
1767. Here they established the Mainas missions, which encompassed
most of what is now Ecuadorian Amazonia and the northern portion of
Peruvian Amazonia. The key territorial strategy of the Jesuits was to relocate indigenous groups into large, sedentary *reducciones* (mission towns,
similar to the *aldeias* in Portuguese Amazonia) along the major rivers of
the region, where the natives were to be evangelized, learn agriculture,
give up their so-called savage customs, and, in general, become civilized
within the European mold of the time. The Jesuit program of establishing sedentary villages based on agriculture represented a major shift in
the settlement patterns of the native Amazonian groups, which were
much more mobile than the sedentary groups of the Lower Amazon
Basin. These indigenous groups lived from a vital mix of nomadic hunting, fishing, and foraging and temporary sedentarianism for the planting of their gardens.

Another crucial effect of the mission towns was the forced grouping of
different indigenous societies, a situation that provoked a breakdown of
internal indigenous social organization, usually based either on kinship
ties or ties to a shaman-headman, as well as of the territorial use-area of
each of the indigenous groups. Golob states that "violence was the usual
method for bringing the Indians to the missions," principally through
the mechanism of armed capture (1982, 159). Though some indigenous
groups voluntarily cooperated with the Jesuits, primarily to acquire tools
or seek protection from the Portuguese slave traders, most opted for
strategies of "open resistance, flight into the interior uplands or the formation of larger groups among distinct subgroups in order to better
resist their capture" (32). This set in motion a host of migratory movements, which were also influenced by the commercial and slaving interests of Spanish and Portuguese traders, that completely transformed the

ethnic makeup of the Upper Amazon Basin and led to the destruction of many groups and the creation of new ones.

The policy of forced settlement in large, sedentary reductions also facilitated the spread of fatal diseases among the native population. The height of epidemiological destruction of native Amazonians in the Upper Amazon occurred during the second half of the seventeenth and the first half of the eighteenth centuries, precisely when the Jesuits were most active. The Jesuits' own records note six epidemics of smallpox and two of measles between 1642 and 1762 (Golob 1982, 198). The dramatic demographic decline during the sixteenth and seventeenth centuries of the Omagua populations, who had dominated the riverside areas of the Middle Amazon and Napo Rivers, was due both to their early exposure to European diseases, which spread rapidly throughout their concentrated settlements, and to "a startling increase in the amount and frequency of warfare" (173), which resulted from the exogenous pressures exerted by the Europeans and the new resource demands that they fomented.

This decline in population created a territorial vacuum that was filled by the Encabellados, along the Aguarico and upper Napo Rivers, and the Záparos, who moved into and controlled a large swath of territory between the Bobonaza and Napo Rivers (Moya 1992, 19). In the late 1600s the Záparos were in a state of demographic and territorial expansion and were believed to number eight thousand to ten thousand. The Shuar (Jívaro), located further to the south, were able to maintain themselves in relative isolation from these movements because of both their reputation for fierceness and head shrinking and the mountainous terrain of their homeland. They succeeded in surviving into the twentieth century as one of the few populous indigenous groups of the Upper Amazon Basin (Harner 1972).

A notable ethnic change within the area of the Jesuit Mainas missions occurred in the Canelos region, located near what is now the Ecuadorian city of Puyo, which served as a "refuge zone" for individuals of Quijos, Záparo, Jívaro, and Andean indigenous origins who were fleeing from "the *encomenderos* as well as the mission priests" (Naranjo 1977, 156). Their subsequent mixing and the adoption of the Quichua lingua franca used by the missionaries sparked "the emergence of a formative culture . . . 200 to 300 years ago," which became the Canelos Quichua (Whitten 1994, 98). This group, forged from the situation of colonial encounter, is an example of what Whitten calls "ethnogenesis" (1976,

281–85), and it corresponds to what Taylor calls "neo-colonial tribes" (1994, 32).

The ethnogenesis process, which resulted from the previous centuries of ethnocide, was fostered by Jesuit use of Quichua as their missionizing language. The emergence of the Canelos Quichua group, for example, is part of the larger process of "Quichuaization" of the Upper Amazon Basin, which Hudelson defines as "the spread of the Quechua language and Quichua transitional culture" (1981, 4).[11] He defines three major phases in this process. The first phase (1560–1780), which began in the mid-sixteenth century with the founding of the Spanish towns in the upper Napo River Basin, was characterized by the use of the Quichua language as the basic "religious pedagogy" within the many Jesuit missions. The second (1800–1940) and third (1940 to present) phases will be discussed later.

The emerging Quichua society also developed its own social and territorial structures centered on the *muntun*. For the Quijos Quichua, Macdonald describes the *muntun* as "residential groups composed of several overlapping stem kindreds" (1967, 74). Historically, these "had fairly well established territorial boundaries which were given legitimacy by their cosmology and were defended against intruders" (37) and were often "named with reference to noticeable geographical features close to the settlement" (108). In sharp distinction from other seminomadic groups of the region, the Quichua *muntun* established territories within which members had exclusive rights to hunting, fishing, and gold mining. Macdonald notes that, while there was usually "intermediary buffer space which was open to all" between the *muntuns*, "when conflicts arose . . . , rigid boundaries became established" (47). Here we see a mixing of indigenous kinship structuring with nonindigenous concepts of the exclusivity of territory.

Early Attempts at an Ecuadorian National Cosmography

In 1830, after years of struggling for independence from Spain, Ecuador became a republic with the splintering of Gran Colombia into Ecuador, Colombia, and Venezuela. This division, made in negotiations among the triumphant *criollo* elite, did not take into account the territories of indigenous Amazonian groups. In the case of the Amazonian portion of the border between Colombia and Ecuador, both the Cofán and the

Siona societies were split in half by the international border established along the San Miguel River.

During the remainder of the nineteenth century, the Ecuadorian government was engaged in incessant disputes between the opposing political and economic interests of the elite of the Pacific coastal plain (headquartered in Guayaquil) and the Andean highlands (centered in Quito), which hindered the creation of a unified nation-state (Rivera and Little 1996). In this struggle, the vast Ecuadorian Amazon region, which on paper extended all the way to the Marañón (Amazon) River, was almost completely neglected by the country's political leaders. This marginality from the republican centers of power meant that the history being created in the Upper Amazon Basin, which was based on "brief cycles of rapid acceleration followed by long periods of slow evolution," in no way depended on the more dynamic "Quito-Guayaquil axis" (Taylor 1994, 17). Thus, a large portion of the Upper Amazon Basin, while formally part of Ecuador, had little interaction with the rest of the nation for nearly a century, a situation that made it all the more difficult for Ecuador to incorporate the region into its national territory in the twentieth century.

The first time Amazonia, known locally as the *Oriente* (literally "the East," since it lies to the east of the Andes), was formally recognized as a part of the country by the Ecuadorian government was in the Constitution of 1861, which established the Province of the Oriente (Ruiz 1991a, 298), though for many years the governor of this province was headquartered in Quito, far from the day-to-day problems of the area. In 1899, the new Special Law of the Oriente sought to modernize the administration of this area, but it suffered from the "absence of governmental authorities necessary for its effective implementation throughout this extensive territory" (Restrepo 1991, 143). It was only in 1920, ninety years after the founding of the republic, when the Amazonian provinces of Napo-Pastaza and Santiago-Zamora were created and Amazonia finally began to be integrated into the political-administrative structure of the Ecuadorian state.

This history of neglect is also to be seen in the lack of government-built infrastructure in Ecuadorian Amazonia. Between 1860 and 1912 twenty projects for the construction of roads connecting the Oriente to the Highlands were proposed, yet none of them were ever built (Ruiz 1991a, 298). In 1937 the first road into the region was completed, connecting Ambato with Puyo, and this was constructed by the Shell Oil Company as part of its petroleum exploration in the jungle. The proposal to build a railroad into the region was publicly debated in the early 1900s, but this plan was ridiculed by the press, neglected by government leaders, and denounced by coastal cocoa growers, whose economic fortunes were being made on the readily accessible coastal plain, far from the hostile, abandoned jungle. Even on a symbolic level, the Oriente was not considered to be an integral part of the nation. Almeida indicates that the Ecuadorian national symbol shows a snow-covered Andean peak with its waters flowing down into the wide coastal plain, while the Amazon Basin, located behind the Andes range, is strikingly absent.[12] In the symbol designed to represent the entire Ecuadorian nation, the Oriente simply does not exist.

Yet another indication of lack of interest in the area during this epoch is the fact that, around 1880, fewer than three hundred whites were believed to be permanently residing in Ecuador's Amazonian region (Taylor 1994). The García Moreno government (1861–65, 1869–75) tried to reactivate the area through return of the Jesuit missions, but this effort was fraught with problems and the Jesuits were again expelled from the region by the newly triumphant Liberal revolutionary government in 1896. A government attempt to set up a colonization program in 1884 also ended in failure (Muratorio 1991). It was only with the return of other missions in the 1920s, both Catholic and Protestant, that religious evangelism reentered the region in force and took its present form.

Meanwhile, tensions between Ecuador and Peru over control of the Amazonian lands between the Andes mountains and the Marañón River had simmered throughout the nineteenth century, starting with the signing of the Mosquera-Pedemonte Protocol in Lima in 1830, which ceded most of this land to Ecuador. During the succeeding decades, Peru gradually encroached on this land, moving up the tributaries of the Marañón for commercial reasons, a process consolidated by Peruvian control of the rubber trade. The nearly total neglect of this area by both highland and coastal Ecuadorian government leaders made this encroachment all the easier, as demonstrated by the Ecuadorian signing of the Herrera-García Treaty in 1890, in which Ecuador ceded control of the Marañón River to Peru. This treaty was rejected by the Peruvian Congress with the argument that it *did not cede enough* territory (Sampedro 1992, 42).

In 1900, Liberal Ecuadorian President Alfaro sent the first military contingent into the region, entering by mule through the Quito-Baeza-Tena route and traveling down the Napo, where they were met by Peruvian troops at the mouth of the Aguarico River. This was "the first time that Peruvian armed forces had ever seen Ecuadorian soldiers" in the Amazon (Sampedro 1992, 44). Military skirmishes in 1903 (in Angoteros) and 1904 (in Torres Causana) resulted in the defeat of Ecuadorian troops. In 1904, Ecuador signed a treaty with Brazil ceding a tract of land in what is now the northwest corner of the Brazilian state of Amazonas. In 1916, the Ecuadorian government ceded a large tract of land south of the Putumayo River to Colombia, an area that Colombia had controlled during the rubber boom and that was subsequently ceded to Peru in 1922. All of Ecuador's treaties with its neighbors were land cessions and greatly diminished the amount of territory to which the country could formally lay claim. The repeated losses of territory by Ecuador created a national trauma among Ecuadorians, which formed the basis for an emergent national identity founded on the effective control of its territorial borders.

Mercantile Cosmographies of Agave, Rubber, and Cattle

While the Ecuadorian state demonstrated a general lack of interest in its Oriente, the forces of the world market were operating throughout the region, showing that the market and its social agents were willing and capable of penetrating areas lacking significant government control. The demand for forest products from the Upper Amazon increased dramatically during the nineteenth century and included such products as gold, agave (*pita*), vanilla, wild cocoa, resins, quinine, tagua, and sarsaparilla. In the upper Napo River basin, agave, from whose fiber cord was made, was the most important product harvested before the rubber boom. It was primarily extracted by indigenous peoples and used as an important source of trade in the northern Oriente during much of the nineteenth century, particularly in the Archidona area. Often it was used as payment (along with gold dust) in commercial transactions (both forced and voluntary) between indigenous peoples and whites (Muratorio 1991, 81–83).

Yet it was the rubber boom, which gained strength in the Upper Amazon Basin starting in the 1880s and continued until its dramatic demise in 1913, that would produce profound transformations among the numerous indigenous peoples still living in the area. The source of greatest impact was the incessant need for Indian labor to find, collect, and harvest rubber for the powerful rubber traders (*caucheros*), and brutal methods, including slavery and wanton killing, were used to secure this labor force. While the devastation caused by the rubber boom was massive, its effect on indigenous peoples varied from area to area. Among the hardest hit were the Huitoto of the Putumayo River Basin (Taussig 1987; Pineda 1993) and the once numerous Záparo,[13] who were driven into near extinction, as were numerous smaller indigenous groups who had resisted incorporation into the market structures of the Amazonian region up to that time.

Ecuador's Oriente was spared some of the harshest effects because it "had less rubber and of an inferior quality compared with Peru, Colombia, or Brazil and also a smaller indigenous population" (Muratorio 1991, 109). Nonetheless, this area did experience "the forced mobilization and exploitation of thousands of indigenous laborers by a small group of Ecuadorian and foreign adventurers and traders" (106). Many of these laborers were Quichua speakers who "had a definite advantage over other native groups" (Hudelson 1981, 215) due to their long history of interactions with whites, their familiarity with the mechanisms of the market economy, and their use of Quichua, the lingua franca of the Upper Amazon Basin. As a result of renewed Jesuit missionizing and numerous interpersonal contacts due to the rubber trade, epidemics returned to plague indigenous groups. Between 1869 and 1924, Jesuit and official Ecuadorian government documents recorded eighteen distinct epidemics in the Oriente of smallpox, measles, dysentery, dengue, flu, tertian fever, and malaria (Muratorio 1991, 249).

The rubber in the Upper Amazon Basin, which was known as *caucho,* came from the *Castilloa elastica* tree and was of inferior quality when compared to the rubber from the various *Hevea* species found primarily in Brazil. The exploitation of the *C. elastica* tree caused greater damage to the forest than did the use of *Hevea* trees, since *Castilloa* was rarely tapped; rather, the latex was gathered after the trees were felled. This difference meant that the Upper Amazon *caucheros* did not lay permanent claim to large tracts of land, as was the case in Brazil with the *seringais;* instead, they were engaged in a constant and expanding search for new stands of the rubber tree, which extended the rubber trades' social network and increased environmental damage.

The rubber boom also produced a rapid expansion of Peruvian interests into large parts of Amazonia formally claimed by Ecuador. This led to a gradual loss of effective Ecuadorian control to the Peruvian military and to rubber traders who operated out of the town of Iquitos, which was under Peruvian control. The fact that all the rubber was exported downriver through the port of Iquitos and that almost all consumer goods were imported via these same fluvial routes consolidated Peruvian presence in the region and helped incorporate it into the Peruvian economy. This situation was aggravated by difficult access to the Oriente from the Ecuadorian highlands due to the lack of basic infrastructure. The territorial gains that Peru would make in the 1941–42 war coincided almost exactly with the area under their regular control gained during the rubber boom.

After the collapse of the Amazonian rubber market, cattle ranching gained force as an economic alternative. The *hacienda* (ranch) system, which had been established during the latter half of the nineteenth century, spread rapidly during the early years of the twentieth century. The spread of this system, together with the rubber trade, characterizes Hudelson's second phase in the ongoing process of Quichuaization of the Upper Amazon Basin (Hudelson 1981). With the establishment of ranches in new regions, the white ranchers brought their indentured Quichua workers with them. This introduced Quichua-speaking peoples into the Aguarico, San Miguel, and Putumayo River areas, while it consolidated their presence on the lower Napo River as they filled the territorial vacuum caused by the demographic decline of the Záparos.

The Quichua transitional culture was a type of "culture broker" (232) that provided a means of preventing a total loss of identity by indigenous groups who were faced with the prospect of rapidly assimilating to non-Indian culture. Yet another factor that facilitated the rapid expansion of Quichua culture among other indigenous groups was that the Quichua were the only group capable of translating power relations between Indians and whites into shamanistic terms familiar to indigenous groups, thus providing them yet another role as "cultural intermediaries" (Taylor 1994, 60). The cattle boom was interrupted by the Great Depression, not so much because of the lowering of cattle prices, but rather because of the sharp increase in the price of gold, which diverted the economic efforts of the ranchers almost exclusively to gold extraction. This was followed by the resurgence of rubber production during World War II, an activity that lasted until 1945 (Muratorio 1991, 157–60).

Petroleum Exploration and the Ecuador-Peru War of 1941–42

With the possibility of finding oil, the Upper Amazon became of strategic interest to foreign oil firms. Exploration for petroleum began in the Ecuadorian Oriente in 1921 when two contracts were given out by the Ecuadorian government: one to the Leonard Petroleum Company, a subsidiary of Standard Oil of New Jersey, for 20,000 hectares, and the second to the Canadian firm Amazon Corporation Limited, for 15,000 hectares. These contracts were terminated in 1937, and in this same year a new one was signed, this time with the Anglo Saxon Petroleum Company, a subsidiary of Royal Dutch Shell, covering a concession of 8,345,610 hectares (Villacrés 1963, 280). Though no oil was found at this time, the search for oil had become intense because of rising international pressures, which would soon erupt into World War II. When Standard Oil obtained Amazonian concessions from Peru and Shell Oil was granted concessions from Ecuador, the stage was set for a clash between these two competing oil giants for control and exploitation of these vast tracts of land.

During the 1930s, the Peruvian military had begun to prepare for a military takeover of this area, which was already under their de facto control. Now, with the promise of oil revenues on the basis of the Peruvian government's concession to Standard Oil, the Peruvian military put their plans into action. In July 1941 Peruvian armed forces launched a surprise two-pronged attack on Ecuador, with one front along the southern border between the two countries and the other in Amazonia. "Following the routes of the *caucheros,* the Peruvian army thrust up various Oriente rivers, using some Jivaroan and Cocama troops" (Whitten 1976, 234). After suffering military defeats on both fronts, Ecuador was forced to sign the Rio de Janeiro Protocol, in which it ceded to Peru 200,000 square kilometers of Amazonian land, nearly half the total surface area of the nation at the time and most of its Amazonian area. The new borders coincided with the oil concessions given out by the two countries, a fact Galarza uses to support his claim that this war was first and foremost an oil war between two of the Seven Sisters,[14] with the Ecuadorian and Peruvian governments serving as proxy armies (Galarza 1983). With this war the territorial dynamic of the Oriente was extended well beyond the interactions and conflicts among indigenous groups and between these groups and whites to include an international dispute between two nation-states under the influence of powerful international corporations.

The international border established by the Rio de Janeiro Protocol in 1942 divided the territories of the western Tukanoan (Secoya) peoples and the Jivaroan (Achuar and Shuar) peoples. Now these members of the same indigenous societies would become citizens of two different nations that had long neglected their interests. The defeat by Peru also brought changes in the makeup of the Ecuadorian army, particularly in the Oriente, where increasing numbers of Quichuas were recruited as soldiers and used to patrol the border. This policy was later expanded to include Shuar troops in the southern area of the Oriente. In addition, the war provoked the northwesterly migration of some of the Ecuadorian ranchers who had settled along the lower Napo River and who preferred to maintain their formal presence in Ecuador. In short, the new border fractured the Upper Amazon by cutting off the historical flows that had given it a regional unity.

The constant loss of Amazonian territory and the apparent lack of petroleum there (after thirty years of exploration) led Ecuadorian President Galo Plaza to announce in 1949 that "the Oriente is a myth." With this phrase he seemed to indicate that perhaps the chronic neglect of Amazonia shown by Ecuadorian leaders was justified, since it had little economic value and was a constant source of problems. During the 1950s, however, this attitude shifted radically. For the new leaders, the humiliation of the 1941–42 war with Peru represented a turning point in their national history and, for the first time, the Oriente entered their consciousness as an integral and important part of the Ecuadorian nation. By 1960, the Ecuadorian government had adopted the slogan "Ecuador has been, is, and will be an Amazonian nation" and placed it on its official letterhead. This new attitude served to diminish the bipolar coastal-highland makeup of Ecuadorian politics by adding a third region. Although still marginal, Amazonia was soon to step into the forefront of Ecuadorian development. It was only in the mid-twentieth century that Ecuador emerged as an integrated nation-state (Rivera and Little 1996).

The Aguarico River Region

The Aguarico River Region is nestled at the northern edge of the Upper Amazon Basin and encompasses the entire lowland portion of the Aguarico River watershed. The Aguarico River has its source in the snowmelt from Cayambe Mountain, which at nearly 6,000 meters above sea level is the world's highest point along the Equator. Within a span of 100 kilometers, these mountain waters drop 5,700 meters down the eastern slope of the Ecuadorian Andes before leveling out at an elevation of a mere 300 meters above sea level in the tropical Amazonian lowlands. At the edge of the Andean escarpment, several streams come together to form the muddy Aguarico River, marking the western edge of the Aguarico Region delimited here. From this point the Aguarico proceeds slowly for another 350 kilometers until it enters the Napo River. Midway in its course through the rain forest, the Aguarico receives from the northeast the clear, black waters of its largest tributary, the Cuyabeno River, which drains a large area of flat swamplands and interconnected lakes.

Strategically located between the Putumayo River (to the north) and the Napo River (to the south), both tributaries to the Amazon River, the Aguarico River Basin has long been an important transit area for indigenous societies. For centuries native Amazonians have used these waterways in making contacts, trading, and migrating and as fluvial highways connecting the Andes Mountains to the Amazon River. The Aguarico Region was affected both directly and indirectly by these demographic, social, economic, and cultural movements of the Upper Amazon Basin.

Since the sixteenth century, the Aguarico Region has been dominated by two indigenous societies: the Encabellados and the Cofanes. The lower Aguarico River basin and parts of the Putumayo and Napo River basins were controlled by the numerous Encabellados, a group famous for their powerful shamans and named for the long hair worn by both men and women. The Encabellados are part of the western Tukanoan linguistic group, which is believed to have split from the eastern Tukanoan group some fifteen hundred to two thousand years ago. The Encabellados are direct ancestors of the contemporary Siona, Secoya, and Tetete groups and, "at the time of European contact, speakers of Western Tukanoan occupied an area of 82,000 square kilometers along the Napo, Putumayo and Aguarico rivers," with an estimated population of sixteen thousand (Vickers 1994, 306–7). Though the Encabellados were first contacted by the Jesuit missionaries in 1599, it was only after a 1683 royal decree granting the Jesuits the right to missionize this area that the Jesuits established a significant presence through the founding of seventeen missions in the Aguarico-Napo River Basins.

The Encabellados suffered from many of the forces of depopulation, with diseases taking the heaviest toll. Fewer than five hundred Sionas and a similar number of Secoyas existed by the mid-twentieth century. The Ecuadorian portions of the Siona subgroup, now split in two by the Colombian-Ecuadorian international border, and the Secoya subgroup, now split in two by the Peruvian-Ecuadorian international border, had joined together to form a single ethnic group, a move designed to enhance their chances of survival. This union was spurred in part by the Ecuador-Peru war. As tensions between Ecuador and Peru increased in mid-1941, a group of Secoya migrated to the northeast from their home at the mouth of the Santa María de Guajoya River (a tributary of the Napo River) and joined their (western Tukanoan) Siona kin in Ecuador at their settlements along the Aguarico River. The Siona-Secoya lived in several communities along the middle Aguarico River and maintained a large community at Puerto Bolívar along the Cuyabeno River.

In his study of historical and contemporary Siona-Secoya territoriality, Vickers describes their patterns of resource use based on shifting cultivation, hunting, fishing, and collecting along with their "pattern of patrilocal, patrilineal extended households located at different sites" (1983, 459), while emphasizing that each of these local communities operates under the influence of a prominent headman-shaman and that they are noted for their easy fissionability. In comparing data concerning the territorial size of historical Encabellado and contemporary Siona-Secoya communities (calculated as the area exploited by members of each community), Vickers notes the remarkable closeness of the two estimates (1,124 and 1,149 square kilometers, respectively), which "derives from certain fundamental technoenvironmental similarities that characterize both the modern Siona-Secoya and their Encabellado ancestors" (464). Finally, he notes that the periodic migrations of the Siona-Secoya have historically occurred within particular sections of the Aguarico and Napo Rivers.

The Cofanes, who are believed to come from Chibcha linguistic stock (Borman 1982; Moya 1992, 36),[15] have long inhabited the area to the west of the Encabellado groups, along the upper Aguarico and San Miguel Rivers. They are believed to have come into this basin from the north, in a migratory movement along the Amazonian lowlands that hug the Andes escarpment. Aristazábal locates their "traditional" territory as encompassing the area between the Guamués River (Colombia) and the Aguarico River, an area bisected by the San Miguel River, the "river that unites the Cofanes" (1993, 143). Their closeness to the Andean range placed them along the route of possible pre-Columbian highland to lowland (or vice versa) migrations and trade routes. Their first contact with the Jesuits came in 1599, during the first of ten Jesuit *entradas* (reconnaissance trips) made into the area from 1599 to 1632. The mission of Padre Ferrer was established among the Cofanes on this first trip, and he became a martyr of the early missionaries when in 1607 the Cofanes cut the bridge on which he was walking and he fell to his death (Moya 1992, 24–25). Indigenous resistance to missionary activity often began at the moment of first contact.

Their location to the north of the main entrance route into the Upper Amazon Basin (Quito-Baeza) kept the Cofanes partially protected from the devastation of continual contact with the invading Europeans. Nonetheless, over the centuries smallpox proved to be a formidable enemy and, by the mid-twentieth century, the Cofán population had been reduced to about one thousand individuals. The Dureno community located along the Aguarico River was the largest Cofán community within Ecuador. Relations between the Cofanes and the Encabellados, who shared two ends of the lowland Aguarico River Basin, were friendly and marked by exogamic marriages.

The Tetete, another western Tukanoan group, by mid-twentieth century had fewer than twenty-five members. They lived in isolated areas between the Cofán and Siona-Secoya groups scattered along the upper Cuyabeno River and possibly the upper Guepi River. Along the lower Aguarico River near its mouth with the Napo River, a group of Quichuas established the community of Zancudo as a companion village to the Ecuadorian military base set up there to patrol the Ecuador-Peru border. The Quichua also had larger populations to the north, along the San Miguel and Putumayo Rivers, and to the south, along the Napo River. The Huaorani occupied a large territory to the south of the Napo River, along the Cononaco and Curaray Rivers in a region distinct from the Aguarico one, though there is toponymic evidence that they once occupied portions of the Aguarico River Basin and were pushed out by the Encabellados (Trujillo 1986).

In the 1940s and 1950s, new commercial networks were established in the region, this time for animal hides and fish. In the Cuyabeno River basin, for example, jaguar and manatee hides were in high demand, as was the delicious *paiche* fish (*Arapaima gigas*) that abounded in this black-

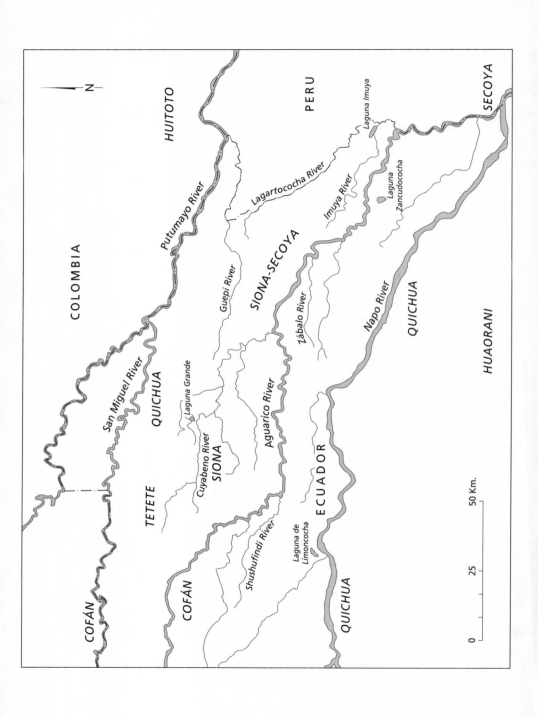

water system. Three river traders regularly bought hides and fish from local Siona-Secoya inhabitants and shipped them downriver to be sold in Peru. This trade demonstrates the resilience and flexibility of market mechanisms in Amazonia and shows how political borders are of little consequence in the fulfilling of market demand. While national leaders were signing treaties and armed forces were engaged in combat, river traders continued to extract forest products wherever they could be found and to ply their wares to whomever would pay the best price. This trading network would be revived by other social actors in the 1970s and 1980s with the contraband trade in liquor and drugs in the Colombian-Ecuadorian-Peruvian jungle triangle.

Interregional trade brought on Hudelson's third phase of Quichuaization, since many of these traders were descendants of Quichua-speaking peoples. They were not, however, directly tied to the *muntun* system of territorial organization and tended to speak Spanish rather than Quichua, thus turning them into a "type of 'river mestizo' . . . similar to the [Brazilian] *caboclo*" (Hudelson 1981, 212). The inhabitants of the Playas de Cuyabeno Quichua community, established during the 1950s at the mouth of the Cuyabeno River, express many of these traits. Today they are a Spanish-speaking community with diverse origins, though the initial migrations seem to have come from the San Miguel River basin, an area that had been populated by Quichua speakers during the first half of the twentieth century (Chavez).

The 1950s brought a new social actor to the Aguarico Region: the Summer Institute of Linguistics (SIL). In 1954, the Johnson husband-wife missionary team landed in an aquatic airplane on the Laguna Grande (Large Lagoon) in the Cuyabeno Lakes district and began mission work with the Siona-Secoya located at Puerto Bolívar. Farther up the Aguarico River basin, the Borman missionary couple began evangelizing the Cofán in the community of Dureno. One of the special missions of this evangelical organization was to work with isolated indigenous peoples with nonwritten languages. Upon making contact with an indigenous group and establishing a presence in the area, one of SIL's first tasks is to learn the native language, give it a written script, and then translate the Bible into the native tongue. Parallel with these linguistic activities are evangelical ones, such as establishing a church, making converts, eliminating

The Aguarico River Region: Indigenous Homelands circa 1950 *(opposite)*

Antonio Yori, ex–river trader and current nature guide, 2000

"heathen" or "pagan" beliefs, and prohibiting the use of hallucinogenic drugs, alcohol, and tobacco. A different set of activities, designed to integrate the indigenous groups into Western societal structures, included the establishment of trade schools and small health clinics.[16]

Circa 1950, the Aguarico Region was occupied by four indigenous groups—the Siona-Secoya, the Tetete, the Cofán, and the Quichua—that were each settled in scattered communities. The territorial control of this region by these indigenous groups was loosely defined, since their relatively small demographic presence did not create enormous resource pressures, nor did it provoke direct territorial conflicts between the differing groups. Long distance travel was still limited to fluvial networks, since the area was not traversed by any roads, although air traffic in small prop planes would soon become a limited means of entry.

The Aguarico Region also was home to a smattering of Ecuadorian ranchers, Catholic and Evangelical missionaries, Amazonian river traders, and Ecuadorian soldiers, many of whom came from local indigenous communities. There was a notable absence of Ecuadorian government officials, since they mainly operated out of Tena, the provincial capital, well to the south of this region. The Ecuadorian military had outposts at Nuevo Rocafuerte (Napo River), Puerto El Carmen (San Miguel River at its mouth with the Putumayo), and Zancudo (lower Aguarico River). The river traders of this time did not have a fixed territory (except in terms of their range of operations), the ranchers were in economic decline, and the religious missions were directly tied to the territories of the indigenous peoples.

Tipishca/Puerto El Carmen

Tipishca appears on almost all maps of Ecuador as a principal port along the San Miguel River and the terminal point of the petroleum road opened in the 1980s. Upon arriving there, I found that it consisted of just four buildings—a warehouse, two abandoned houses, and a restaurant. My colleague Roberto and I decided to get a bite to eat as we waited for the daily boat that would take us to Puerto El Carmen, five hours downstream. Waiting and eating with us in the restaurant were four Carmelite sisters who worked as teachers and missionaries in the various Quichua communes along the San Miguel. Shortly, four Petroecuador oil workers stopped to eat. Including the couple who owned and operated the restaurant, none of the twelve people present was a native-born Amazonian. At first this struck me as odd—here I was in the middle of Amazonia and, of a dozen people, none was from there. Yet all of us were directly tied to the region either through work, residence, or personal interest. This eclectic presence of outsiders was not new: for centuries, missionaries, traders, explorers, scientists, and developers had passed through this area and probably gathered at riverside restaurants not too different from this one at Tipishca. All of these people were, and are, an important part of Amazonia and its long history of globalization, and they need to be considered in the telling of this history.

Later that day, upon arriving at Puerto El Carmen, a sleepy municipal seat located at the confluence of the San Miguel and Putumayo Rivers along the border with Colombia, we interviewed the Mother Superior of the Carmelite high school that served the lower San Miguel River. After we introduced ourselves and explained our interest in the town and its history, this nun launched into a twenty-minute tirade against Mobutu Sese Seko, the corrupt and brutal dictator of Zaire. As it turns out, she had just been transferred to Ecuador after fifteen years of missionary work in Zaire, and her heart was still filled with the problems of that African country. The connections between a Zairian village and Puerto El Carmen are certainly remote but, as this encounter showed, they do indeed exist.

Upon leaving the school we headed into town to get a soft drink. In a chat with the owner of the local store, she told us of a pressing problem: Coca-Cola had not arrived in Puerto El Carmen. Of course, neither had a road, or telephone lines, or regular mail service, or a small airport, but this was not her immediate concern. Coca-Cola had launched a nationwide promotional campaign in which one could win valuable prizes by collecting Coke bottle caps. All the kids in town, who knew of the campaign via radio, were complaining to her because she didn't sell Coke and they couldn't collect bottle caps. My long-held assumption that Coca-Cola had arrived just about everywhere now had a new angle: here was a case of anticipated, but unfulfilled, cocacolonization.

This brief excursion brought home to me the varied ways in which the world, with its multiple, distant, and often obtuse connections, has been acting on Amazonia and the way its peoples, from wherever they may hail, have been responding.

Indigenous and *Caboclo* Territories in Comparative Review

The massive depopulation of Amazonia caused by warfare, slavery, and disease precipitated major territorial changes in the Jari and Aguarico Regions. In both cases, armed warfare was an almost immediate result of initial contacts between Europeans and indigenous peoples, with the latter suffering the greatest number of deaths, while smallpox was the disease that devastated the largest number of indigenous peoples, followed by measles. Furthermore, the rate of indigenous dying in both regions was most intense during the seventeenth and the first half of the eighteenth centuries, leaving major portions of the jungle depopulated. Significant differences in the resultant creation of social territories in the two regions are partially explained by their differing demographic and societal makeup.[17]

The Jari Region, as with much of the Lower Amazon Basin, was one of the most densely populated areas of the entire Amazonian biome because of the widespread presence of fertile floodplains and marshlands, two of the most productive habitats for humans in Amazonia. These biophysical conditions allowed the establishment of large, sedentary chiefdoms based on intensive use of these habitats' resources. This demographic density allowed a greater total number of indigenous deaths in the Lower Amazon when compared with the Upper Amazon, although the dead were not necessarily a greater percentage of the region's total population. In the Jari Region, the large populations of indigenous societies of Tucujús on the mainland and Aruãs and Nheengaíba on the delta islands did not survive as territorial societies. However, many individual members and their racial stock did survive, providing a substratum of people that would form the *tapuio* population and the indigenous component of the subsequent *caboclo* one. The biophysical richness of this area, together with its relatively easy fluvial access, made it an attractive site for the establishment of villages and towns by outside settlers, and over time the Lower and Middle Amazon Valleys would become wholly nonindigenous areas (Galvão 1960; Melatti 1995).

The lowland tropical forest habitat in the Aguarico Region fostered a more extensive use of the forest by indigenous groups and had a far lower demographic density. The groups that inhabited this area had smaller populations, allowing a larger number of autarkic indigenous societies, each with its own form of territoriality. Small societies offer much less demographic resistance to depopulation pressures and were the first to be pushed toward or into extinction. At the same time, their isolated, seminomadic mode of subsistence and the mobile, fluctuating territories they maintained made it easier for them to take flight and move away from the areas of greatest European pressure. And, while the total number of indigenous *individuals* who died in the depopulation waves of the Upper Amazon was less than in the Lower Amazon, the total number of *societies* that became extinct was greater.[18]

Since Cofán and Siona-Secoya groups were located off the major Amazonian river highways and had fairly large populations (for the area) at the time of the initial European invasions, they were able to survive into the twentieth century, though only as a remnant of what they once had been. By this time, these groups had a greatly reduced population, were hybrids of many influences, lived according to altered social structures, and were being threatened by other indigenous groups such as the Quichua. The Shuar, another large Upper Amazonian group, lived amid difficult mountain terrain, where they survived in much larger numbers than did the Cofán or the Siona-Secoya. The Záparos, on the other hand, in spite of their relatively large population, were located on major trade and slaving routes and were nearly totally extinguished.

From a very early stage of the European invasions of Amazonia, the entire biome functioned as a socionatural entity united by numerous pan-Amazonian interhuman connections. The voyage of Orellana, which left from Quito, began its fluvial expedition from the upper portion of the Napo River in the heart of the Upper Amazon Basin and sailed down the length of the Amazon River before arriving at the Amazon Delta. The expedition of Pedro Teixeira, nearly a century later, reversed the direction of Orellana's voyage but followed the same route. The Teixeira expedition was launched in response to the surprise arrival in Belém of two Spanish Franciscan priests and a dozen Spanish soldiers who were fleeing from an attack on their group by Encabellados along the Napo River at the other end of Amazonia. When Teixeira and his expedition arrived at the Napo, they launched punitive raids on the Encabellados, a group that had not had previous contact with the Portuguese.

The indigenous depopulation of large areas of Amazonia caused by European invasions served to intensify the struggles between the Portuguese and Spanish Crowns to appropriate this biome as part of their respective monarchical domains. During the colonial era, Amazonia represented a single, contested space divided into numerous regional frontiers, each with its biophysical and social specifics. The fact that the Portuguese were able to gain control of well over half of this continental watershed in direct affront to the 1494 Treaty of Tordesillas, which ceded the entire watershed to Spain, is partially rooted in the geography of the Amazon River Basin. The Portuguese entered the region from the river's mouth, where they had the advantage of direct, easy fluvial access to the ocean and Europe. The Spaniards entered the region from the rugged heights of the Andes range, where they pushed through dense mountain and jungle vegetation until they were able to gain access to navigable rivers.

In spite of this relentless push to conquer indigenous peoples and control vast geographical areas, both colonial powers were interested less in lands than in riches, or, more precisely, in lands that would produce riches. This was in keeping with the mercantile system that dominated the expanding European economy of that epoch. To produce riches one needed labor, and the principal means of producing riches in Amazonia was control over Indian labor. In this category, the Portuguese once again had an advantage over the Spanish because of the much larger riverside populations readily accessible to their invading troops. These social and geographical factors help explain why, by the time of the Treaty of Madrid of 1750, the Portuguese had gained effective control over the heart of the Amazon River Basin.

Conquering indigenous tribes and claiming vast Amazonian lands for the Spanish or Portuguese Crown was one phase of the process of multiple conquests, but physically occupying this land and imposing new cosmographies was a different and in some respects more difficult task. The *encomiendas* in the Upper Amazon, modeled on those given out by the Spanish Crown in the Andean highlands, never functioned well in the jungle environment and were gradually abandoned. A similar fate met the *sesmarias* handed out by the Portuguese Crown to explorers and conquerors. The main interest of these individuals was not to settle the land and found new nations, but to extract riches as quickly as possible. Neither the Spanish *encomiendas* nor the Portuguese *sesmarias* survived as viable territorial entities, though they played an important part in the indigenous depopulation process.

During the colonial era the notion of *terras devolutas* was first used by the Portuguese Crown to maintain dominion over large geographical areas. Land that had been given out by the Crown but was no longer effectively occupied, exploited, defended, or preserved was returned to royal dominion. This kept large tracts of land under nominal monarchical control. In general, during the entire phase of colonial rule, control over land was guided by the "concept of the covenant—that actual possession (*uti possidetis de facto*), not legal title (*uti possidetis de jure*), takes precedence" (Tambs 1974, 68).

The territorial restructuring of Amazonia that succeeded the destruction or drastic reduction of the territorially based indigenous societies was provoked by the installation of new cosmographies by the Jesuits, the settlers, national governments, and, later, the rubber barons. The Jesuits, missionizing in the Lower or Upper Amazon or in other parts of

South America, formed a single religious order structured according to clearly established, hierarchical Roman Catholic principles and shared a common religious ideology and practice. The territorial mandate underlying the *reducciones* in the Upper Amazon and the *aldeias* in the Lower Amazon was based on the same practice of forming large, riverside, mission villages where indigenous peoples of widely differing ethnic backgrounds were gathered to be Christianized, to become civilized, and, most importantly, to work for the Jesuits. This provoked demographic, adaptational, and ethnic alterations among local populations and had major territorial consequences.

In both regions, the forced resettlement of indigenous peoples in permanent villages greatly disrupted their traditional forms of subsistence and settlement. The forced mixing of different indigenous societies in mission towns radically transformed the existing ethnic boundaries between the groups, while proselytizing had strong cultural effects by partially suppressing local beliefs and imposing new ones. The missions presented indigenous societies with a mission cosmography, with its own forms of settlement and adaptation all justified by a religious ideology, that was superimposed on indigenous cosmographies with highly diverse results. The missionary work of the Jesuits in the Upper and Lower Amazon covered a similar period of 150 years, while their respective expulsions from Portuguese (1759) and Spanish (1767) America came within eight years of each other. During the most intensive phase of Jesuit activity—the mid-seventeenth to the mid-eighteenth centuries— this religious order was the richest economic entity in both areas and operated as the principal system of government, although their control of the Mainas missions in the Upper Amazon was greater than their control of Portuguese Amazonia, where they had to contend with a vociferous settler population.

The Portuguese Amazonian settler population, while rarely able to escape their harsh living conditions and being at an economic disadvantage when compared with their Jesuit contemporaries, still managed to support a thriving extractivist export trade in forest products, which was possible only because of their continual exploitation of Indian slave labor. With the expulsion of the Jesuits, the settlers became the demographic and economic anchor of the colonial, and later national, government reforms that sought to incorporate this area into their effective political domain, an effort that was ultimately successful.

The size of the settler population in Portuguese Amazonia stands in direct contrast to the lack of a sustained colonial and republican settler population in the Upper Amazon in general and the Aguarico Region in particular. Starting with the Ecuadorian republican era in the early nineteenth century, the Archidona-Napo Region, located just to the southwest of the Aguarico River Basin, was the central political headquarters for the Ecuadorian Oriente, but even in this capacity it never became a major population center and the settler population remained low until well into the twentieth century. This coincided with a general lack of interest on the part of both colonial and republican political leaders to incorporate the Oriente into lands under their effective control. Settlers and traders who did live and work in the area were able to maintain a small, highly volatile extractive economy that fluctuated between different extractive booms. Ecuador made several unsuccessful efforts at incorporating these lands into their national economies and policies in the nineteenth century, such as scattered colonization attempts, but these were thwarted by lack of infrastructure and government disinterest.

The varying sizes of the settler population played a significant role in the way that the processes of ethnogenesis evolved in the two regions. In the Upper Amazon, the ethnogenesis process centered around the Quichuaization of the indigenous population, in which the use of Quichua as a common language served to unite remnants of many small indigenous societies. The Quichua groups established their own territorial system and were able to survive as a distinct indigenous group and enter into a process of territorial expansion during the nineteenth century, a process that continues today.

In the Lower Amazon, the first wave of depopulation, coupled with the ethnic mixing in the Jesuit mission villages and the settler slave trade, gave rise to a large *tapuio* population comprising full-blooded Indians from many ethnic groups who adopted the *língua geral* as their new language, one that was gradually extinguished during the nineteenth century. This outcome stemmed from several causes. First, the larger settler population in Portuguese Amazonia provided an important colonial presence in the process of consolidating Portuguese and later Brazilian control of the Amazon River Basin. Second, this same population and a small but significant black population gradually mixed with the *tapuio* population, making their indigenous racial stock ever more diffuse. Third, the Cabanagem rebellion, which could have offered the *ta-*

puios a chance to establish themselves as a distinct political and cultural actor in the region, was poorly organized and brutally crushed, effectively aborting this ethnogenesis and transforming it into the cabaclization process. In this case a racially mixed, rural Amazonian society with a distinctive cultural and adaptive system emerged, but under the aegis of the Portuguese language and predominantly Catholic customs.

The Brazilian *caboclo* population, in contrast with the Ecuadorian Quichuan one, had weak collective identities that obstructed their establishment of communal territorial units. They maintained marginal contacts with the market economy while eking out a living from their family productive units using traditional subsistence means. And while the Quichua fulfilled important intermediary roles in the Upper Amazon, controlling many of the region's trade networks and brokering relations between the indigenous societies and whites, including those with the rubber traders, the Brazilian *caboclos* of the Lower Amazon retreated to their riverside habitats, where they were gradually subsumed by the larger forces of the rubber trade and turned into a type of indentured extractivist with the *aviamento* system.

The continual superimposition of mercantile cosmographies in Amazonia would prove to be one of the most powerful and enduring forces of territorial change in the histories of both the Jari and the Aguarico Regions. The desire of the European invaders to exploit the Amazon jungle was evident from their first excursions into this biome. Europeans at first looked for products with which they were familiar, most notably gold. The few mini–gold booms of the late sixteenth and early seventeenth centuries quickly depleted alluvial deposits, and the European invaders were generally disappointed not to find the El Dorado they so desperately sought. Beginning in the late sixteenth century, other natural resources and new products never imagined by the early explorers emerged in Amazonia as the result of the conjunction of native Amazonian knowledge and technologies and the nascent scientific, experimental worldview of Europe. This little-appreciated contribution of indigenous Amazonian knowledge to world development shows that intercontinental contact, for all of its destructive qualities, was also a two-way exchange of knowledge and ideas. Many Amazonian resources were highly valued because they were endemic to this biome.

From this point onward, the Amazonian economy was directly connected to extracontinental demand for its products and, hence, to world markets, thereby strengthening the incipient process of the globalization of Amazonia. Market forces stimulated the establishment of new forms of adaptation based in intensive mono-extraction of resources, producing differential effects ranging from the total depletion of some resources to selective, long-term harvesting of fruits of the forest. A short list of some of the most salient resources extracted from Amazonia would include cinnamon, agave, cascarilla, chinchona bark, barbasco, clove, cacao, sarsaparilla, guaraná, vanilla, Brazil nuts, rubber, and a wide variety of oils, resins, seeds, hardwoods, and animal hides.

The spatiality of resource distribution, which ranged from high concentration to widespread dispersion, generated specific harvesting strategies, brought new social groups into the jungle according to world demand, produced specific relations with local indigenous populations, and structured settlement patterns, often determining their geographical locations. To the degree that social groups participated in this adaptive dynamic, the existence of flexible mercantile cosmographies can be detected. These cosmographies are founded on a common set of market mechanisms but change as new products are extracted and new social groups emerge to extract and market them.

Just as resources were being extracted out of Amazonia, new products were being introduced into it, producing far-reaching effects. European manufactured goods such as fish hooks, metal knives, machetes, axes, firearms, and munitions radically altered how indigenous peoples adapted to their environment and rapidly became part of their new lifeways. In addition to these tools, products such as salt, woven cloth, pots and pans, needles and thread, and matches were incorporated into the daily life of native Amazonians and quickly turned into necessities. While one can speak of market *intrusions* into the jungle, one must also mention market *seductions,* with the use of new products to gain access to new areas. One of the more pernicious of these products was liquor in its many forms, which was often used in transactions not only as a means of trade but also as a way of cheating indigenous people through negotiations or trade conducted while they were inebriated.

The two-way commerce of resources extracted (in large part) by indigenous peoples in return for their access to manufactured goods established entire new trade networks in Amazonia and empowered those social groups, both indigenous and European, who were able to control them. At the same time it disrupted, and in some cases destroyed, the old, interindigenous networks and the alliances upon which they were founded. A great deal of indigenous labor was contracted, and many slaves were bartered for, in exchange for manufactured goods imported from Europe.

Of the many mercantile cosmographies installed in Amazonia, the rubber boom of the late nineteenth and early twentieth centuries produced the most significant territorial effects. The Amazon River Basin was the exclusive worldwide site of extraction of high-quality rubber, thereby creating a biophysical monopoly on this highly valued commodity. The rubber boom mobilized thousands of people to extract it; enslaved indigenous peoples throughout the region; gave birth to the *caboclo* rubber tapper as a distinct social group; reconstituted Amazonian trade networks; swelled the Amazonian port cities of Iquitos, Manaus, and Belém with migrants; and generated fabulous fortunes among a small elite. While the trade in rubber greatly expanded the extractive export model that had been functioning in Amazonia throughout the past two centuries, the ecological differences between the harvesting of *seringa* from *H. brasiliensis* and *caucho* from *C. elastica* created different territorial patterns in the two regions.

In the Lower Amazon and throughout Brazil, the rubber barons controlled large, relatively fixed *seringais* from which rubber could regularly be extracted, while in the Upper Amazon the harvesting of rubber by felling of trees caused a constant search for new stands to be exploited, making territorial control of the areas less permanent. In both cases, however, the rubber barons did not own these areas in the strictly capitalist sense, nor did they maintain capitalist wage relations with those who collected the rubber. Thus, by the beginning of the twentieth century, after four centuries of European invasions, the main economic activity of the Amazon Basin had not consolidated into a clearly demarcated private property system, as had occurred in other parts of the continent. Amazonian territories were still vague and would continue to be contested throughout the twentieth century. Indeed, after four centuries of different frontier waves, these lands would continue to generate new frontiers.

With the establishment of the Brazilian Empire in 1822 and the independence of the Andean Spanish colonies in 1822–24 came new relations between the newly created imperial and republican governments and the Amazonian indigenous peoples and their lands. National cosmographies, which introduced notions of sovereign control over territory by nation-states, began to be applied to Amazonian lands. Disputes erupted between governments over their international Amazonian borders because of their great distance from the nations' capitals, the presence of indigenous peoples with nonnational claims to territory, and the general absence of geographical information about these areas. These disputes placed Amazonia at the heart of the process of nation building for each of the nation-states with Amazonian lands.

These political disputes were often linked with economic ones, as can be seen in the nationalist territorial dimensions of the rubber boom. Border disputes between countries erupted in spite of the fact that the rubber trade was essentially an international process whereby the rubber was extracted from Amazonia and exported directly to international markets with very little participation by national governments, except in the collection of export tariffs. In Brazil, the rubber boom represented the last phase of that country's expansionary effort to control a greater part of Amazonia and led to a consolidation of their current borders. The 1895 "Contestado" war between Brazil and France over lands between the Araguari and Oiapoque Rivers in northern Amapá was decided in Brazil's favor in 1900, and the current northern international border with French Guiana was established after more than two centuries of squabbling. Three years later, tensions between Bolivia and Brazil sparked armed conflicts that were settled in the Treaty of Petrópolis of 1903, in which Bolivia ceded Acre to Brazil in return for a cash payment and the construction of selected infrastructure. Treaties with Ecuador in 1904, Colombia in 1905, and Venezuela in 1907 settled differences with those countries and gave Brazil its present territorial dimensions (Tambs 1974).

From the national territorial perspective of Ecuador, on the other hand, the rubber boom was disastrous. Ecuador formally ceded land to Brazil, land over which it had no effective control, and the rapid expansion of Colombian and Peruvian rubber traders into lands formally claimed by Ecuador led to the loss of effective Ecuadorian control over them, a situation that later translated into a loss of formal control. In 1916 Ecuador ceded a large swath of land along the Putumayo River to Colombia (which six years later ceded it to Peru), and in 1942, after the disastrous war with Peru, they lost control of the entire central and eastern portions of their Oriente, lands that Peruvian interests had occupied during the rubber boom.

The ability of one nation-state to expand its territorial control in Amazonia and the penchant of another for diminishing this control are directly related to the interest that these two national governments placed in these Amazonian lands. The will of the Brazilian government to control these lands was expressed just thirteen years after Brazil became independent, with its quelling of the Cabanagem rebellion. Shortly afterward, in 1850, Brazil split the Amazonian province of Pará in two to create the province of Amazonas, in an effort to facilitate administrative control over its Amazonia. In contrast, the Ecuadorian government let its Oriente languish in neglect throughout the nineteenth century; it became of interest to political leaders only with the first petroleum concessions of 1921. Just a year earlier, the government had established two Amazonian provinces and begun to exercise minimal administrative control of the area.

Early explorations for petroleum heralded efforts at industrial extraction of resources in Amazonia during the second half of the twentieth century. By 1949, however, Ecuador had once again lapsed into pessimism and become disinterested in its Oriente when nearly thirty years of petroleum explorations had failed to find deposits, provoking President Galo Plaza to call the Oriente a myth. This contrasts starkly with Brazil, where President Getúlio Vargas, just nine years earlier in Manaus, had announced another conquest of Amazonia and embellished it in terms of creating a new civilization. New government-sponsored social and health programs and the installation of an industrial manganese-mining complex in the heart of Amapá represented important steps toward implanting a modern developmentalist cycle in this tropical biome.

To sum up, the repeated, centuries-long superimposition of distinct cosmographies installed by distinct social actors who established territories tied to historical epochs was a key result of numerous regional frontiers. The long history of historical frontiers radically changed indigenous peoples and their cosmographies through processes of conflict, interpenetration, and accommodation, yet five centuries of superimpositions have not completely eliminated these peoples nor their claims to Amazonian homelands. Many indigenous societies were decimated or exterminated, but many others survived.

Emerging from this process was a set of territories that differed markedly from the relatively autarkic indigenous societies with symbiotic relationships with neighboring societies; the new territories had hybrid characteristics that incorporated elements of other cosmographies. Mission cosmographies of diverse Catholic orders, which waxed and waned over a two-century period, left their distinctive mark on indigenous peoples in the form of radically altered settlement patterns and the tumultuous process of depopulation, coupled with widespread ethnic, racial, and linguistic mixing. Mercantile cosmographies, which over the centuries had been installed in connection with particular resources, also provoked powerful changes in the constitution of new social groups and the territorial claims made on the frontiers they created. Trade with distant markets, often of worldwide scope, became a mainstay of numerous Amazonian societies, although the degree of market articulation and interaction varied greatly from society to society.

This long and diverse process of historical frontiers resulted in the establishment of what can be considered the homelands of the indigenous and *caboclo* peoples of the Aguarico and Jari Regions, respectively. These groups, whether dating from pre-Columbian times or emerging from the ethnocide/ethnogenesis process in the colonial era, will be referred to as Amazonian traditional peoples based on several characteristics.[19] Historically, these peoples have roots in Amazonia: They were born there, have ancestors from the region, have a long history of occupation there, and identify with this region as their homeland. Ecologically, the forms of biophysical adaptation of indigenous and *caboclo* peoples are based on intimate knowledge of Amazonian ecosystems and are finely honed to match its natural cycles, providing long-term sustainability. Territorially, these peoples have developed collective forms of access to and use of geographical space, which places their territorial claims outside the market realm of private property; the claims of the traditional peoples are founded on collective rights, prior presence, and effective occupation. A type of territoriality that Almeida (1989) calls "common lands" was constructed around collective forms of use and access to land and resources outside the sphere of market relations. The delimitation of these homelands tends to be "socially recognized, even by their neighbors" (163). In this sense, these homelands are social territories and represent a unique type of control that is not readily classified as either private or public.

The effective occupation of these lands by these traditional peoples provides yet another set of important claims to their territories. Throughout the history of Amazonia, the actual possession and continual use of a geographical area have been a key means of justifying control over large parcels of land. Yet these claims house unresolved issues stemming from the ethnogenesis process on historical frontiers, which blurs the boundaries of who is and who is not aboriginal and makes it difficult to determine whose historical claims to a homeland are the most legitimate. In the Aguarico Region, the historical claims to territory must be differentiated among four indigenous groups. The small Siona, Secoya, and Cofán populations view themselves as the legitimate aboriginal inhabitants of the Aguarico River Basin, which was subsequently invaded by an expansive, colonizing, demographic movement of Quichuas, while the Quichuas appeal to their common identity as indigenous peoples with aboriginal rights.

In the Jari Region, the situation is different but no less complex. The local *caboclo* population has biological and cultural ties to earlier indigenous and *tapuio* peoples. These ties are difficult to trace, given the enormous degree of mixing over the centuries. Since the late eighteenth century, racial mixing has added a black component stemming from contingents of escaped black slaves and the *quilombos* that were established in Amapá. Their specific claims to the land in this region, however, date back to the beginning of the twentieth century, when their direct *caboclo* ancestors permanently settled the area and established their *colocações* while performing extractivist work for José Júlio de Andrade. Throughout the remainder of the twentieth century, this region experienced constant migratory flows of Amazonian *caboclos,* most of whom were moving between the Jari Region and the nearby Delta Islands Region.

The notion of traditional homelands clashed with national cosmographies installed in these regions starting in the early nineteenth century with the emergence of nation-states. The consolidation of these nation-states was founded on the establishment of national homelands (*patrias*) housing a single "national" people and claiming exclusive territorial rights based on the concept of sovereignty. The existence of other homelands based on tribal, kinship, ethnic, ecological, or first possession criteria was left unresolved, generating a new set of territorial questions. How do traditional peoples' homelands fit into the notion of national homelands? What happens when the former are dissected by the latter? How many types of homelands exist in Amazonia?

By the mid-twentieth century, the approximate closing date for this chapter on historical frontiers, the claims to territory made by traditional peoples were not legally recognized by their respective national governments. In Ecuador, the legal modality of communal titles for indigenous peoples came into existence in 1937, but these titles were given to separate *communities* and not ethnic *societies*. Furthermore, this modality was primarily applied to indigenous communities in the Andean highlands and would begin to be used (and in an extremely limited form) for Amazonian groups only in the 1960s. The formal recognition of *indigenous nationalities* (the term used in Ecuador today to refer to Indian societies) would have to wait until the 1980s (see CONAIE 1989).

In Brazil, the government made a distinction between squatters (*posseiros*), who claimed land rights grounded in historic occupation and use but only in rare cases possessed formal individual land titles, and "wild forest peoples" (*silvícolas,* later changed to "Indians" in the 1988 Brazilian Constitution), who were wards of the state and under the control of the Indian Protection Service (SPI) and, after this agency was extinguished, the National Indian Foundation (FUNAI).[20] By the mid-twentieth century, indigenous peoples resided along the northern fringe areas of the region, with the heart of the area being occupied by extractivist *caboclo* populations. In most cases, the *caboclos* still lived under the control of local *patrões* and their territorial rights were not formally recognized by the government.

CHAPTER TWO

Taming the Jungle

Development Cosmographies in Amazonia,
1945–1995

During the first half of the twentieth century, a gestating development ideology was giving signals as to how it would deal with the immense Amazonian watershed, which seemed to evade the growing path of planned, rational "progress." By the 1920s, voices were being raised about the need to once again conquer the Amazon. As incredible as it may seem, more than four hundred years after Yáñez Pinzón took the first indigenous captives at the mouth of the Amazon and after centuries of wars, conquests, colonization, migrations, fortune building, and the like, Amazonia still needed to be conquered!

Presumably, the new conquest would be different. The historian Nash confidently affirmed that the "weapon with which to attack the Amazon is . . . modern collectivism armed with the keen-cutting weapons of science. . . . I envisage the conquest of the Amazon . . . [in which] every inch gained will be consolidated by an army of agriculturalists, herdsmen, and mechanics" (1926, 390–91). Two decades later another North American, the engineer and geographer Hanson argued forcefully for the creation of a "new frontier" in the Amazon, led by "men and women who want to make new homes for themselves by carving a new civilization out of the wilderness" (1944, 5). This, according to Hanson, would be best done with "white settlers," though he admitted that it would most likely be achieved "at first with Latin American settlers who are more adaptable than Europeans and North Americans in that they do not demand as high a standard of living" (69).

By the 1950s the discourse of conquest had infiltrated Latin American technicians and political leaders. In *The Conquest of Amazonia,* the Brazilian Carneiro urged that Belém "should serve as a trampoline from which to penetrate and ultimately occupy the vast unknown territory that lies to its west" (1956, 39). By the 1960s this discourse had taken on a strong nationalist tinge, as "the settlement of Amazonia has become

our most preeminent challenge that should agitate the national consciousness, fill responsible men with passion, and even provoke insom-
nia among our government leaders" (Rabelo 1968, 89).[1]

In Brazil, the process of implementing major infrastructural works
began during the Kubitschek administration (1956–60) with the construction of the Belém-Brasília highway, the first road connecting Brazilian Amazonia with the rest of the country. In 1966 the state-run Superin-
tendency for the Development of the Amazon (SUDAM) was created and
began financing the development of immense cattle ranches. During the
seventies two National Integration Plans (PIN I and PIN II) opened up
major new roads in the jungle and promoted its massive colonization. By
the eighties, the state's development interests had shifted to mining with
the construction of the Grande Carajás Mining Complex in Pará and the
announcement of the *Calha Norte* (North Corridor) national security
program.

In Ecuador, major Amazonian development programs began in the
sixties with exploration for petroleum and subsequent building of roads
and pipelines. Agricultural colonization programs in Ecuadorian Amazonia were also initiated in the sixties and greatly expanded during the
seventies. By the eighties, this expansive drive included the development of several large African palm plantations and a major wave of industrial logging.

Enclave Territories

The establishment of a massive tree plantation and wood pulp factory in
the Jari Region in Brazil and of the petroleum industry in the Aguarico
Region in Ecuador began in the late 1960s and radically transformed the
existing indigenous and *caboclo* territories. Regional frontiers that had
been opened and closed in the past would be reopened with the arrival of
new social actors, who installed development cosmographies, introduced new technologies and markets into Amazonia, and created new
types of territories. These two large-scale development projects established *enclave territories* and represent a particular territorial result of the
implementation of development cosmographies. The concept of enclave
comes from political geography, where it refers to "discontinuous territories of states which are located within the territory of other states"
(Melamid 1968, 60).

Economic enclaves, such as foreign mining operations (silver, copper, tin) and agricultural plantations (bananas, sugar, coffee), are productive enterprises with their administrative headquarters in one country and their physical production process in another. Enclave territories have direct ties to groups or institutions located outside the host country or geographical region. Thus, while economic enclaves are insulated from their direct territorial neighbors, they are linked to larger entities beyond these neighbors. By cutting across different geographical regions and articulating them within a particular structure, economic enclaves can simultaneously function at local, regional, national, and international levels.

Enclave territories require a relatively large territorial base of operations and depend upon exclusive control of extensive areas of land within another country or geographical region (e.g., mines, plantations, ports). Late-twentieth-century large-scale development projects are a unique, historical incarnation of development cosmographies that require direct state intervention and major infusions of international capital. Their location in isolated areas "facilitates the extension of power of the corporation: the establishment of a *controlled territory* that obeys the logic of the production of the project" (Ribeiro 1987, 12). This also allows the enclave to control access to the area, an important element in the control of any territory.

Furthermore, Amazonia offers the distinct advantage of "appropriating large portions of space. This possibility is facilitated by its territorial expanse, its low population density and its weak social organizations which are not capable of resisting this new appropriation" (Becker 1989, 11). To the degree that national governments are involved in this process, rather than just foreign governments or transnational corporations, the establishment of an enclave in Amazonia implies a particular relation of power over this region based upon relations of "internal colonialism" in which "colonial relations become internalized" within a country (Chaloult 1978, 36). Whitten's analysis of Ecuadorian Amazonia has shown that "processes of internal colonialism . . . provide differential and unequal technological and administrative advantage to the dominant cultural sector, to the escalating disadvantage of other sectors" (Whitten 1976, 277).

The extractive nature of these enterprises is another important dimension of enclave territories in Amazonia. Large-scale development projects continue a centuries-long history of extraction geared to meet the demands of ever-changing international markets (see Bunker 1985). The territorial dimension enters not only through the location of resources but in the way that they represent "islands of syntropy" (Altvater 1993), that is, sites of concentrated energetic order. To prosper within the world economic system structured by the ever-changing demands of the world market, one imports syntropy and exports entropy. Amazonia, for its part, has long been a site of the export of syntropy and the import of entropy, with often devastating results to its economy and environment, as the cases of gold and petroleum extraction clearly attest.

The industrial nature of these enterprises was wholly new to the region and represented a radical break with all of the previous forms of tropical forest adaptation in terms of both the scale and the effects of operations. With industrial extraction and production, major infrastructure works are built, which facilitate the arrival of large populations. Some of these workers are directly recruited by the project and enter the territorial realm of the enclave, while others migrate on their own accord in search of work, do not have direct access to the enclave, and are forced to create their own migrant territories.

The Jari Project: A Wood Pulp and Mining Enclave

On 24 March 1967, U.S. billionaire Daniel Keith Ludwig (1897–1992) bought an enormous tract of land in Brazilian Amazonia, where he would establish what would become one of the most polemical development projects in the history of Amazonia. Ludwig was a reclusive, enigmatic, self-made man who at the time was one of the richest men in the world. He had begun to accumulate his fortune in the thirties with the purchase and remodeling of several ships, an enterprise that had culminated in his pioneering development of the petroleum supertanker during the forties and fifties. By the sixties he was one of the world's leading shipping magnates and had expanded his empire to include a modern shipyard in Japan, a salt production plant in Mexico, a cattle ranch in Venezuela, an oil refinery in Panama, hotels and casinos in Mexico and the Bahamas, coal mines in the United States and Australia, iron ore mines in Australia and Brazil, agricultural plantations in Panama, Paraguay, and Honduras, and real estate scattered throughout the world (Sautchuk et al. 1979, 19–27; Silveira 1980, 17–30; Lins 1991, 126). Ludwig, as an individual, maintained controlling interests over most of these enterprises, giving him personal decision-making authority over any aspect of their operations, an authority that aides claim he used frequently and impetuously. It was precisely this style that he would bring to the Jari Project.

In the 1960s Ludwig correctly surmised that the demand for paper would grow rapidly over the coming decades, thus guaranteeing rising prices for this commodity and for related products such as wood pulp. This economic foresight motivated him to seek a venue where he could develop a tree plantation, a wood pulp mill, and a paper factory. He needed an area of land (and a country) that united several characteristics: tropical climate; abundant, inexpensive land; cheap labor; direct shipping access to the sea; and a stable government willing to dole out tax breaks and fiscal incentives. Ludwig was brought to Brazil by Roberto Campos, then national finance minister (and formerly ambassador to the United States, where he first met Ludwig) and an avid promoter of multinational investments in Brazil, and Augusto Trajano de Azevedo Antunes, a Brazilian mining magnate who, through his association with Bethlehem Steel in a manganese mining operation in Serra do Navio, Amapá, "turned what had been a minor mining company into the biggest mineral-based empire in Brazil" (Evans 1979, 112; see also Silveira 1980, 107; Pinto 1986, 10; Arruda 1978, 15).

After several months of negotiations, in March 1967, Ludwig bought the three Portuguese-controlled firms operating in the Jari Region under the name of his Brazilian-registered firm Entrerios Comércio e Administração Ltda.,[2] which was a holding company for his wholly owned Universe Tankship Inc. Ludwig paid $3 million in cash and agreed to pay an additional $1.7 million during the following three years. The principal activity of the Portuguese firms had been the extraction and processing of Brazil nuts. During his first years in Jari, Ludwig continued the Brazil nut operations but, after a series of subcontracting disputes and harvesting shortfalls, he abandoned all collection and processing of Brazil nuts in 1975. After all, Ludwig did not come to Brazil for its nuts; instead, he sought to transform the jungle through the creation of modern industrial enterprises using the most advanced technologies.

The centerpiece of this economic endeavor was to be a large tree plantation that would furnish raw material for a wood pulp (cellulose) plant to be built by the time the first round of planted trees was ready for harvesting. As Ludwig himself put it, "I always wanted to plant trees like rows of corn" (quoted in McIntyre 1980, 701). Beginning in 1968, the melina (*Gmelina arborea*) tree, a species native to southeast Asia but whose seeds were airshipped in from stands in Africa, began to be planted on a massive scale. This rapid-growth species, however, did not adapt well to the sandy soils of Jari and, to make matters worse, was attacked by a fungus, which further inhibited its productivity. These problems led to the first plantings of pine in 1973, which were followed by the first plantings of eucalyptus in 1979. By 1980, the Jari Project had cleared and planted 106,142 hectares of land, with the melina species occupying 67 percent of these plantings (Lins 1991, 146–51). These homogeneous plantings were ingeniously called *reforestation* by the company,[3] a term that hides the fact that all of these lands had first to be *deforested* of their native, Amazonian species before being planted with industrially useful, homogeneous ones.

A year after the purchase of the land, the company discovered a vast kaolin deposit,[4] the largest in the world, and soon afterward began to extract this product in a large open-pit mine, process it in a factory constructed in the Jari industrial park located at Munguba, and export it to paper factories in various parts of the world. Another of Ludwig's grandiose ideas was to plant rice over a 14,000-hectare area of Amazonian marshlands in São Raimundo, where—through the use of imported, genetically improved strains; aerial planting, fertilization, and pesticide spraying; the installation of an advanced system of dikes, canals, and pumps that would permit at least two harvests per year; and combine harvesting machinery—he hoped to produce as much as 140,000 tons of rice per year. Throughout its decade-long existence, this project was plagued with problems, including soil toxicity, insect plagues, rice diseases, weed invasions, technical failures, and labor problems (Fearnside and Rankin 1979, 610; 1983, 1149–51). At the height of its operation in the late 1970s, only 3,500 hectares were under cultivation, and production never exceeded 32,000 tons annually, less than a quarter of the projected goal (Kupfer 1981, 26).

Other extensive Amazon River marshland areas were used by the Jari Project to graze water buffalo, while beef cattle were raised in upland areas. By the early 1980s, seven thousand head of water buffalo and three thousand head of beef cattle were being raised, most of which were used to feed the thousands of workers of the various economic endeavors of the Jari Project (Fearnside and Rankin 1985, 127).

The Jari Project gained an added dimension with the arrival in 1978 of twin factories—a wood pulp mill and a wood-fueled power plant—which had been built in Ludwig's Japanese shipyards at a cost of $319 million and towed by barges 25,000 kilometers through the Pacific, Indian, and Atlantic Oceans and up the Amazon and Jari Rivers to Jari's Munguba port, where they were anchored and assembled for operation. Production began a year later, with the first wood pulp exports made from wood harvested on the Jari tree plantation (McIntyre 1980; Sautchuk et al. 1979, 41). A sawmill, fed by the trees felled to create the plantations, produced cut lumber and the wood necessary to run the power plant, which generated electricity for the pulp mill.[5]

All of these activities transformed the Jari Project into a major industrial complex and created a multifaceted, territorial enclave that will be analyzed here according to connections that it maintained (1) with the world outside Brazil, (2) with the rest of Brazil, and (3) within the enclave itself. The Jari Project's connections with the world outside Brazil were based on two interrelated sets of networks: sectorial networks tied to the paper (wood pulp and kaolin), timber, cattle, and rice industries and financial networks that formed Ludwig's corporate empire. Each of Ludwig's Jari operations was structured according to the specifications and demands of the worldwide industries of which it was a small part, but it was their union as part of the unique Ludwig fortune that personalized the Jari Project and tied it most closely into the world economy. The Jari Project partially replicated the Ludwig structure of enterprises scattered throughout the globe. The fractal nature of this replication can be seen in the contingent, unpredictable paths that it took because of forces present at this scale of reproduction, especially those biophysical conditions of the Jari Region that complicated the project's productive plans and the political forces in Brazil during its development/national security era, which diverted its development plans. Only when these factors are taken into account can Ludwig's monumental failure in the Jari Project be explained, given that virtually all of the other endeavors throughout his life had been economically profitable.

Another set of connections involves direct commodity flows between the Jari Project and the world at large. During Ludwig's reign over the Jari Project, numerous pieces of equipment—airplanes, tractors, automobiles, water pumps, chain saws, and so forth—were imported directly into the project without the payment of import taxes, a process that culminated in the direct importation of two complete factories built in and shipped from Ludwig's shipyard in Japan. This flow of goods was contrary to the Brazilian "law of similarities," which stipulated that an item could not be imported into the country if a similar, nationally produced item was available. In spite of vociferous criticism by Brazilian industrialists, Ludwig was able to circumvent this law when he gained the explicit authorization of the ruling generals, using the argument that, while some of the items needed for the factories were manufactured in Brazil, entire floatable factories were not currently being built in the country (Sautchuk et al. 1979, 71–72).

Another important concession that Ludwig received from the military government was the elimination of current restrictions on the exportation in bulk of goods from the Jari Project by ships flying foreign flags (in this case Ludwig's own ships). This permitted Ludwig to export wood pulp, kaolin, and rice in his own ships directly from Jari's Munguba port to different parts of the world without any supervision by Brazilian authorities (Pinto 1986, 29). These and other concessions were justified by the top generals of the dictatorship, who considered the Jari Project "to be of pressing interest to national development" (Garrido 1980, 85). The Jari Project was also connected to world opinion through a series of glowing reports in the U.S. press about the visionary development endeavor that Ludwig was implementing in the wilds of the Brazilian jungle. *National Geographic,* for example, published a feature article that heaped awestruck praise upon "the biggest one-man private-development project on earth" (McIntyre 1980, 694).

The physical connections between the Jari Project and the rest of Brazil were not nearly as fluid as those with the rest of the world, while the social connections were marked by numerous confrontations, accusations, and misunderstandings. During the Ludwig phase of its operation, the Jari Project was not connected to the rest of the country by road, with access being limited to planes and boats owned and operated by the company. Getting in and out of the enclave required the tacit authorization of company officials, since one needed to gain permission to use these company-owned vehicles. The main demographic flows into the region from other parts of Brazil were labor recruitment drives operated by private firms (*empreiteiras*) subcontracted and supervised by the Jari Project. This limited the number and type of people who entered the area; in the long term, however, the Jari Project had difficulty controlling people after they arrived. In the short term, workers were placed under strict control through the use of a locally based police force and private jails established by the company (Martins 1981, 57–65).

The reclusion of the enclave was also evident in the eruption of a meningitis outbreak in January 1974, which was kept secret not only from the rest of the nation, but also from the workers themselves. After intensive measures, which included the shipment of vaccines directly from New York (once again showing the fluidity of the Jari enclave/world connections), the outbreak was finally quelled, although the number of deaths from this disease was never publicly revealed. This incident demonstrates that the reclusion of the enclave was not complete, since the disease itself was brought to the Jari Region by a worker who had been recruited from the state of Maranhão (Pinto 1986, 95–96).

The hermetic nature of the Jari enclave can also be seen in the "discoveries" that Brazilian journalists regularly made concerning the project. One such discovery came during the visit of ruling Brazilian General Médici in March 1973, which gave the Brazilian press corps its first opportunity to report firsthand from the area. During this visit, workers staged a protest over their miserable working conditions. Although the protest was squelched before it could reach Médici, it caught the interest of the press corps. As reporter Marcos Gomes wrote, "To the bad luck of Jari, the press discovered . . . the deplorable conditions of life and work of the five thousand *peões* (low-paid workers) who were employed in deforestation work, without having any formal ties to the Company" (quoted in Loureiro 1992, 147). This created the first of several national scandals involving the Jari Project and led to a follow-up visit by the ministers of labor and the interior and the establishment of a "Provisional Worker's Card Applicable in Amazonia" (Martins 1981, 60–62).

Another press discovery came in 1981, when *Fortune,* a prestigious U.S. business magazine, ran a cover story chronicling in detail the economic difficulties faced by Ludwig's Jari Project (Kinkead 1981), revealing facts of which few Brazilians were aware (Kupfer 1981, 24). The Brazilian press lacked access to the Jari Project, and Ludwig refused to give interviews and ordered on-site directors not to speak to the press about company matters. Indeed, poor press relations within Brazil had long marked the Jari Project and were only aggravated by gruff responses from Ludwig. To a reporter who asked, "What do you have to say to the Brazilian people?" Ludwig replied, "I don't have anything to say to the

Brazilian people. I don't have anything to say to anyone. I don't give interviews to the press. You can go to hell. I'm busy" (quoted in Arruda 1978, 20).

The administrative arm of the Brazilian government also lacked a presence in the Jari Project. By 1979 Jari's Monte Dourado headquarters was the largest town within the Almeirim municipality of the state of Pará, but neither the municipal nor the state government had any representation there (Sautchuk et al. 1979, 72).[6] The relationship with the municipality of Mazagão, located in the Federal Territory of Amapá, where the other part of the Jari Project was situated, was marked by tension. Mazagão gained very little tax revenue from the Jari Project, since most of its productive operations, its headquarters, and its port and industrial sector were located across the Jari River in the state of Pará. Furthermore, Mazagão received the brunt of the social demands created by the poor populations housed on the left bank of the Jari River in Amapá.

The connections between the Jari Project and the ruling generals of Brazil experienced a dramatic transformation over the seventeen years that Ludwig owned the enterprise. Ludwig had direct access to and unqualified support from General Castello Branco, the first of the generals to rule Brazil (1964–67) after the 1964 military coup. It was he who said, "Come to our country, Mr. Ludwig. Today, Brazil is a secure country" (quoted in Arruda 1978, 15). This support was continued by Generals Costa e Silva (1967–69) and Médici (1969–74), but began to wane under the rule of General Geisel (1974–79). By the late 1970s, a strong nationalist trend had taken hold of the nation, affecting both the dictatorship and its leftist opposition. General Figueiredo, the last of the ruling generals (1979–84), would consummate this trend, in which the land controlled by the Jari Project would be an important site of contention.

Internally, the Jari Project functioned as a self-contained enclave controlled by the company that had built, owned, and maintained it. During the Ludwig years, control depended upon Ludwig himself, who visited the area three or four times a year. He would give out a series of directives, authorize major capital investments, and, often, change directors. In the seventeen years of Ludwig's ownership, the Jari Project had sixteen different directors (Lins 1991). The town of Monte Dourado, on a high bluff overlooking the Jari River, was built in its entirety by the company. The housing there is organized into divisions that reflect the hierarchical social structure of work relations: one section has complete homes with garages and is designated for top management; a second has duplexes used by engineers, teachers, and other technical staff; and a third has dormitories where other permanent workers bunk. Temporary workers and unskilled labor do not have access to company housing and must fend for themselves in the riverside shantytowns of Beiradão and Beiradinho across the river from Monte Dourado and Munguba, respectively.

Monte Dourado is a complete company town that for years was totally owned and operated by the company. A supermarket, hospital, church, two clubs, two schools, several restaurants, and a jail were all built by the company, and access to some of these facilities was limited by status within the company: one club was for management and professional staff, the other for workers; one school had a Brazilian curriculum, the other an international one with instruction in English; the restaurants were accessed according to status, with the quality of food varying correspondingly. The company also built and maintained basic infrastructure in Monte Dourado, such as streets and sidewalks, running water, a sewage system, garbage collection, telephone lines, and spraying to control mosquitoes. Other housing sites within the enclave include Planalto and São Miguel, two *silvi-vilas* (forest towns) that have a population of approximately two thousand people each and were constructed to house forestry workers near the tree plantations; a small residential area next to the port and industrial park of Munguba; and a town in São Raimundo near the rice project, which functioned for a few years and was subsequently abandoned.

While transportation between the project and the rest of Brazil was minimal, within the enclave transportation exploded as thousands of kilometers of new roads were built, hundreds of vehicles were imported, a railroad line was constructed, an airport was established, and a modern port facility was built. The 4,000 kilometers of primary roads, together with another 7,000 kilometers of secondary roads and logging access trails, facilitated the movement of both logs and people within all parts of the enclave. The 68-kilometer railroad connected the port of Munguba with two different areas of tree plantations. In spite of this extensive internal transport network, an all-weather road connection to the municipal seat of Almeirim was not completed until the 1980s, and the construction of a shorter route is being resisted by the company for fear that it will promote invasions of its property by municipal residents.

Eucalyptus logs and rail line near the Jari cellulose plant, Munguba, 1995

Of all the scandals and polemics that have surrounded the Jari Project in its checkered history, none has been as important as the issue of control of land and the precise territoriality of the project. Over the past century in the Jari Region, land has been bought and sold on the open market, ostensibly placing it within the realm of private property and the rights that go with it. Yet the way in which this private property has been acquired and transferred has created serious problems in establishing with any degree of certainty the specific parcels of land being marketed and controlled. Among the factors that have complicated this process are the concentration of land titles by a single holder, the confusion of the land titling process, the strategic importance of the area, and the question of national sovereign control over the region as a whole.

The question of the concentration of land by a single property holder dates back to the era of José Júlio de Andrade and his "ownership" of more than three million hectares. José Júlio secured most of this land through purchases from the municipality of Almeirim, yet for years he was the person who ruled over that very municipality, calling into serious question the validity of the sale of land to an individual who is at the same time the person in charge of managing the lands being sold. When one also considers the political power that he wielded as a senator and the economic power he had as boss of a prosperous extractive Brazil nut estate, the legitimacy of these purchases are, at the least, questionable. This enormous tract of land was sold in 1948 to the Portuguese firm Empresa de Comércio e Navegação Jari Ltda., which nineteen years later sold it to Ludwig.

In addition to the issue of the legitimacy of these massive land sales, there is the question of the contiguity and compactness of the land being transferred. Ludwig claimed that he bought contiguous parcels of land that are compacted in a single block with no empty spaces between them, thereby avoiding the existence of a so-called checkerboard pattern. To judge the validity of this claim, one must analyze the titling process, which over the past one hundred years has been highly confused for several reasons. First, many of the titles overlap either partially or wholly, producing situations in which two people can claim legal title to the same plot of land. Second, many titles are extremely vague in the way that the limits of the land are described. This vagueness is compounded by references in some of the titles to markers that are no longer in existence (e.g., a ranch house, a fence) or to geographical features that have changed over time (e.g., the course of a river, a clump of trees). Finally, the confusion is increased by the existence of false titles that have been used over the years to invade and control lands via a process known in Brazil as *grilagem*.[7]

Ludwig apparently believed that he was purchasing over three million hectares. However, after floating several figures during the early years of operation, the Jari Project finally claimed formal ownership of 1,632,121 hectares. In calculating this figure, the Jari Project used the concept of "natural limits," whereby it claimed continuous and compact ownership of all land between the Paru River to the west and the mouth of the Cajari River to the east and from the Amazon River to the south to the *Paredão* (canyon wall) to the north. Studies made by INCRA, the federal agrarian reform agency, however, recognized legitimate title to only 600,000 to 1 million hectares, thereby creating a legal impasse (Pinto 1986, 117–37; Silveira 1980, 91–97; Sautchuk et al. 1979, 61–65).

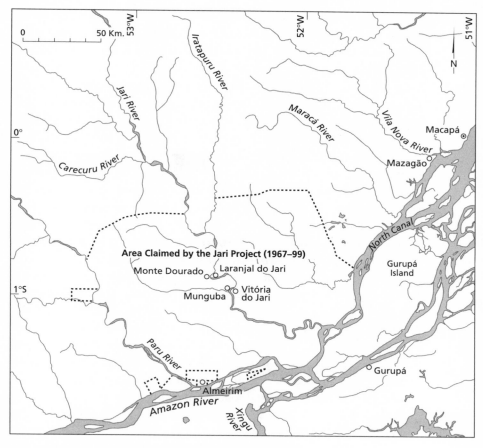

The Jari River Region: The Jari Project and Urban Development

This situation was further complicated by the plethora of land laws and decrees that had never been fully applied or interpreted to the changing land situations that Amazonia presented during its developmentalist phase. One of the most controversial of these laws, which had a direct bearing on the Jari Project, was law 5709 (11 November 1971), which limited the amount of land that foreigners could hold in Brazil. In 1974, three years after it was passed, this law was finally given its specifications (decree 74965, 26 November 1974), which stipulated in its fifth article: "The sum of rural areas owned by foreign persons or companies cannot exceed one-fourth of the total area of the municipality in which they are located" (quoted in Loureiro 1992, 148). The military leaders in power preferred to exempt the Jari Project from this norm, since it appealed to the even higher principle of the integration of Amazonia into national development.

The continuing national debate over the Jari Project raised a different set of principles that went to the heart of concerns that have traditionally been the domain of the armed forces: the strategic importance of this area and Brazil's sovereignty over it. The issue of the geopolitical role of Amazonia in world affairs grew each year because of the large number of strategic resources it contained, especially minerals, whose economic value was increasing in the world economy. A second strategic aspect of the Jari Project was its location near Brazil's northern international borders with Suriname and French Guiana. Brazilian military leaders have long maintained a special concern for the question of borders, particularly in Amazonia, where borders are difficult to demarcate.

The sovereignty of Brazil was thought by many to be placed in check by Ludwig's single-handed control over a vast tract of land that functioned as a hermetic territorial enclave. This theme caught hold of the congressional opposition to the military regime and of the left in general. Throughout the literature published about the Jari Project during this period, whether in the press, academic journals, or the Brazilian Congressional Record, one finds impassioned tirades against the Jari Project: as "a threat to national sovereignty which makes it impossible to guarantee that our natural resources will be used for the benefit of the people" (Arruda 1978, 22); as a threat to "the security of the nation, its people, its territory, and its riches" and as a "cultural cyst [where] all its inhabitants, regardless of their origin, should be required to adopt the Brazilian language, behaviors, and customs" (Silveira 1980, 112, 110); and as "an American invasion" where "the central issue lies in the threat represented by the control of this area by foreign capital" (Sautchuk et al. 1979, 65).

To add fuel to the fire, in 1979 the Brazilian press learned that five years earlier Ludwig, who did not have heirs, had willed the Jari Project to the Ludwig Institute for Cancer Research headquartered in Switzerland. No one knew what would happen to Ludwig's controlling interest in the institute, but it was feared that the Swiss government, which held a small interest in the institute, would indirectly gain control of a tract of Brazilian land, further compromising the nation's sovereignty.

This had repercussions in the Brazilian Congress, where a congressional subcommission was formed in 1979 to scrutinize the Jari Project. Under the leadership of Modesto da Silveira (1980, 61–114), the commission issued a scathing critique of the project which, after heated debate, was unanimously approved. Two years later, a full-scale congressional investigation was conducted on the topic of the internationalization of Amazonia, the phrase used in Brazilian political discourse to refer to multinational corporate penetration into Amazonia and the perceived threats that this posed to national sovereignty.

In 1980 the Executive Group of the Lower Amazon (GEBAM) was created to resolve the Jari Project dilemma along with other land and sovereignty issues of the region. GEBAM's mandate included the "coordination of actions to strengthen the presence of the Federal Government along the left bank of the Lower Amazon River, to monitor development and colonization projects in that region, and to propose measures geared to solve its land tenancy problems" (quoted in Almeida 1984, 57). This agency was under the direct supervision of the National Security Council and was headed by Admiral Gama e Silva, self-described as "an extreme nationalist, but not a xenophobe" (1987, 198), who represented the nationalist faction within the Brazilian armed forces that had begun to take hold of the upper reaches of the dictatorship during General Figueiredo's mandate. After an initial visit to the Jari Project, during which Gama e Silva refused to speak English in his discussions with the Jari management and declined all offers to use the project's vehicles, GEBAM drafted a report urging that the Jari Project fulfill to the letter of the law the requirement limiting the amount of land that a foreign person or firm could hold within a single municipality.

By this time, the constant annual operating losses the Jari Project had experienced since its inception were beginning to affect Ludwig's debt payment obligations, and his eighty-three years of age were also impinging upon his ability to manage the project with his usual vigor and interest. In addition, serious environmental problems, most notably the difficulties encountered with the melina tree and the rice project, raised doubts about the feasibility of the project as a whole. In March 1981, Ludwig floated the idea of selling the project to his old friend Azevedo Antunes, one of the very people who had encouraged him to invest in Brazil in the first place. The pace of negotiations accelerated among three sets of social actors: Ludwig and the Jari Project management, a consortium of Brazilian industrialists headed by Azevedo Antunes, and representatives of the military government. This led to the so-called nationalization of the Jari Project when the military government invited CAEMI, a consortium of twenty-three nationally owned firms, to buy the project from Ludwig while using the offer of massive government loans and other guarantees to entice the industrialists to accept. This solution was preferred by the military. From their point of view, "the important point was to not have any more foreigners in the region. The definition of the size of the land controlled by Jari, now without Ludwig, was no longer an explosive issue, and could be dealt with later with more leisure" (Pinto 1986, 192).

By January 1982 the details of the sale had been completed as Ludwig sold his interests in the project (except for the rice project, which was sold two years later) to the CAEMI consortium. Ludwig lost a good deal of money on the whole process, but since he had no heirs and had always viewed his business dealings as a gamble, he could write it off as simply one of the bets on which he lost.[8] The Antunes Group put up 40 percent of the private capital used in the purchase, including control of the profitable kaolin mine, while the other twenty-two firms invested the remaining 60 percent. Yet again Antunes used his strategic position as a broker between multinational firms, Brazilian industrialists, and the Brazilian government to advance his personal fortune, showing that "Antunes needs the multinationals as a group, but they are dependent upon him as well" (Evans 1979, 158). In this transaction, private capital represented less than a third of the total amount paid, since two state-owned banks, the Bank of Brazil and the National Development Bank (BNDES), put up the remaining two-thirds of the capital, making this a unique deal in which the Jari Project was *privatized* with predominantly *state* capital, all in the name of *nationalization.*

The new owners set up separate companies to run the tree farm and wood pulp mill (Companhia Florestal Monte Dourado) and to operate the kaolin mine and processing plant (Caulim da Amazônia S/A). In 1984 the Brazilian owners bought Ludwig's rice project, his last stake in the area, but had no more luck with it than he had. By the late 1980s this ill-fated project had been completely deactivated; it was eventually sold to a financial group with plans to turn it into a tourist resort, though these plans were never implemented. During this time refractory bauxite, used in the manufacture of aluminum sulfate and for the lining of industrial furnaces, was found within the domain of the Jari Project. By the early 1990s extraction, calcination, and export of this resource was fully operational and was placed under the management of a third company (Mineração Santa Lucrécia).

By the early 1980s, environmental concerns were beginning to be voiced about the Jari Project. The pioneering reports by Fearnside and Rankin (1979, 1982, 1983, 1985) were the first to propose that the Jari Project should (and could) be evaluated in terms of its environmental sustainability. In all of the debates up to this time, no one had questioned the feasibility of turning heterogeneous, native Amazonian tropical forests into an immense homogeneous tree plantation, nor had anyone envisioned the environmental effects that might be caused in the long term.[9] The Fearnside and Rankin studies over a ten-year period were important because they analyzed from a biological viewpoint the problems and possible negative influences of each of the economic activities of the Jari Project—tree plantations, industrial mining, cattle ranching, rice irrigation—which had thus far been evaluated only in economic terms by both Ludwig and the new Brazilian owners. Their warnings that "long-term problems are likely to include soil degradation from erosion and soil compaction, and decline of nutrient stocks relative to newly cleared areas" (Fearnside and Rankin 1985, 129; see also Fearnside 1988) would be heeded in a systematic way only by new owners with the formation of a separate Environmental Division in 1991. By this time the Jari Project was responding as much to worldwide concern over the destruction of the Amazon rain forest as to specific environmental problems. Indeed, this department functioned simultaneously as the environmental watchdog of the economic enterprise and as the company's primary public relations division, since by then most criticisms of the Jari Project were related to environmental issues.

The territorial assumptions maintained by the Jari Project over the years have varied little between international and national ownership. Both relied upon the capitalist principle of absolute control over the land subject to change only through the mechanisms of buying and selling on the market. The national, private owners claimed legal ownership over the same contiguous, compact 1,632,121 hectares that had been claimed by Ludwig, land claims that had been vociferously contested by the Brazilian government. By this time, however, the issue of the control of land had greatly dissipated. Within the nation as a whole, the Jari

Project had virtually disappeared from view, since the perceived crucial issue of sovereignty had seemingly been resolved. The nationalist-tinged sovereignty issue was used by Brazilian industrialists (who were directly induced to do so by the military regime) to gain control of this vast tract of land, with a significant infusion of public monies, without having to change their privatizing mentality.

The lack of interest in questioning the new Jari ownership's claims was also reflected within GEBAM, which ostensibly had been created to settle the land claims but did not deal with the issue during the remaining years of its existence. After the sale of the Jari Project, GEBAM concentrated its efforts on mineral exploration in the area, which by the early 1980s had captured the imagination of Brazil's military rulers and development planners as the most profitable use of Amazonia. GEBAM's President Gama e Silva, in referring to the Lower Amazon Basin, stated afterward: "It became clear that the best use of that area was in minerals, or better yet, in industrial mining" (1987, 198). With the end of the dictatorship in 1985 and the resumption of civilian control over the Brazilian government, GEBAM was decommissioned in 1986.

The territorial claims made by the Jari Project in all of its incarnations covered both surface and subsurface rights, allowing for its multiple uses as a tree plantation, a cattle ranch, a mining site, a port, and an industrial zone. When these varied economic activities are combined, the desire to assert control over a large, compacted parcel of land makes sense, since this facilitates constant expansions of the homogeneous tree plantations and cattle grazing and because the specific location of mineral reserves is unknown. This capitalist, all-inclusive viewpoint worked contrary to the claims of the *caboclos* who had lived in the area over the past century and practiced Brazil nut extraction under the dominance of José Júlio, the Portuguese firm, or Ludwig's Jari Project (until 1975), while at the same time maintaining small plots of land under cultivation and hunting and fishing in the area.

None of the bosses and owners of the various Jari enterprises recognized the land rights of the *caboclos*. Their *colocações* were located in this region, and they claimed control over them through the Brazilian law of possession, which granted them rights to the land because of their continuous physical occupation of the land. These possession rights were a constant source of conflict, which was never given its due by the national press or by the government, both of which were more concerned with the issues of sovereignty and geopolitics. Meanwhile, both the traditional *caboclo* inhabitants of the area and the Jari Project were being assaulted by a third force—people coming into the area in search of work. Though the entry of these people was strictly controlled for years through exclusive access by company-owned boats and firms subcontracted to recruit workers, once their temporary jobs had been completed many workers chose to stay. Most of these people lived in the riverside shantytowns of Beiradão and Beiradinho, which will be analyzed later in this chapter, but others decided to stake out rural plots on lands that belonged either to the Jari Project or to the traditional *caboclo* inhabitants, depending upon one's point of view. From the squatters' point of view, these lands belonged to no one and were ripe for the taking.

In summary, the social, economic, and environmental effects of the Jari Project, which began in 1967, greatly restructured the Jari Region. The industrial nature of the interventions, which included the introduction of numerous high-energy technologies, altered the biophysical environment in a variety of ways. The major environmental impact stemmed from the clearing of more than 100,000 hectares of heterogeneous, native rain forest and its conversion into homogeneous tree plantations in a process euphemistically called reforestation by the company. The social effects were equally acute, as the population of the Jari Region soared from approximately two thousand people in the mid-1960s—mostly extractivist *caboclos*—to over sixty thousand people just three decades later. The story of this growth will be told within the scope of the migrant territories that were established in the Jari Region.

Petroecuador: A Petroleum Enclave

After the multiple deceptions of the 1940s—loss of large tracts of Amazonia to Peru followed by the pullout of oil companies without having found oil—the 1950s was a decade of rising nationalism in Ecuador, buttressed by an emergent developmentalist discourse based upon the reigning notions of progress and modernization. In 1960 the revival of interest in Amazonia by Ecuadorian political leaders was further stimulated by President Velasco Ibarra's official pronouncement of his country's unilateral nullification of the Rio de Janeiro Protocol of 1942 amid great nationalist bombast. In 1964 new petroleum exploration concessions, encompassing 1,431,000 hectares of Amazonian lands, were granted to a consortium comprising the Texaco and Gulf Oil companies. When oil spurted out from Lago Agrio well 1, on 29 March 1967, in what was then the Napo Province, the oil age finally arrived in Ecuadorian Amazonia. During the succeeding five years, the construction of the 500-kilometer trans-Ecuadorian oil pipeline—stretching from the Amazonian lowlands up and over two Andean mountain ranges before descending to the Pacific Coast port of Esmeraldas—culminated in Ecuador's first oil exports in August 1972 (Vega 1980, 91–92).

In February of that same year, just months before the oil began flowing, Army General Rodríguez Lara engineered a coup d'état, and the armed forces gained control of the state apparatus, initiating seven years of military rule. Rodríguez Lara represented the nationalist, developmentalist faction of the Ecuadorian armed forces and began implementing his "revolutionary nationalist" program, which sought to "achieve national integration and sovereignty; to improve the living conditions of all Ecuadorians, especially the poorest sectors; and to stimulate economic growth through a more rational use of resources and territory" (Isaacs 1993, 38).

This program of "authoritarian modernization" included the gradual nationalization of the oil industry (58), starting with the creation of the Ecuadorian State Petroleum Corporation (CEPE) in 1972, and the reassertion of national ownership of all petroleum deposits in the country.[10] Between 1973 and 1976, Ecuador's oil income nearly quadrupled, and petroleum rapidly became the staple of yet another export-led economic cycle of boom and bust, which has characterized the economic history of the country for the entire twentieth century. With the completion of a modern state-owned oil refinery near the coastal city of Esmeraldas in 1976, the Ecuadorian state dominated all sectors of oil development in the country. The nationalization of the oil industry was backed by an upsurge in nationalist feeling that caught hold of Ecuadorians from the right, center, and left of the political spectrum, creating an implicit consensus around the concept of national development during the 1970s. This ideology was reinforced with Ecuador's entry into OPEC in 1973, a move followed by the naming of Ecuadorian Minister of Natural Resources General Jarrín Ampudia as OPEC's rotating president in 1974.

In January 1976, the authoritarian, national security faction of the armed forces executed a bloodless coup and established a military triumvirate of hard-line generals who promptly imposed policies modeled on a national security state, including the promulgation of a National Security Law in August of that same year. The Amazonian oil fields were declared a national security zone, providing a new role for the armed forces, which were now charged with defending the nation's most important strategic resource against either internal or foreign subversion. The seven years of military dictatorship were of a double "oil and debt boom" (Jacome 1992), in which the military leaders engaged in an unprecedented spending spree, sometimes applying this money to infrastructural and other development projects and at other times squandering it on expensive weapons systems. The military called elections in 1979 and, with the election of Jaime Roldos as president, turned control of the state to civilians. With this move, the armed forces showed opportunistic foresight as they "intervened on the eve of an oil boom and withdrew to the barracks before the economic crisis of the 1980s struck" (Isaacs 1993, 64).

In 1982, as the international debt crisis began to affect the Ecuadorian economy, signaling the beginning of the so-called lost decade in Latin American economies, the government of President Oswaldo Hurtado opened up the oil industry to foreign investments. With the election of León Febres Cordero to the Ecuadorian presidency in 1984, an entire set of neoliberal policies began to be implemented in the economy, including an intensive effort to entice foreign oil firms to (re)enter Ecuadorian Amazonia to conduct oil explorations using their advanced seismic and drilling technologies. In 1985, the first of seven rounds of international bidding held over a decade awarded exploration rights to select 200,000-square-kilometer oil concessions.[11]

These expansive moves were temporarily waylaid by a devastating earthquake in March 1987. The epicenter was in the Reventador volcano along the eastern slope of the Andes, and the quake shut down the trans-Ecuadorian pipeline and the road connecting the northern Oriente with Quito for several months. The administration of President Rodrigo Borja, which came to power in 1988, transformed the CEPE-Texaco consortium into the wholly state-owned company of Petroecuador, which subsequently took complete control of the trans-Ecuadorian pipeline and of all of the consortium's oil production activities. The Amazonian province of Sucumbíos was created in 1989 out of the northern portion of the Napo province to shore up administrative control of the nation's principal oil-producing region.[12]

By the early 1990s, domestic oil consumption accounted for over half of total national production and was increasing at an accelerating rate, thereby reducing the amount of oil available for export. A 1991 report by Luis Román, then president of Petroecuador, projected that by 2005 the country would consume all of its national production and by 2020 all of the nation's oil reserves would be depleted (Román 1991). Sixto Durán Ballén, elected to the presidency in 1992, implemented a new wave of neoliberal reforms and in 1993 withdrew Ecuador from OPEC so that it could export oil above the limits established by the cartel, a move criticized by Jarrín (1994, 100), one-time president of OPEC, as being "against the true national interest." Nonetheless, by 1995, in spite of a decade of oil exploration by foreign firms and two waves of neoliberal reforms, 95 percent of the nation's total oil production came from Petroecuador, showing the continued dominance of the state sector in the oil industry.

The petroleum industry in Ecuadorian Amazonia was centered in the northeast corner of the country, just south of the international border with Colombia, in the Amazonian lowland portion of the Aguarico River Basin, lands occupied by small groups of Cofán, Siona, Secoya, Tetete, and Quichua peoples. Since the oil industry was expanding in the name of national development and hailed as being beneficial to all Ecuadorians (supposedly, all Ecuadorians wanted development), the national government simply ignored the existence of indigenous peoples' homelands and did not formally recognize their historically based territorial rights. The occupation of indigenous lands by the oil industry was considered to be, rather than encroachment, a type of manifest destiny, this time launched under the banner of development, which granted the nation the "right" to colonize its "own" lands (Whitten 1976).

The Cofanes suffered directly from this occupation, since the first oil wells were located in the heart of their homeland, just a few kilometers from the Dureno community, an important center of Cofán activity. Oil wells were being installed, roads and pipelines were being built, settlers were arriving in hordes, and Cofán lands were being occupied. This greatly curtailed their freedom of movement and made hunting and fishing in the area increasingly difficult. For the first time in their history, the Cofanes came face to face with a new enemy, one that would grow as the years went by—water and soil contamination caused by oil production. Though some Cofanes found employment with the expansion of the oil industry onto their lands, this rarely compensated for the negative effects suffered by their communities. By the early 1980s the situation had grown so bad that a group of young Cofanes headed down the Aguarico River to get away from oil industry–induced disruptions in their lives and to embark upon a life based upon traditional means of subsistence. The group settled along the lower Aguarico River near the mouth of the Zábalo tributary, well away from oil activity, in an area where game and fish were still abundant.

The Quichua, in general, displayed a different initial response to the arrival of the oil companies. Ever since the first explorations in the 1920s and throughout the explorations of the 1930s and 1940s, Quichua men had been employed as guides and trailblazers for the seismic crews working in the area (Muratorio 1991). This same pattern was repeated in the sixties when seismic crews entered the area. Given the long history of relations with white invaders and their adaptability to new inputs (which gave rise to the Amazonian Quichua as an ethnic group), the arrival of the petroleum crews was seen as an opportunity for jobs and income by many local Quichua. This attitude changed over the following decade as Quichua communities suffered severe consequences of continual expansion of the oil industry onto their lands and acute contamination of the ecosystem.

The initial effects of the oil industry on the Siona-Secoya were centered in the community of San Pablo, located to the east of Shushufindi, a major petroleum-producing area and the site of a gas refinery. The predominantly Siona community of Puerto Bolívar, located along the Cuyabeno River, was out of the range of the first wave of petroleum development, leaving their hunting and fishing grounds intact. Though some Siona-Secoya did work for the oil companies in the early years, they, too, began to see gradual encroachment on their lands as the oil industry continued to grow and pollute. Meanwhile, another western Tukoanan group, the Tetetes, who by the 1960s had been reduced to a few survivors, was pushed into extinction when the oil companies expanded onto their lands.

The coming of the oil industry to the Aguarico Region reopened the Aguarico regional frontier through the arrival of social actors who constructed new territories. The petroleum industry united under one activity the actions of the geologists who do the seismic explorations, the engineers who drill the wells, the pipe fitters who construct the pipelines, the road crews who build roads, the workers who pump the oil, the truckers who transport materials, the accountants who keep the books, the managers who run the operation, and a host of support personnel. Another key social actor in the region was the military personnel who had been installed in this newly christened national security zone to defend the nation's oil.[13]

At a worldwide level, the Ecuadorian petroleum industry can be seen as part of a larger system that operates in numerous countries, utilizing people of diverse nationalities connected by the use of a particular realm of scientific knowledge tied to a specific set of technologies (e.g., seismic exploration, well drilling, oil and gas separation and refining, various transport technologies) toward the common goal of extracting oil. The relationship of the Ecuadorian Amazonian oil enclave to this worldwide oil structure is fractal, in that the social, productive, and territorial practices of the oil industry are reproduced in partial and unpredictable ways. Petroleum knowledge, technologies, and practices were often applied to Amazonia without the unique social and biophysical conditions of the tropical rain forest being taken into consideration. Amazonia just happened to be the place where oil was to be found, and the existent technology was brought to bear in the same way as in the Arabian desert or the Alaskan tundra. Nonetheless, since local, regional, and national factors almost always shape this enclave in historically and geographically unique ways, each regional enclave is a recognizable offshoot of the worldwide network but far from being a clone of it. A glimpse at the social organization and infrastructure of the Ecuadorian Amazonian oil enclave can show how it is unique while at the same time being related to larger structures.

The Petroamazonas compound, located next to the town of Lago Agrio, is one of several such petroleum compounds in the Oriente and houses the permanent work force of managers and technicians of Petroecuador. The large, fenced-in compound, which also houses an oil refinery and an airport, was originally built by Texaco in the late 1960s, and the lodging quarters still exude a Holiday Inn–style architecture reminiscent of the era. All buildings have electricity, internal plumbing, hot water, air conditioning, and satellite dish television, all luxuries in Amazonia today and even more so in the 1960s and 1970s. All services of the compound are free and include a large cafeteria serving three meals a day, laundry and maid service, tennis courts, a soccer field, and a recreation hall complete with a small movie theater, bowling alley, and bar.

The rest of the compound consists of neatly manicured lawns and gardens more reminiscent of a golf course than the dense tropical jungle that once grew on this land.

Access to and use of the compound depends upon one's rank within the oil industry hierarchy. Managerial staff and oil technicians, the upper echelon that makes up 25 percent of the total work force in the oil industry, have complete access to the compound. As a rule they live in Quito and are flown directly into the compound on a weekly basis by Petro-ecuador's air-taxi service. They work for seven straight days and then receive a week off. The next echelon includes workers subcontracted by specialty firms to do service work: cooks, waiters, maids, cleaning staff, groundskeepers, accountants, secretaries, chauffeurs, and maintenance staff. They work for fourteen straight days and then get a week off. Though much of this work is done within the compound, these workers are prohibited from living there. The lowest echelon is made up of day workers, occasional laborers, and other nonpermanent staff who work twenty-one straight days and receive a week off. This group has no access to the compound. Since the oil fields are spread over a wide area, the oil industry has a series of compounds dispersed throughout the region and therefore has avoided the establishment of a single, large company town in the Oriente, though Lago Agrio is by far the most important concentrated settlement in the area.

The territories that the oil industry constructed in Ecuadorian Amazonia were of a qualitatively different order than any that had come before. The use of advanced geological knowledge and seismic technologies afforded this new social actor access to parts of Amazonian lands never before explored, the extreme depths of its subsoil. Since petroleum and gas, both located in underground deposits, are the resources sought by the oil industry, the territorialities that the industry imposed upon this region were vertical as well as horizontal. The subterranean territorialities were based upon access to and control of the subsurface hydrocarbons that lie beneath a particular surface land area.[14]

These subterranean territories have taken the legal form of oil concessions, now standardized into 200,000-hectare rectangular blocks. The entire Oriente region (as well as the coastal off-shore region also believed to have petroleum deposits) has been subdivided into petroleum blocks, mapped out and then superimposed over the land, irrespective of who was currently occupying the surface. Since the Ecuadorian state claims

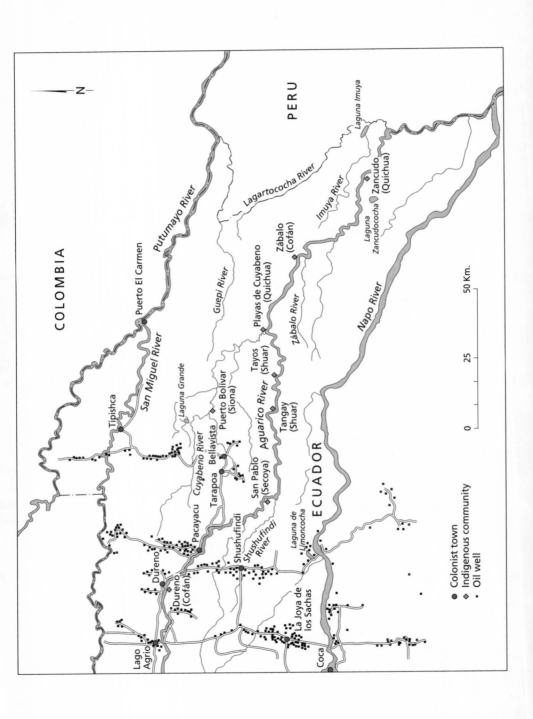

all subsurface rights in the country, it has granted itself the right to divvy up the subsoil and parcel out concessions to the highest bidder. This generates a unique type of overlapping territorialities, since one person or group can occupy or own the surface area while another can control the subsurface of the exact same area. A problem is created when an oil company seeks to gain access to these subsurface resources, since this can only be achieved from the surface.

The exploitation of subterranean territories requires surface access that inevitably impinges upon the surface territorialities of other peoples. Surface access to the petroleum deposits is manifested in a widely dispersed set of oil wells tied together by a single, complex network of pipelines and roads built, owned, and operated by the oil companies. These surface territories do not form a single, contiguous territory, as is common in other large-scale projects. Because of the dispersion of the well sites, many areas between them are not directly used by the oil industry, allowing these lands to be taken over by colonists. When mapping out the territorialities of the oil industry, one must simultaneously plot the subterranean territories represented by the petroleum blocks and the surface ones representing their effective control over and use of the former. This web of connections forms the internal structure of the petroleum enclave within the Aguarico Region, yet remains isolated from the rest of the jungle and its peoples by strict rules of access and use of petroleum facilities.

The connections between this enclave and the outside world, on the other hand, are extensive. First and foremost are the liquid connections provided by the pipelines. The oil pumped out of each well is piped to larger pipelines that eventually merge into a single pipeline. The trans-Ecuadorian pipeline pumps the crude out of the jungle and over the Andes to the Pacific Coast, where it is refined in a state-owned petroleum refinery and then shipped to various parts of the world. A similar pipeline system transports natural gas. Within Amazonia, gas is piped to the Shushufindi gas refinery for processing and then directly to Quito via a 300-kilometer gas line. Every pipeline is accompanied by a road built at the same time and used to service the pipeline and the wells and to transport products and people in and out of the area. This road network

The Aguarico River Region: Petroleum Development and Colonist and Indigenous Settlements *(opposite)*

Oil storage tanks with a colonist dwelling in the foreground, Tarapoa, 2000

is connected to a main highway that links the jungle with Quito. Roads and pipelines make up a single, isomorphic network of connections: they were built simultaneously and operate under the same logic of facilitating the flow of oil and gas out of the jungle.

Airstrips built and operated by the oil industry represent yet another source of connections between the petroleum enclave and the non-Amazonian world and are used to transport workers and equipment. Oil-company planes are able to go from Quito to Lago Agrio in just a half-hour, a trip that takes ten hours by bus. Finally, there are communications connections, which include satellite dish television, installed in the early 1970s long before it was commonplace, and direct telephone service. This telephone line is noteworthy, since the oil compounds have a direct line to Quito. If, however, one wants to call from the Petroamazonas compound in Lago Agrio to the town of Lago Agrio just 1 kilometer away, one must make the connection through Quito, 300 kilometers away. In most cases, the connections between the enclave and the outside world are far better and more frequent than those between the enclave and Amazonia.

The effects of the oil industry upon Ecuadorian Amazonia and the Ecuadorian economy have been enormous, though they are starkly different depending upon the level of analysis used to evaluate them. From a national viewpoint, the oil industry has greatly transformed the economy by infusing it with export income that has fostered the emergence of a middle class of technicians and technocrats, fueled a construction boom of modern high-rise office and apartment buildings in the nation's two largest urban centers, Guayaquil and Quito, and spurred the growth of the Ecuadorian state apparatus. The military also has greatly benefited from this boom through the law established during the dictatorship that granted them 30 percent of all state oil revenues, funds that have been used to buy arms and for personal enrichment. Oil-led economic growth has not been of a redistributive nature, however, and has tended to widen existing divisions within the country. This tendency was evident as early as 1977, when the Ecuadorian Catholic Church declared that "rapid economic growth due to the discovery of oil deposits has not yet benefited, in a egalitarian manner, all Ecuadorians; rather it has made the inequalities even greater, both in the countryside and the cities, as well as between geographical regions and, above all, social classes" (Conferencia Episcopal Ecuatoriana 1977).

Throughout the entire era of petroleum development, the Amazonian region, which generated this wealth, has suffered greatly. The arrival of thousands of poor migrants has created poverty zones where previously only jungle existed. The oil industry has been a notorious polluter and is responsible for hundreds of oil spills; by 1991 they totaled 16.8 million barrels of oil, a sum 50 percent greater than the oil spilled by the *Exxon Valdez* oil tanker in Alaska's Prince William Sound in 1989 (Kimerling 1991, 69). To these damages one must add unknown amounts of water, soil, and air contamination, deforestation, and enormous social effects, especially with regard to indigenous peoples. Finally, the level of consequences and the intensity of conflicts on this frontier have been greater than those on any previous regional frontier.

The achievement of economic growth in the nation's urban areas at the cost of negative social and environmental effects in the Amazonian region, where the oil is extracted, is typical of "development by pillage" (Little 1992), a common outcome of internal colonialism whereby certain sectors of the national society exploit other regions of the country. The territorial foundation of this exploitation is found in the establishment of enclaves that allow one area to be exploited while benefits are accrued in another region. That this national development came at the social and environmental expense of Amazonia was irrelevant to some and heroic to others. As early as 1980, the economist Vega would write: "Petroleum has allowed for the *true* conquest and colonization of *our* Oriental Region" (1980, 92, my emphasis). Once again, Amazonia was being conquered, this time supposedly for keeps and in the name of people who did not live there. The oil in the depths of Amazonian subsoil now belonged to the Ecuadorian nation, as represented by the Ecuadorian state, which as the long history of the country has shown, was rarely concerned about the Oriente and its peoples.

Several similarities between the enclave territories of the Jari and Aguarico Regions can now briefly be discussed. In the case of the Ecuadorian oil industry, one had public land with private concessions, while in the case of the Jari Project, one had private land with public concessions. In both cases, the complex intertwining of public (read *state*) and private interests is a hallmark of large-scale development projects in general (Ribeiro 1994). In the Ecuadorian situation, dispersed oil territories could be established because the state maintained control over all subsurface rights and could therefore establish surface territories wherever it wanted. In the case of the Jari Project, private land was at stake, increasing the need to maintain direct control over large, continuous parcels of land. Neither the national nor international owners of the Jari Project have been willing to cede an inch on the land issue. Finally, in both regions, the territorial rights of previous occupants were not just ignored, they were directly suppressed.

Although the initial launching of these two enterprises within five days of each other in March 1967 can generally be described as a chronological coincidence, it produced a series of similarities tied to their parallel development during the same moment of Latin American and world history. The nationalist sentiment that emerged within the development discourse and was promoted by military governments in both countries directly affected how both projects were handled and eventually nationalized. Both projects were fractal entities that jumped across numerous levels of social scale in irregular ways, though in both cases their articulation to world markets controlled by multinational corporations was essential to their functioning. Structural similarities can be noted between the company town of Monte Dourado and the oil industry compounds; both were planned, well-maintained, tightly controlled housing sites in the middle of the jungle with poor shantytowns on their outskirts.[15] The presence of U.S. corporations in both cases also produced architectural similarities, as seen in the sixties-style suburban motifs in these housing sites.

Petroamazonas Petroleum Compound, Lago Agrio

My colleague Gerardo and I gained access to the Petroamazonas Petroleum Compound to interview an ex–college classmate of his who was now working as an accountant with Petroecuador and who was responsible for the compound's equipment inventory. After discussing various topics related to the internal operation of the company, we moved on to the topic of its inventory. At this point, our informant told us that, when the fleet of cars and trucks of the company reaches a certain mileage, these cars are buried in the jungle and a new fleet is purchased. The same fate awaits broken computers and other damaged equipment. Noting our astonishment at this revelation, our informant offered an explanation for this seemingly irrational behavior: "The only thing the company is interested in is pumping oil. It doesn't want to be bothered with inventory problems."

Here is a case of enclave thinking in one of its more brazen forms. The fact that Ecuador as a nation, and particularly its Amazonian region, suffers from severe shortages in public transportation and education for which this equipment, regardless of its age or condition, could be useful, does not enter into this logic. An enclave doesn't want or seek connections with the country that surrounds it. The most important connections of the Ecuadorian oil enclave are with oil companies and buyers in other countries, and since these old pickup trucks and damaged computers are not useful to them, they are simply buried in the Ecuadorian jungle.

Migrant Territories

Internal (i.e., within country) migrations have been a hallmark of Latin American societies ever since the colonial era. Their scale and frequency,

however, increased dramatically after World War II and reached unprecedented proportions during the sixties and seventies. Most of these migrations stemmed from the burgeoning "rural exodus" experienced by Latin
American nations as they rapidly transformed themselves from pre-
dominately rural societies to urban ones (Wood and Wilson 1984, 143–
45). Peasants abandoned the countryside because of acute processes of
land parcelization (*minifundización*) and soil erosion; semifeudal, repres-
sive land tenure structures; high relative population pressure; stagnating
food supply; and lack of income-producing opportunities (Schuurman
1980, 106). Government programs designed to modernize agriculture,
principally through mechanization and the cultivation of cash crops,
together with policies geared to expand their nation's industrial sector,
also encouraged migration to urban centers.

This process was particularly strong in Brazil. In the twenty-year period of 1960–80 alone, 30 million Brazilians left the countryside for the
city (Torres 1991, 302), turning the urban centers of Rio de Janeiro and
São Paulo into two of the most populous megalopolies in the world. In
Ecuador, major urban migrations to the industrializing centers of Guayaquil and Quito began in the fifties and continued unabated during the
next forty years, creating urban problems of a magnitude never known
before in the country.

Not all of these migrants went to urban centers, however, for there
was a significant amount of rural-to-rural migration as peasants sought
new areas to settle where land was available and demographic pressures
were slight. Government leaders throughout Latin America encouraged
the creation of agricultural and industrial fronts on reopened regional
frontiers in Amazonia as part of a nation-building strategy geared to
integrate these marginal, forested tropical lands into the larger national
economy and to resolve some of the pressing agrarian and demographic
pressures faced by these national societies. Colonization programs, unplanned rural migrations to Amazonia, and the urbanization of the
jungle were understood by military leaders concerned with national security as a viable strategy for the creation of living borders. Under this
conception the people who lived along international Amazonian borders would have national identities that claimed allegiance to their respective national governments. Thus, the armed forces could count on
these colonists to claim this sparsely populated area as truly a part of the
national territory, a key concern of nation building, since "territory is at
the heart of national identity and cohesion" (Murphy 1990, 531).

The principal means of advancing agricultural fronts into Amazonia was through the mechanism of colonization in which peasant families would settle these lands and place them into immediate agricultural production. In this variant of frontier expansion, land becomes the main resource that Amazonia has to offer. The logic of colonization that guided national leaders contrasted Amazonia, which contained large parcels of so-called empty lands (i.e., not in agricultural production), with the intense land distribution pressures existing in other parts of the country. Perhaps the most succinct expression of this logic is to be found in Brazilian ruling General Médici's dictum of sending "people without land to the land without people." The mechanisms used to accomplish this varied between small-scale, directed and semidirected colonization programs and massive, unplanned colonization, with the latter supplying the greatest number of colonists in all of the Amazonian countries.

In Ecuador two agrarian reform and colonization laws were passed in 1964 and 1973 by military governments. Though the redistribution of land was one of the stated goals of both laws, they were essentially designed to eliminate the last vestiges of feudalism in the countryside, represented by the *huasipungo* system, through restructuring and modernization that would place agriculture firmly within capitalist relations of production (Velasco 1979). Agrarian reform in Ecuador was intimately tied to the promotion of colonization of forested lands, as expressed in the names of the laws—agrarian reform *and* colonization. In practice, however, "colonization no longer constituted a complementary policy to agrarian reform, but rather its substitute" (Trujillo and Ruiz 1982, 10). During the developmentalist epoch of Brazilian politics from the 1960s to the 1980s, massive colonization of Brazilian Amazonia, whether planned or unplanned, was facilitated by the opening of roads into the jungle from other parts of the country. Within a two-decade period (1955–75), three principal road corridors were built—the Belém-Brasilia highway, the Cuibá–Porto Velho highway, and the Transamazon highway—each of which brought thousands of settlers in search of plots of land that they could farm and call their own.

By pushing land-hungry peasants onto Amazonia, however, national leaders were not resolving the land concentration issue at the heart of the land reform issue, but rather deflecting it to another part of the country. The issue of justice, which was one of the driving forces behind the push for land reform, also was deflected, since large landowners would be left untouched, while highly vulnerable and economically marginal traditional Amazonian peoples would have their homelands invaded. The settlement of Amazonian lands by citizens of the national society was conceived as a safety valve that was supposed to relieve social pressures in other regions of the nation, pressures that were potential hotbeds of subversive resistance to the military regimes. The military reasoned that, "through colonization, politically dangerous sectors of the population can be neutralized," though in practice what often occurred was "nothing more than the spatial displacement of poverty within the country" (Chirif 1980, 189). These policies once again opened regional frontiers, provoking a new set of conflicts that rapidly turned the struggle for land into a national security issue (Almeida 1984).

These policies essentially precluded indigenous and *caboclo* Amazonian peoples as valid members of the national society, implying that they were somehow a threat to national sovereignty. The policies failed to recognize these peoples' claims to the lands they had historically occupied and explicitly encouraged the invasion of these lands in the name of some vague notion of territorial security. This philosophy pervaded the armed forces of all the Amazonian nations to widely varying degrees. In Brazil, Lima clearly expressed this sentiment when he argued that the "rapid peopling of non-Brazilian Amazonian areas, by the neighboring countries that possess them . . . could result in pressures on our borders. For this reason, the occupation of Amazonia constitutes a challenge to our generation that cannot be refused. The Government of President Médici has launched this patriotic battle and this very President has taken on the leadership of these actions" (1973, 54). In Ecuador, the takeover of Amazonian lands by Peru was a historical fact, rather than just a rhetorical argument, which gave even more urgency, within the Ecuadorian armed forces, to the notion of living borders. In this context, the colonization of Amazonian lands was seen as an issue of patriotism and territorial self-defense.

The policy of expanding the agricultural frontier was founded upon the capitalist principle of granting individual titles to the migrating farmers in what would represent a massive transfer of public lands to private control. The expansion of the agricultural frontier was part and parcel of a broader capitalist logic of private ownership of land and sought to bring new parcels of Amazonian land into the capitalist productive sphere. In practice, this policy was subverted by capitalist firms in other parts of the country, which accumulated large parcels of land in

Amazonia not for productive purposes but as a means to obtain large profits through state subsidies and land speculation. These firms directly benefited from the opening of roads and government investments in infrastructure as well as from colonization schemes because these things increased the value of their land holdings (Sawyer 1984, 186–90; Martins 1990, 251–54).

The industrialization of Amazonia, on the other hand, was founded upon the policy of installing large-scale development projects in rural areas, expanding the existing industrial sectors of urban areas, creating free trade zones, and building hydroelectric dams to provide the electric power needed for industrial development. All of these efforts required the movement of large numbers of people to Amazonia, where they would serve as a cheap labor force for these varied projects. In this variant of frontier expansion, jobs become the main resource that Amazonia had to offer. The creation of a stable work force required the concentration of large numbers of people in one place, which created the need to urbanize the jungle. As Becker points out, "The project of the integration of Amazonia was predicated upon urbanization as the logistical base of its settlement, justified by the necessity of offering attractive living conditions to the migrating population" (1989, 17).

None of these strategies or policies could have been implemented without the active participation of the migrants themselves, the key social actors in the creation of what are called here *migrant territories*. In many cases, the migrants were implementing personal or family adaptive strategies that led them to migrate from their previous homes into the unknown (to them) lands of Amazonia (see Moran 1981; Lisansky 1990). Given the limited options for poor peasants in Latin America due to their lack of wealth and political power, migration to another region of the country represents an alternative to fatalistically accepting their current undesirable living conditions. While the reasons for migrating are diverse, common factors cited by the migrants include the desire for material betterment and the effort to escape economic, political, or environmental hardships in their land of residence. At the same time they are often cognizant of their role in the development discourse, which places them at the center of national and military strategies. Implicitly or explicitly, migrants are carriers of a development cosmography founded upon beliefs in social progress, technological modernization, and integration into market forces.

The two cases of migrant territories analyzed in this section—Sucumbíos and Laranjal/Vitória do Jari—are both directly tied to the installation of large-scale development projects. The waves of improvisational migrations from other parts of the country were made possible by the new transportation and communication networks established by the development projects, though they produced rural colonization in one case (Aguarico Region) and urbanization in the other (Jari Region).[16] The enclave territories of Petroecuador and the Jari Project and the migrant territories they helped create represent two complementary modalities of a development cosmography based upon its differential appropriations by distinct social actors, since these migrations to Amazonia occurred within the broader context of national development programs and the nationalist developmentalist ideologies that were in full vigor during this period.

Sucumbíos: Improvisational Colonization

Throughout the twentieth century, acute land pressures in the Ecuadorian highlands fomented rural-to-rural migrations. In the 1930s and 1940s, the country experienced small-scale migrations to the southern Oriente areas of Morona Santiago and Zamora Chinchipe as people who went to extract gold and quinine eventually settled in the area (Brown et al. 1991, 11–12). In the 1950s the focus of colonization shifted to the Santo Domingo area along the western slope of the Andes, where migrants participated in the banana boom that increased national exports of this product from 13,881 tons in 1944 to 802,705 tons just fourteen years later (Martínez n.d., 90; see also Bromley 1980). By the 1960s the rural-to-rural migration had shifted back again to the Oriente, this time to the Puyo-Tena area, where the *naranjilla* (*Solanum quitoense*) fruit was the principal market crop (Casagrande et al. 1964, 290–303).

Starting in the early 1970s, the colonization of Ecuadorian Amazonia took on nationalistic and developmentalist tones during the Rodríguez Lara military government. Whitten narrates highlights of the five-hour speech that the general gave in the Oriente town of Puyo in 1972, at the beginning of his four-year regime, when he "urged poor colonists to work with IERAC to secure titles to land, loans from banks, and to clear away the jungle and plant such marketable crops as rice, cacao, corn, and grain, and obtain and care for cattle and swine. He promised that mod-

ern pesticides and defoliants would be made available through government programs of education aimed at conquest of the forest" (1976,
266).

This emphasis was linked to the building of transportation infrastructure in Amazonia, a process that was most advanced in the petroleum-
producing areas of the Aguarico Region, and it is not surprising that this
region experienced an explosion of improvisational colonization. The
road connecting Lago Agrio to Quito was completed in 1971, giving the
rest of the country modern land access (i.e., other than by foot or mule)
to this region for the first time, and the oil industry opened up an extensive network of roads within the area to build pipelines and gain access to
the wells. This new land access was promptly utilized by thousands of
colonists who were eager to lay claim to tracts of land where they could
farm and ranch. The resultant first wave of colonization in this area
lasted throughout the 1970s.

Roads are fundamentally important to the colonist enterprise because
they provide direct and easy access to the land and facilitate the marketing of crops. Colonist settlements, which take "the form of a rather hap-
hazard ribbon development along newly constructed roads" (Bromley
1980, 181), are intimately tied to the expansion of the oil industry into
the area such that the geographical areas occupied by both activities are
practically isomorphic. With the expansion of the oil industry eastward
from Lago Agrio into the newly created (1979) Cuyabeno Wildlife Production Reserve and onward to the San Miguel River Basin along the
Colombian border in the 1980s, a second wave of colonization occupied
these hitherto indigenous lands, which were the hunting and fishing
grounds of the Siona-Secoya and the Tetete.

The relationships between improvisational colonization and the oil
industry are not only geographical, but also function on an economic
level. While the oil industry imports all the technical workers it needs to
pump the oil and houses them in compounds, it also requires a large
number of low-paid day laborers to do a host of manual tasks, such as
cutting away forest underbrush, building fences, painting buildings,
cleaning up oil spills, hauling pipes and other materials, and maintaining roads. The colonists represent a ready-to-use work force already living in Amazonia and, as such, do not have to be fed or housed by the oil
industry. All of these factors mean that the salaries paid by the oil company can be kept low. In spite of low wages, the colonists readily accept

these jobs, since they generate much-needed cash income, especially in the first few years while their perennial crops come to maturity. As one young colonist put it, "I work for the [oil] company to earn my 'potatoes.' If I don't work, I don't eat."

The colonists who settled this area came in large measure from the Andean highlands, especially the Loja and Bolívar provinces, with a sizable minority coming from the coastal plains, principally from the Manabí and Los Ríos provinces. The Lojanos were by far the most numerous group of settlers to arrive through immigration, which was sparked by a severe drought suffered by Loja in the late 1960s together with a high degree of land parcelization and increasing soil erosion there. Access to large tracts of forested lands where rainfall was abundant proved to be enticing to these desperate peasants eking out a living on their dwindling plots. Similar processes of desertification in the coastal Manabí province also encouraged migrations to these rain-drenched lands. Colonists from the highland Bolívar province and the coastal Los Ríos province often cited brutal working conditions as one of the main reasons for their migration (Little 1992).

These empirical conditions alone are not sufficient to explain why these particular peasants decided to migrate while many of their neighbors, who suffered from similar conditions, chose to stay. To explain this, one needs to locate a specific set of attitudes toward life as characteristic of this social group. Casagrande et al. describe the Ecuadorian colonist as "an entrepreneur of sorts, and a rather independent one at that" (1964, 292). The colonist who sets out to settle a land unknown to him, establishes himself on a plot of land, and then sends for his family so that together they can set up a new life in the jungle exhibits a certain set of pioneer attitudes that play an important role in the decision to migrate.[17] These attitudes include an adventurous spirit, the willingness to take risks, a strong hope for a better material life, the desire to will land to one's children, and confidence in one's psychological and physical ability to adapt to new and difficult conditions. This combination of pressing material living conditions and a set of personal attitudes toward life is what spurs improvisational colonization.

Land is the principal resource sought by the colonist in his migration to the jungle. For the colonist, Amazonia does not represent a tropical jungle, nor a set of forest extractive products, nor a potential gold mine, but a place where land is available. And this land exists for agriculture, since that is the main function that the colonist has used to make a living.[18] The agriculture that these peasants had practiced in their place of origin was not strictly of a subsistence nature, but rather had strong ties to regional and national markets, thus placing them firmly within a cash-based market economy. Upon arriving in the jungle, colonists seek to establish market ties as soon as possible. Occasional work with the oil companies provides much-needed cash income, but this is at best an expedient; the goal remains to gain cash income from the agricultural production of the farm. And though subsistence crops are grown, the goal of the farm is to produce crops to be sold on the market.

This agricultural market emphasis, along with the minimization of subsistence concerns that requires an extensive knowledge of the tropical jungle ecosystem, represents an important environmental difference between the colonist and the indigenous populations of the area. This, of course, must be added to the enormous cultural and historical differences between these two groups. These differences also help explain why the colonist does not see himself as an invader of indigenous lands. From his agriculturally based market perspective, this land is essentially unused and exists in sufficient quantities to support Indians and colonists alike. Since colonists do not practice or understand the extensive environmental bases of indigenous adaptation, these are seen as inefficient, resulting in exaggeration of the amount of land needed by a small indigenous community to support itself. If a colonist family can support itself on a small farm, it is reasoned, then why can't the Indian do so as well? The colonists are reinforced in these beliefs by the government agencies that encourage colonization and by the oil industry, which seeks access to the hydrocarbon resources located under indigenous lands.

The first act of environmental appropriation made by the colonist after establishing his plot is to clear a parcel of the forest and begin to work the land. Forested land is considered to be unworked land of little value. Land gains value for the colonist only when it produces crops in an orderly and regular fashion. In this agricultural logic, deforested land is potentially productive land, and cutting down the forest is one of the major ways of increasing land value. Though some of the wood cut down is used to build the colonists' homes and other wood is sometimes sold, these uses represent nothing more than side benefits to the overall goal of farming cleared land. In most cases, the forest is cut down and burned on site so that planting can begin immediately.

At the scale of the family farm, the deforestation process is gradual, since the colonist clears a small plot to plant and tends to that plot. Only after that plot is in production will the clearing process begin again to expand the amount of land in production. At the microregional scale, however, deforestation is extensive and rapid, since thousands of individual colonists are simultaneously clearing small parcels of land. In areas where colonization has existed for twenty years, such as the Joya de los Sachas area near Shushufindi, total deforestation rates have reached as high as 66.4 percent of the original forested area. Between 1976 and 1987 the annual deforestation rate in the Aguarico Region was 2.63 percent, one of the highest in Latin America (Toro 1991).

The economic strategy of the first wave of colonists was to plant coffee, a perennial crop that takes three to five years to begin to produce, as the principal market link and a source of cash income. In the meantime, quick-producing crops such as bananas, corn, and manioc were planted and small farm animals were purchased and raised to provide for daily subsistence needs. Coffee has proved to be a problematic crop for several reasons. First, Amazonian soils and climate are not apt for the production of the higher quality Arabian coffee, so the lesser quality robusta coffee was planted, which generates far less income. Second, transportation is a constant problem, forcing colonists to sell their produce at the low prices offered by those who transport the coffee. Third, the coffee borer entered the region in the late 1980s and destroyed the harvest of many colonists. Finally, low international coffee prices during the late 1980s and early 1990s did not provide a high income for the colonists.

Given these problems, during the 1980s some colonists turned to the planting of rice as a market alternative to coffee. This option was adopted readily in the Tarapoa/Bellavista area because of its extensive swamplands, which allow rice to prosper. The introduction of cattle onto colonist farms often follows the consolidation of a crop production scheme. Cattle fetch consistently high market prices and are a highly liquid capital investment, which is important for the colonist. The environmental disadvantages of cattle raising are enormous, since cattle require extensive cleared lands and rapidly exhaust the soil (see Hecht 1985, 1993).

The territorial strategies of the colonists are founded upon the family farm, which is the mainstay of their livelihood. The actual appropriation of the land is structured according to a long colonist tradition. Upon arriving in the area, the colonist will either squat upon or purchase from a former squatter a 50-hectare tract of land. The layout of this tract of land is structured in relationship to the road of access to the area. These tracts are 250 meters wide along the road and have a depth of 2 kilometers, a shape that permits a large number of colonists to maintain prized access to the road. The tracts along the road are the first to be taken and form the first line of colonization. As more colonists arrive, new tracts are settled directly behind this first line and, since they take the same dimensions, extend from 2 kilometers to 4 kilometers from the road, forming a second line of colonization. This process continues as ever more colonists arrive. In the areas of earliest colonization in the Aguarico Region, up to eight lines (16 kilometers) of colonization have been made.

The first organizational strategy of the colonists is to form pre-cooperatives, a nonlegal entity that gathers together twenty to fifty farms with the principal objective of applying for legal titles to the land from the government land titling agency. Upon gaining titles, the pre-cooperative is transformed into a full-fledged cooperative and is registered as a legal entity under Ecuadorian law. The experience of cooperatives among Ecuadorian Amazonian colonists has shown them to be a weak mechanism for organizing production and credit. In many instances, upon gaining free title to the land, the cooperative rapidly falls apart, giving evidence to the claim that the key function of the pre-cooperative/cooperative structure is to secure land titles for individual members.

The importance to the colonist of individual land titles cannot be understated. Land titles grant legal recognition of the squatting enterprise, are a source of family security, provide needed collateral for bank loans, and can be sold if the colonist decides to abandon his farm or needs quick capital. Land titles also reaffirm the individual (or family) nature of the colonist enterprise. Though extended family social networks are used to inform family members of the existence of settlement opportunities and are relied upon during the actual process of settling the land for the first time, each nuclear family seeks its own tract of land and the title to it.

The emphasis on individual land titles precludes categorizing the cooperative as a *collective* territorial claim. Rather, the cooperative is a collective strategy used to consolidate *individual* territorial claims that are the object of personal adaptive strategies simultaneously adopted by numerous individuals. This lack of collective territorial claims of the cooperatives is seen in the almost universal refusal of colonists to accept collective title to the land through their cooperative, a modality that has been repeatedly suggested by various environmental groups. Collective titling does not permit the buying and selling of individual farms (or at least makes it extremely difficult), a key element in the entrepreneurial aspect of colonist migration. This aspect represents yet another distinction between colonist and indigenous groups living in the Aguarico Region.

Some colonists even specialize in the initial phase of opening up forested lands as they squat a tract of land, put it into production, sell the tract to newly arriving colonists, and then move on to squat another plot of land in an area just being opened to settlement. What is in fact being sold in this situation is not the land per se, since few colonists gain free title so quickly, but rather the "improvements" made on the tract, which often include the existence of a house (often nothing more than a hastily assembled one- or two-room shack), the amount of forest cleared, and the number of crops in production. These full-time squatters must be distinguished from land speculators who do not work the land at all, but exclusively dedicate themselves to the buying and selling of tracts of land in newly settled areas. Though colonists are aware that land speculators often exploit them through inflated prices, given their existential demand for tracts of land they accept their presence as a necessary evil. They prefer the existence of exploitive land speculation to areas where land is simply not available at all. In many cases, the colonist prefers to "buy" a farm rather than begin the squatting process from scratch, since this reduces the time necessary before the land can be put into production and begin generating income.

At a microregional level, the demographic settlement patterns of the colonists can be classified according to the concepts of entrepôt, frontier town, nucleated settlement, seminucleated settlement, and dispersed settlement (Casagrande et al. 1964). Lago Agrio serves the dual function of an entrepôt, which "provides the vital link between the area of colonization and the metropolitan area," and the frontier town, which "serves as the jumping off point for new colonists entering the area" (312). The town of Lago Agrio grew up around the Texaco-CEPE petroleum compound and oil refinery and quickly filled with people seeking to provide services to the oil workers. Since workers in the petroleum industry (as well as the soldiers stationed in Amazonia to defend the wells) tend to be predominantly male and either single or separated from their families while they are stationed in the Oriente, the off-work services that they seek helped create an unruly population center noted for its raucous bars and cabarets, its free-flowing contraband whisky, and its many prostitutes, who came from other parts of the country as well as from neighboring Colombia. Lago Agrio gradually became the hub of a new socioeconomic region growing up around the oil industry.[19] Nonetheless, two decades after its founding, it still suffered from a severe lack of basic services—potable water, schools, hospitals and clinics, paved streets, and a reliable source of electricity—even though it had grown to a population of just over ten thousand people. During the nineties the city installed several new infrastructural works, but in the same period its population mushroomed to more than twenty-eight thousand people and Lago Agrio remained sorely underequipped to handle this new influx.[20]

La Joya de los Sachas, Shushufindi, Dureno, Pacayacu, and Tarapoa each can be classified as a nucleated settlement that has "one or more small stores which provide for the minor needs of its colonists and those of the immediate vicinity," along with "a church, a school, and perhaps other municipal facilities" (Casagrande et al. 1964, 313). Seminucleated and dispersed settlements are scattered throughout the entire area, though they tend to be most prevalent in newly settled areas. All of these categories have been modified by the presence of the oil industry, as the settlements correspond not only to colonists' needs but also to those of the oil industry.

The main territorial implication of this phenomenon at a national level is the creation of ever-smaller political-administrative units within the state. The Ecuadorian government is divided into three distinct, nonautonomous political-administrative levels: province, canton, and parish. One of the principal means used by colonists in newly settled areas to increase their political power is to petition for the creation of new provinces, cantons, and parishes so as to gain greater local control over their internal affairs. This process is also a springboard for gaining access to economic and political resources offered by the national government and increases colonists' voting power within the governmental system.

In moving onto forested lands, the colonist needs political support. The colonist is poor, in most cases lacks formal education, is located in a hostile biophysical environment, needs credit, and seeks land titles. The lack of economic and political power makes colonists ripe for the implementation of clientelist political practices by politicians seeking to construct power bases of voters loyal to them. In return for such loyalty, the colonists gain a voice for their concerns in the governmental apparatus. The most important political resource they have is the vote, and this gains in strength in direct proportion to the demographic base that they have created in the area. The rapid colonization of a particular area represents an implicit political strategy by the colonists, since it increases their demographically based voting power. They claim and use these voting rights as citizens within a national body politic, rights carried with them from their place of migration.

In 1989 the province of Sucumbíos was created from the northern portion of the Napo province, since the colonist and petroleum populations had grown sufficiently to justify the establishment of a new province. While colonists considered this to be an important political victory, it was achieved only partially by their lobbying. The existence of the majority of the nation's oil reserves in its subsoil made the creation of a distinct oil province an important factor. While the national government was primarily looking after strategic interests, these coincided with the regional interests of the colonists, demonstrating yet another link between the development cosmographies of these two social actors. By the 1990s, however, this population was greatly dissatisfied because of the lack of national government attention to the province, and a series of provincewide protests erupted.

At a local level, this struggle is waged over the creation of new cantons and parishes. In the parish of Tarapoa, for example, the most important annual festival is not Christmas, nor Holy Week, nor national independence day, but the date of the creation of the Tarapoa parish in 1985. The creation of the parish promoted Tarapoa from a seminucleated settlement to a nucleated one and increased political power within the Lago Agrio canton and the province of Sucumbíos. The creation of ever-smaller political-administrative units gives the colonists closer contact with their political leaders and increases the possibility of local colonists gaining positions of power. This is seen in the election of Eliseo Azuero as prefect of Sucumbíos in 1992, the first locally born person to occupy the post. His mandate has been marked by a clear interest in the needs of the colonists, who are the most populous group in the province, far outnumbering both the indigenous population, which has been drastically reduced over the centuries, and the oil industry technicians and managers, most of whom reside permanently in Quito.

Soccer championship inauguration, Tarapoa Parish Day, Tarapoa, 1991

The existence of a national space of demographic movement is an important aspect of internal colonization. Over the decades, internal migratory movements have helped foster a decidedly national identity. When migrants moved into Amazonia, they created new regional social spaces as part of the larger national social space. Colonists who move within their own country are leaving behind a particular regional identity to enter an area with immigrants from all parts of the country. While some migrants tend to group together according to their province of origin, the broad mix of migrant origins makes this a limited, or at least temporary, aid. In the long run, it is their identity as Ecuadorians that becomes the lowest common denominator capable of grouping them all into one political identity. This identity is emblazoned in the consciousness of the colonists as they struggle for their rights. In interviews with colonists of the Aguarico Region, one phrase cropped up repeatedly when asked about their identity: "We are all Ecuadorians here."

This identity is therefore linked to the nationalist development ideology, which has been appropriated by the colonists as part of their personal adaptive strategies. The colonists in the Aguarico Region know that

they serve the function of creating living borders and express this sentiment in statements such as, "Before we colonists settled here, this land
wasn't Colombia, it wasn't Ecuador, it wasn't Peru. It wasn't anything."
In spite of the lack of recognition of indigenous land rights that this
expresses, it does reflect quite well the living borders strategy of the
military, a strategy that has been successful to the degree that these colonists express a clear identity as Ecuadorians. Many colonists have also
adopted the notion of expanding the agricultural frontier as one of the
services that they are providing to the nation (and to God, as one colonist from the town of Bellavista emphatically claimed: "God put this
land here to farm"). Finally, they express the development ideology in
local events. Dances, soccer championships, school meetings, and other
community events are often preceded by speeches by local officials and
politicians who invariably invoke developmentalist themes. As one local
colonist leader of the community of Tarapoa affirmed, "Tarapoa is developing! It may be at a snail's pace, but it is developing nonetheless."[21]

Laranjal and Vitória do Jari: Improvisational Urbanization

Brazilian Amazonia experienced not only large waves of rural-to-rural
migration, but also rural-to-urban migration that, during the 1980s and
1990s, became the predominant form of migration into this region.
While many of these migrants moved to already existing cities such as
Belém, Manaus, Santarém, or Macapá in search of work, others created
totally new towns and cities. A major impetus behind the creation of
towns and cities in Amazonia was the implementation of large-scale
development projects.[22] The emergence of the towns of Beiradão, formally known as Laranjal do Jari, and Beiradinho, formally known as
Vitória do Jari, in the Jari Region is a direct result of Ludwig's Jari Project
during the late 1960s and the 1970s. The creation of these two towns is
an expression of a development cosmography as it has been appropriated and implemented by thousands of poor migrants. However, these
towns have generated their own territorial dynamic, one that is markedly different from and increasingly in opposition to that of their pro-
genitor and benefactor, the Jari Project. By tracing the history of the
creation of these two towns, we can clarify these interrelated dimensions
and reveal how improvisational migration can give birth to urban centers where formerly only jungle existed.

The town of Laranjal do Jari, initially called Zona Franca (Free Zone), began in 1968 with a few scattered houses built on stilts over the flood-plain of the Jari River in typical *caboclo* style along the eastern side of the river in what was then the Federal Territory of Amapá. In 1971 the ad-ministration of Ludwig's Jari Project decided to raze this settlement, since these settlers were considered to be illegal squatters on company land over which the Jari Project claimed exclusive rights to the authori-zation and building of any houses. The Jari Project police force was sent across the river and demolished all the houses. The government of the Federal Territory of Amapá expressed its anger over and opposition to the destruction of the houses, located on land over which the territory claimed political jurisdiction. This began a series of disputes that would last for decades between the inhabitants of Beiradão and the Jari Project. In these and ensuing conflicts, the government of Amapá was one of the few defenders of the migrants to the area.

The early years of the 1970s brought about intense deforestation of native jungle as the Jari Project began massive planting of the melina tree. Though initially tractors and bulldozers were used to clear-cut the native jungle, this heavy machinery overly compacted the soil and obstructed the successful planting of the plantation species. The com-pany switched to manual deforestation by chain saws, which required the importing of thousands of temporary hired hands. Since the imme-diate area was only sparsely populated by *caboclos,* who were involved in their own extractive and agricultural activities, the company looked be-yond the Jari Region for a labor force willing to do the backbreaking work of deforestation for subsistence wages.

The state of Maranhão, which lies half in Amazonia and half in the northeast, is extremely poor. During the thirty-year period from 1960 to 1990, Maranhão "expelled" nearly one million workers (one-fifth of its total population) in search of jobs and decent wages (Sawyer 1993, 153–55). The Jari Project set up recruiting stations in several parts of Maranhão and began to import workers. These workers were brought to the area in company-owned boats and hired for three- to six-month stints of cutting down the forest, after which they were shipped back to Maranhão. This recruitment was not done directly by the company, but rather by a subcontracting firm set up by it, which rapidly gained notori-ety for its unscrupulous practices. The recruiters were known as *gatos* and had a reputation for abuse of the potential workers, who were promised good pay and excellent working conditions only to find, upon getting to Jari, that the labor situation was considerably worse than had been presented. Nonetheless, these men were desperately in need of work and income, and so they signed up in droves. At the peak of the deforestation effort, the Jari Project employed four thousand to five thousand temporary workers located at different sites.

The grouping of thousands of poor, young, and single (or temporarily separated) men in one place creates a ready market for two things: liquor and sex. It did not take long for word of this demand to spread, and once again people began settling along the floodplain of the east bank of the Jari River, just across from the headquarters of the Jari Project in Monte Dourado. Bars, cabarets, brothels, and commercial activities were established to serve the needs and desires of this captive, yet festive and horny, labor force. The new town gained the name of Beiradão (literally "big riverside settlement"). Its population increased as some of the workers, upon finishing their labor stints in the Jari Project, chose not to be shipped back. After all, they knew that the same poor conditions they had left in Maranhão would be waiting for them upon their return. Many settled in Beiradão with hopes of finding future employment in the company, while others staked out plots of land in other parts of the area with the intention of setting up small family farms. Beiradão emerged as a social enclave of Maranhenses in the midst of the Jari Region. This has been the source of a constant latent tension between those whose identity lies with the Amazonian area and its rivers and those who maintain a strong Maranhense identity. This tension is exacerbated by the common use of the negative stereotype of the Maranhense as an ignorant, culturally deprived person.

By 1977 Beiradão had a population of 4,866, equally divided among men and women. Among the economically active population, only 39 percent had formal employment, with 41 percent of this group employed in the Jari Project and another 41 percent engaged in agriculture. The majority of unemployed or subemployed people were forced to survive within the thriving informal economy, which had both licit and illicit sectors. Half of the adult population was illiterate or had not completed primary school (ASPLAN 1977, 44–56). The residents of Beiradão also suffered from a host of catastrophes, including the flooding of the town in 1974, a fire that ravished a large part of the town in the late seventies, and the death of four hundred people—many of them from

Beiradão or Monte Dourado—when a ship destined for the area sank on the Amazon River in 1981 (Lins 1991).[23] Beiradão continued its rapid growth and by the late 1990s housed a population of approximately twenty-five thousand people. Most of this growth spread over the floodplain, though by 1990 part of the town had settled on dry, upland areas.

The 1978 installation of the wood pulp and power plants at the port of Munguba, approximately 20 kilometers downstream from Monte Dourado on the western (Pará) side of the Jari River, gave impetus to the growth of another riverside settlement, called Beiradinho ("little riverside settlement"), also located on the eastern (Amapá) side of the river just across from Munguba. Beiradinho was also a type of "unwanted child" of the Jari Project, which tried to stop its growth. This time the company entered into negotiations with the government of the Federal Territory of Amapá, offering to donate a tract of dry upland and to build basic infrastructure for the town, but these two parties could not reach an agreement and Beiradinho grew in improvisational form along the riverside without the benefit of any external planning.

The settlement patterns of Beiradão and Beiradinho are founded upon the traditional *caboclo* architecture of wood structures built upon stilts to allow for the rise and fall of river waters. The construction of wooden piers and ladders permits water to be taken from the river, and washing is done over a slotted wooden sink that extends out from the edge of the house so that the used water falls to the ground or the river. A latrine is erected a short distance from the house, where human wastes are deposited directly into the earth. Trash, which traditionally was all organic material, is generally thrown in a pit located near the house, where it is eaten by pigs or wild animals or simply left to decompose.

An analysis of the architectural structures and settlement patterns of Beiradão shows how irregularities and undesirable effects emerge when these structures and patterns are reproduced at a larger social level of articulation within the same biophysical scale (i.e., a single watershed). This architecture has for centuries been adequate for *caboclos* living in isolated areas along riversides throughout Amazonia, but when twenty thousand people, densely packed together over a single floodplain, adopt this settlement pattern, numerous problems are created.[24] The building of a city on stilts has meant that access from house to house must be by elevated walkways. These boardwalks have become the streets of Beiradão. The direct discharge of human feces onto the floodplain (which during half the year is dry) in such a concentrated area causes serious hygiene problems, creates a breeding ground for flies and other insects, and imparts an unpleasant odor to the city. The high concentration of population makes malaria a serious problem during the dry season, when stagnant water is abundant. The daily throwing of trash onto this same floodplain greatly increases the problems of hygiene, insects, and stench. Much of this trash now consists of plastic, tin cans, and other non-biodegradable objects, making the town unsightly as well. Yet people continue to go to the river to bathe, to wash clothes, to swim, to clean fish, and to perform a host of other water-related activities. When this traditional mode of settlement, which was well adapted to the region, was reproduced in Beiradão on a much larger scale, it quickly became dysfunctional and created health hazards for the inhabitants.

Beiradão does have its enchantment. The narrow boardwalks and wooden houses could be considered quaint and picturesque, if one were disposed to ignore the carpet of trash below them, the stench of the place, and the poverty of the inhabitants. Also, the town has lots of vitality, stemming from its thriving trade and commercial activity during the day and its clubs, bars, dance halls, and billiard parlors, which come to life at night. This liveliness, however, produces hazards of its own, such as the cycle of violence that is the hallmark of a port area with an inordinate amount of bars, liquor stores, and brothels.[25] Another interesting aspect of Beiradão is the presence of numerous evangelical sects (dominated by the Assembly of God and Seventh Day Adventists) that have placed their churches in the midst of the red-light district. When one walks along the boardwalk at night, the sounds of disco music are interspersed with the wailing of preachers calling upon all sinners to repent.

Both Beiradão and Beiradinho can be characterized by the phenomenon of urbanization by shantytown, which gathers the poorest segments of a region together in concentrated settlements. On one hand, these shantytowns are the mirror image of company towns. While those who maintain steady employment with the Jari Project live in company housing located in Monte Dourado, Munguba, or the two *silvi-vilas,* the temporary and least-skilled workers must fend for themselves across the river in Beiradão and Beiradinho. The mere existence of these towns attracted many migrants who were looking for work and had heard that the Jari Project offered great possibilities. These people, though not recruited by the company and rarely employed by it, nonetheless created a pool of cheap labor that could be tapped when necessary. The arrival of these newcomers boosted the activities of the informal economy since, one way or another, they needed to survive in their adopted home. On the other hand, these shantytowns *cum* urban centers harbor some of the characteristics of frontier towns as described in the case of rural colonization in Ecuadorian Amazonia. Beiradão is a jumping off point for gold miners who pan, dig, and dredge for gold along the upper reaches of the Jari River. It is also the port of arrival for squatters looking for new lands to settle.

Though the emergence of these two towns is directly tied to the Jari Project, once in existence they rapidly entered into a dynamic of their own as urban centers with their own needs and interests, often in opposition to the Jari Project. The growth of Beiradão, for instance, has been spurred by many economic activities no longer directly tied to the Jari Project. First, Beiradão is the largest commercial center in the entire Lower Jari River Basin, which encompasses Monte Dourado, Munguba, Beiradinho, and numerous, small *caboclo* communities. Second, Beiradão is the main market and trading center for Brazil nuts harvested by extractivists throughout the area. Third, it is an important port for the lower Jari River through which flow commercial goods and raw materials not directly tied to the industrial operations of the Jari Project. As a port, Beiradão employs stevedores, warehouse workers, boat builders, mechanics, passenger service staff, and administrative personnel. Fourth, starting in the 1980s, Beiradão has temporarily housed and attended to the needs of gold miners en route to and from the upper Jari River, and it has several established gold-buying firms. Fifth, it has numerous municipal government jobs and many other government employees who work in the post office, the telephone company, schools, public transportation, and sanitation services. Sixth, economic activity revolving around the timber industry provides jobs in the felling of trees, in sawmills and lumberyards, and in the construction of houses and boardwalks.

Many of these economic activities depend upon demographic movement and economic growth, such that Beiradão represents an opposing tendency to that of the Jari Project enclave, where contacts with the outside world are strictly controlled. Beiradão is decidedly anti-enclave: it thrives upon contacts with the outside world and is constantly seeking more. This is to be expected of a port town, a commercial center, a town

The southern portion of Laranjal do Jari along the Jari River, 1995

with nightlife, a trading center, a frontier town, and a growing urban center. Beiradão has moved far beyond being a mere appendage to the Jari Project and is engaged in the larger process of converting the lower Jari River valley into an economic and demographic growth pole in Brazilian Amazonia, capable of offering the local population most of its commercial, cultural, social service, and entertainment needs. To achieve this, it must be open to the rest of the society. Herein lies one of the core reasons why the population of Beiradão was so interested in gaining a road connection to Macapá with the construction of state highway BR-156, a hotly disputed issue that will be analyzed in chapter 4.

The political strategy of the population of Beiradão focused upon the attainment of greater political power through the mechanism of voting. Demographic power plays a crucial role in this struggle, one that serves to encourage further immigration by people from outside the area. The underlying logic of this strategy is that, with more people present in the area, the voting power of the populace is increased and its political presence within the government is expanded. This strategy is directly tied to clientelist politics, in which politicians seek votes from the migrant population in return for favors or promises of infrastructural projects. An urban center established by migrants is invariably deficient in virtually all the basic services that come with full citizenship and a good quality of life: schools, roads, hospitals, telephones, sanitation services, electricity, potable water, sewage treatment, and the like. In such a situation, opportunistic politicians and migrant-originated populations exist in symbiotic relationship.

In this process of political formation, new identities have lessened the tensions between the newcomers, notably Maranhenses, and the local *caboclo* population, whose identity is decidedly Amazonian. As both groups struggle for political representation and citizenship rights, their common plight as marginal and powerless inhabitants of the same demographic area begins to build bonds of unity that tend to diminish previous allegiances to one's place of birth, bonds that are reinforced by the children of the migrants, whose birthplace is now the Jari Region. This new regionalist identity is part of a larger Brazilian one based upon one's membership in a national political community that grants a common set of citizenship rights.

The territorial strategy of these inhabitants is directly related to their demographic power and has focused upon the establishment of new political-administrative units by the government. The inhabitants ostensibly gain greater representation within the government, access to financial resources earmarked for each governmental administrative unit, and greater control over local affairs, since the decision-making bodies are located within the region. In Brazil, this process is carried out at state, municipal, and district levels. A major accomplishment of these efforts was the granting of statehood to the Federal Territory of Amapá in 1988. The historical neglect of the Amazonian federal territories created in the 1940s in Brazil has long been a source of public denouncements (see Lima 1970). By gaining statehood, Amapá made important financial and administrative gains in direct, local control over this isolated piece of land cut off from the rest of the country by the mouth of the Amazon River. State governors began to be elected rather than appointed, and federal financial resources available to states were freed up.

Statehood set in motion a parallel movement for the creation of new municipalities. The tactic here is for local leaders and statewide politicians to enlist the support of the rural populations so that they will then petition the state legislature for standing as a municipality. This process has proven to be fairly easy; from 1988 to 1994, the number of municipalities in Amapá jumped from five to sixteen, with nine more on the docket in the state legislature. The large surface area and low population of Amapá, which is heavily concentrated in Macapá, has resulted in the creation of geographically large municipalities with minuscule populations, some even less than five thousand inhabitants, placing them among the least populated municipalities in Brazil. The municipalization process is rampant with political opportunism, as populist political parties seek to create ever-smaller power bases that offer ample opportunities for nepotism and the buying of favors and that function as launching pads for politicians into the state and federal political arenas.

The Jari Region has been in the forefront of this municipalization process. When the Territory of Amapá was created in 1946, the municipality of Mazagão encompassed the entire southern and western portion of Amapá. With the installation of Ludwig's Jari Project in 1967 and the influx of people that followed, Beiradão became a new population center and the Laranjal do Jari municipality was formed in 1977 from the entire western portion of the Mazagão municipality, with Beiradão serving as its municipal seat. The municipality of Laranjal do Jari comprised a wide strip of land along the left bank of the Jari River, the western border of Amapá, from its mouth into the Amazon River in the south to its source along the international borders with Suriname and French Guiana in the north. One of the principal sources of revenue for the municipality were royalties paid to it by the Caulim da Amazônia S.A. company generated from the kaolin mine located near Beiradinho. Shortly after Laranjal do Jari became a municipality, Beiradinho was granted the status of district, taking the name of Vitória do Jari. The residents of this district then petitioned the state legislature for the creation of a new municipality, in a move fought by the residents of Laranjal do Jari, since they would lose royalties from the kaolin mine. Nonetheless, the territorial logic of creating new municipalities prevailed, and Vitória do Jari became a municipality in 1994 by lopping off the entire southern portion of the Laranjal do Jari municipality. The ease with which municipalities formed, not only in Amapá but throughout Brazil, began to be questioned at a national level, and pending federal legislation would, if passed, require the National Congress to approve the creation of all new municipalities.

A review of the migrant territories of Sucumbíos in Ecuador and Laranjal and Vitória do Jari in Brazil reveals several core processes operating

in both, though with local variants. A basic difference in settlement
patterns is evident, since the bulk of the population in Sucumbíos was
rural, stemming from massive improvisational colonization of lands,
while the Jari Region was peopled via a process of improvisational urbanization. One began through the dispersed, simultaneous arrival of small
farmers on small parcels of land, while the other grew out of the concentrated, simultaneous arrival of workers who settled into shantytowns.

In both cases, however, the growth of industrial enterprises was an
impetus for the arrival of migrants who were functional to the projects
but who were not able to be directly controlled by them. This lack of
control is evidenced in the political and territorial strategies promoted
by these migrants once in their new locale; they used their increasing
demographic voting power to force their respective governments to attend to their needs. Both cases exhibit the creation of new political-
administrative units within existing governmental structures. Amapá
became a state in 1988; Sucumbíos became a province in 1989. Amapá
increased the number of municipalities from five to sixteen in just seven
short years; the area that Sucumbíos encompasses increased its number
of cantons from two to seven from 1982 to 1998. The regionalization of
identities within the framework of national identities also occurred in
both regions and served to reinforce the military intention of integrating
Amazonian lands into the national political body. Finally, multifaceted
development cosmographies, which were appropriated by markedly different social actors during a particular phase of Amazonian history, have
brought about the consolidation of new enclave and migrant territories
in two separate regions.

The *City of Óbidos* / Boat to Laranjal do Jari

The weekly boat from Santana to Laranjal do Jari was packed because of
the closing of the recently constructed BR-156 state highway, as occurred
regularly during the several months of heavy rains in southern Amapá. By
six in the evening, when the boat was scheduled to leave, nearly two hundred passengers had hung their hammocks in three overlapping tiers in
every available open space in the boat. For the next four hours, I watched
as dozens of new refrigerators, televisions, and ovens were loaded into
the bowels of the boat, items destined for Monte Dourado, the headquarters of the Jari Industrial Complex, where they would be used by the
complex's top-level staff. This was followed by hundreds of cases of beer,

scores of tires, and numerous other items of practical use, which would be deposited in towns along the route up the Amazon and Jari Rivers. Meanwhile, people continued to swell the boat. At ten at night, the overcrowded and overloaded *City of Óbidos I* boat finally took off, and there was no turning back.

My first acquaintances on the boat were two teenage prostitutes who had hung their hammocks next to mine. They were heading to Laranjal do Jari, enticed by rumors of the town's booming nightlife and freeflowing money. During the four-hour wait for the boat to take off, I also engaged in a long conversation with a schoolteacher in Laranjal. She came from a thirteen-member family in Macapá who were descendants of a *quilombo* of Amapá. As we talked, she pointed out a former student of hers who had shot and killed someone in a barroom fight and was on leave from jail under military police escort to visit his hometown.

So began the parade of acquaintances I made on this twenty-nine-hour boat ride: a *caboclo* who lived in Jarilânia, where he collected and sold Brazil nuts and raised subsistence crops; two engineers from the southern part of Brazil who worked at the kaolin mine near Munguba; a traveling salesman who sold hardware supplies throughout Amazonia, representing a well-known hardware store in Belém; a young man who had been recently converted to the Assembly of God sect and was openly evangelizing to an unreceptive audience; a Brazilian soldier who was on leave to visit his family in Laranjal. In short, the travelers on this boat were a snapshot of the variety of people behind the improvisational development that the lower Jari River had experienced during the twenty-five years since Ludwig began installing his grandiose Jari "dream." This snapshot, however, was limited to the poorest segments of that development, that is, those who had to put up with the dangerous, overcrowded conditions of this old boat. The managers of the Jari Complex, the businessmen and politicians of Laranjal do Jari, and other big shots in the development drama had it much easier: they flew in and out of the area in small planes that serviced the Jari Complex in Monte Dourado.

CHAPTER THREE

Saving the Rain Forest

Environmental Cosmographies in Amazonia, 1970–1999

The emergence of a worldwide environmental movement during the 1950s and 1960s and its subsequent consolidation as an important force in world politics during the 1970s and 1980s presented alternative understandings of the human adaptive process and partially challenged the reigning developmentalist paradigm that had gained hegemony during the postwar epoch. Nowhere were these conflicting discourses more evident than in Amazonia. By the late 1980s, the accelerating destruction of the world's tropical rain forests had become one of the central issues of the worldwide environmental movement (see Myers 1984; Caufield 1991; Colchester and Lohmann 1993). The reasons behind the priority given to the rain-forest issue are numerous and diffuse. After all, the large-scale destruction of forests that had been occurring for centuries throughout the world had generated only negligible protest. Why did tropical rain-forest destruction become an issue at all, and why did this occur when it did?

One answer lies in biophysical reality: the scale and speed of forest destruction had increased to levels never before known, creating a sense of urgency among environmentalists. Another underlying reason lies in the emergence of a global ecological consciousness that understood environmental problems within a planetary framework. It was in this context that globalist arguments were put forth for saving the rain forest, some of which were patently false (e.g., the notion that tropical rain forests were the oxygen-supplying "lungs of the earth"), others of which exaggerated the scope of the environmental effects (e.g., the contribution of rain-forest burning to the accumulation of greenhouse gases), while still others were justifiably alarming (e.g., the irrecoverable loss of biodiversity). This global consciousness had its material basis in an increasingly globalized economy in which the extraction of raw materials by large transnational firms headquartered far from the area of environmental destruction made tropical forest destruction an undeniably international issue, a fact highlighted by multilateral lending agencies—such as the World Bank and the Inter-American Development Bank—that financed many of these destructive endeavors in the name of economic development (Millikan 1992).

Of course, the issue of tropical rain forests has specific geographical coordinates (i.e., those countries within the tropics that still have rain forests). Of all of these forested lands, Amazonia represents the largest single block of rain forest in the world, accounting for approximately 40 percent of the world total. Thus, it is not surprising that, within the rain-forest issue, Amazonia became a privileged site of struggle and attention and turned into an issue in and of itself with environmental, social, economic, and historical implications that go far beyond the narrow scope of concern over the destruction of the rain forest. Amazonia was appropriated into the international environmentalist discourse as a world biome, a perspective that posed deforestation, the activity that most radically alters existing ecological relationships, as the most serious problem facing the rain forest. As the rate of deforestation increased dramatically during the 1980s, this topic became the principal cause of alarm and the rallying cry of environmentalists to the exclusion of almost all others.

Throughout the 1980s the identification of the culprits of deforestation and other rain-forest destruction was a topic of much contention among environmentalists and led to a type of demonization of cattle ranchers, gold miners, loggers, colonists, land speculators, and the armed forces as destroyers of the rain forest (see Hecht and Cockburn 1989). Meanwhile, Amazonia's millions of urban dwellers were generally neglected by environmentalists in these debates. In Brazil, for example, 60 percent of the Amazonian population lives in urban centers (IBGE 1994), where they are struggling over such issues as better housing, accessible health care, more schools, good-paying jobs, paved streets, electricity, potable water, and sewage systems, issues not directly related to deforestation.

The naturalist bias of the environmentalist appropriation of Amazonia also gives only secondary importance to the rain forest as a geographical area under the sovereign national control of seven different nations. Indeed, these governments were often placed in the role of the enemy of the rain forest, since many of their policies openly encouraged rain-forest destruction. The increased importance of international groups in the expansion of environmentalism to Amazonia, together with their strong critique of national development policies, encouraged a backlash from nationalist and developmentalist leaders in Latin American nations. This backlash was strongest in Brazil, and the specter of the internationalization of Amazonia, which previously had been directed by leftists against multinational corporations (like Ludwig at Jari) seen as usurping national sovereignty over jungle lands, was now aimed at environmentalists. This time rightist political and military leaders viewed the worldwide environmental concern over Amazonia as a threat to its national sovereignty and asserted that no foreigner had the right to tell Brazilians what to do with their Amazon jungle.

In spite of these countertrends, an environmental front coalesced and grew in strength in Amazonia during the 1980s and the early 1990s, and the diverse set of social actors who composed it began to establish new regional frontiers (Onis 1992, 173–248). Although this front sometimes crosscut national borders, because of a strong emphasis on the implementation of new public policies and programs it usually functioned within national contexts. In all Amazonian countries new environmental programs were established to reverse the deforestation trend and remake Amazonian policies in an ecologically sound mold. In these programs, environmental nongovernmental organizations (NGOs), social movements, and local Amazonian populations entered into a tenuous power relationship with other social actors in an expanded environmental sector that included multinational lending agencies, which by the late 1980s were requiring environmental impact statements for all projects they funded; national governments, which had created environmental ministries and greatly expanded their environmental protection responsibilities; and private enterprise, which was forced to abide by new environmental regulations and began to develop "green" products (Ribeiro and Little 1998).[1]

The environmental front introduced a series of new (and not so new) activities into Amazonia: agroforestry projects, the restoration of deforested lands, the demarcation of Indian lands, the harvesting and marketing of forest products, the application of selective logging techniques, biodiversity prospecting, ecotours, and environmental education seminars. By pursuing their own interests, which in one way or another were related to environmentalism, the diverse social actors of the environmental front created a political space filled with new alliances formed around specific goals, generated new contradictions, and produced the partial overlap of political interests among themselves.

The unique appropriation of the environmental discourse by these varied social actors based on their specific interests has concrete territorial dimensions, thus giving substance to the notion of environmental cosmographies. Two types of environmental territories will be dealt with in this chapter: (1) preservationist territories and (2) sustainable use territories. Each has its own historical and philosophical roots, rules and regulations, and social actors that will be analyzed ethnographically within each of the two regions.[2]

Preservationist Territories

The establishment of governmentally sanctioned protected areas—national parks, wildlife sanctuaries, wilderness areas, forest reserves, and so forth—is a defining practice of the wilderness preservation current of the environmental movement and represents the clearest expression of its territorial dimension. Protected areas are founded on a contemporary notion of wilderness that arose in contradistinction to the industrial, urbanized world that was forming in Europe and the United States and are a modern phenomenon, since "the idea of creating in perpetuity a wilderness enclave of land, plants, and animals would have been unthinkable at the beginning of the nineteenth century" (Oelschlaeger 1991, 3).

One of the premises that underlay the creation of these areas was that the lands should be in a pristine or wild state and needed to be protected from the hands of humankind, which was considered to be intrinsically destructive. Thus, the creation of national parks represented the "only way of saving pieces of nature, which housed great beauty, from the deleterious effects of urban industrial development" (Diegues 1994, 31). The practice of prohibiting people from living in protected areas and exploiting their resources flows from this particular conception of nature, which promotes a hands-off policy whereby human use of these areas would be limited to contemplation, study, and recreation. This policy was designed to keep these lands wild so they can serve as a constant source of inspiration for civilized humans, since only nature in its wild state offers adequate spiritual rejuvenation from the trials and tribulations of daily industrial life.

The wilderness preservationist environmental current, together with its practice of establishing protected areas, arrived in Latin America during the first decades of the twentieth century, when it was applied to natural areas with little modification in its content, in what Diegues calls the "transposition of the 'Yellowstone model'" into a Latin America context (1994, 31). Peru was the first nation to establish protected areas in Amazonia, with the creation of the Pacaya Reserve in 1940 and the Samiria Reserve in 1954, both in the Marañón River basin. The first national park in Amazonia was the Araguaia National Park, established by the Brazilian government in 1959 in what is now the state of Tocantins. The twenty-year period from 1970 to 1990 witnessed the formal installation of this current of environmentalism in Amazonia and is the temporal referent for understanding how these preservationist territories competed with and were superimposed on both enclave territories and migrant territories of development cosmographies, which experienced peak installation during the 1960s and 1970s. Of the eighty protected areas that existed in Amazonia in 1991, sixty-five, or 80 percent, were created during the 1970s and 1980s (27.5% and 52.5%, respectively) (Rojas and Castaño 1991, 65–75).

National protected area systems have conceptual and political ties with the worldwide preservationist current of the environmental movement. A worldwide network of social actors supports and promotes the creation of what can be called *preservationist territories,* which represent a biological cross section of world ecosystems and biomes, each with their distinctive fauna, flora, and geological formations. The creation of protected areas in Amazonia is but one part of this movement, which seeks to preserve ecosystems on all the continents, with each protected area representing a fractal part of this fragmented worldwide network. Amazonia occupies a privileged space within this network because of its record levels of floral and faunal diversity and its enormous tracts of land still under forest cover.

The establishment of protected areas in Amazonia involves a host of specific social actors. National legislative and regulatory agencies are crucial actors, since they are responsible for passing environmental laws that regulate human use of the biophysical environment and for establishing the legal framework within which protected areas must function. Both private and public groups, such as the International Union for the Conservation of Nature (IUCN), the World Wildlife Fund (WWF), and the United Nations Environment Programme (UNEP), have been responsible for the creation of an informal monitoring system of protected areas in all parts of the world, which is coordinated through conferences, seminars, publications, and programs and serves as a common technical and conceptual basis from which to build a unified worldwide approach to protected areas. Scientists are another important Amazonian social actor, since they play leading roles in establishing criteria for the implementation and evaluation of Amazonian policies not only in the environmentalist realm, but also in such areas as agriculture, ranching, mining, and forestry.[3]

This entire set of social actors exercises territorial control over protected areas even though, in many cases, they are both physically and culturally removed from the local populations who live in or near the geographical area to be protected and who usually have longstanding territorial claims to these lands. In addition to visits to the area, they have access to protected areas through the use of technologies such as satellite imagery, scientific studies, and photographs, which permit them to know an area in an indirect manner. Many Amazonian protected areas were drawn on maps and published in federal registers (which is what formally brought them into existence) by bureaucrats who had little, if any, firsthand knowledge of the area where they were established. Since these people have considerable territorial power over this area, a power granted to them through the legal mechanism of the national protected areas system, they must be considered to be Amazonian social actors in their own right.

The implementation of protected areas policies represents a major change in land management techniques, since it turns the issue of territorial control over geographical areas into a bureaucratic and legal endeavor. Nugent places this within a larger framework in which "Amazonia is basically a management problem, a social landscape to which technical expertise can be applied" (1993, 237). In this respect, there is a commonality between development cosmographies, in which national leaders and military personnel draw up and approve large-scale development projects with major territorial implications while rarely consulting local populations, and the establishment of protected areas, which proceeds via a similar bureaucratic route, though with different overall goals. In both cases, development and environmental cosmographies can be promoted by social actors located far from the site of these Amazonian territories, and these social actors can effectively establish new

territories from a distance. The two preservationist territories to be analyzed here—the Cuyabeno Wildlife Production Reserve in the Aguarico
Region and the Jari Ecological Station in the Jari Region—are contemporary examples of these complexities.

The Jari Ecological Station

Just as the final details of the sale of Ludwig's Jari Project to national
industrialists were being finalized in early 1982, the Jari Ecological Station was created along the northern edge of the project by Presidential
Decree 87092 (12 April 1982). The 207,307 hectares set aside by this
station for preservation and scientific research added a new and quite
different layer of territoriality to the Jari Region. The creation of the Jari
Station is tied to two very different federal government agencies: GEBAM
and SEMA, the Special Secretariat for the Environment.

GEBAM, which since its establishment in 1980 had been directly responsible for overseeing all land issues in the Lower Amazon and, as a
military institution, had direct access to the military rulers, was a prime
mover behind the creation of the Jari Ecological Station. It was GEBAM
that suggested to the head of SEMA that the creation of an ecological
station would not only be a good idea but would be supported by the
agency (Nogueira-Neto 1991). From its point of view, the creation of a
protected area just to the north of the Jari Project would partially control
this company's territorial expansions. GEBAM provided important cartographic information in the delimitation of the station, rapidly ushered
the decree establishing it through the federal bureaucracy, and financed
the construction of all its infrastructure (Gama e Silva 1991, 85). The
modern research facilities built at the Jari Station had space for a large
biological laboratory, a kitchen and dining room, and lodging that could
accommodate up to twenty researchers. Nearby was constructed an administrative headquarters with housing facilities for station staff. This
territorial strategy by GEBAM was possible only due to the existence of
an established protected areas program within the country, which, in
fact, had gained in strength during the years of the military dictatorship.

The adoption of a broad-ranging, national forest code in 1965 and a
stringent wildlife protection law in 1967 provided new guidelines for the
management of Brazil's extensive forests. The Institute for Forest Development (IBDF), created in 1967, was charged with implementing

these laws and was given the mandate of overseeing existing federal protected areas and creating new ones. The RADAMBRASIL radar mapping project initiated by the military government in the early 1970s in collaboration with the U.S. Air Force, while geared to meet their strategic, geopolitical interests, also generated a wealth of topographical, geological, soil, and vegetation information that would prove useful in the establishment of preservation and conservation policies for Brazilian Amazonia. In 1973, the Special Secretariat for the Environment (SEMA) was established to regulate and control all types of environmental pollution. In the period stretching from 1975 to 1985, the Brazilian government, with the explicit support of the scientific community, established a large number of protected areas as territorial policies founded in preservationist ideals gained a strong foothold in Amazonian policy making. The negotiations between the eight South American nations with Amazonian lands culminated in the signing in 1978 of the Treaty for Amazonian Cooperation,[4] a document strongly conservationist in tone, which gave further impetus to establishment of protected areas (Barretto Filho 1997).

The policy of creating protected areas was staunchly opposed by the so-called Amazonian regional elites comprising the local bosses and "colonels" who wielded significant political and economic power within their isolated regions. Since much of their wealth had been gained through uncontrolled, predatory appropriation of natural resources such as timber, rubber, Brazil nuts, gold, fishing stocks, or agricultural land, they were opposed to any policies that would limit their access to these sources of wealth and place controls on resource use. In yet another ironic twist of history, the expanding role of the federal government in Amazonian affairs, which was being implemented by a military government that did not allow dissent, reduced the power of these regional elites and helped environmentalism gain a stronghold in Amazonia.

The Brazilian Amazon Conservation Plan, prepared by IBDF during the mid-1970s and published in 1979, applied a nascent environmental cosmography toward the goal of establishing preservationist territories, giving them visibility and scientific credibility in the process. And though IBDF, which was located within the Ministry of Agriculture, was responsible for creating most protected areas (it established fifteen national parks and biological reserves in the four-year period from 1979 to 1982), SEMA, which was within the Ministry of Interior, under the single-handed leadership of biologist Paulo Nogueira-Neto developed a different program of establishing ecological stations throughout the country to provide the natural and infrastructural basis for advanced scientific research in Brazil. One early SEMA document went so far as to claim that the establishment of ecological stations should be imbued with "the same spirit that inspired the construction of a medieval cathedral—a work destined to last centuries" (SEMA 1976, 4).

In spite of this lofty rhetoric, pragmatic considerations were generally used in the selection and establishment of ecological stations so that they would function effectively, thus avoiding the danger of becoming mere "paper parks." For example, many social and intragovernmental conflicts were sidestepped by eliminating from consideration areas with agricultural potential or the presence of Indians. Furthermore, SEMA "declined to incorporate any overarching biogeographic theory into its calculus of value" of the natural areas where the stations were to be established, since Nogueira-Neto was suspicious of their broad-based claims (Foresta 1991, 116–17). Nonetheless, the flexible goal of representing all of Brazil's major ecosystems in the Ecological Station Program was adopted, and Ab'Saber's six morphoclimatic domains of Brazil were used as the basis for establishing this representativeness (1970). This program also focused on smaller areas containing unique vegetation and in this way complemented IBDF's policy of creating large protected areas.

During the first years of its existence, the Ecological Station Program of SEMA functioned without any formal legal guidelines. Only in 1981, with the passage of two laws (no. 6902 of 12 April and no. 6938 of 31 August), were formal guidelines established for creating ecological stations and defining the mechanisms for formulating and applying environmental policies. This legislation stipulated that 90 percent of each ecological station must be left in its unaltered state, placing them within the realm of preservationist territories, while allowing the remaining 10 percent to be altered for the implementation of research activities. Each ecological station was to be equipped with housing for scientists complete with kitchen and dining facilities, a scientific laboratory, land and water transport vehicles, an office and housing for station administrators and guards, and small scientific outposts scattered throughout the station (Bruck et al. 1983, 25). By 1982, SEMA had established thirteen ecological stations in widely scattered parts of the country and was working in close collaboration with university research centers in many of them, strengthening ties between government conservation officials and the scientific community, especially in the southern part of the country where the university system was most firmly established. This research focused on the fields of ecosystem ecology, climatology, limnology, biomass studies, species inventories, hydraulic cycles, and thematic mapping of ecosystems (SEMA 1979).

When the Jari Ecological Station was created in 1982, SEMA was at the height of its powers, having just gained legislation reinforcing its program, and continued to push forward with the creation of new stations. The biophysical conditions offered by the Jari River basin were well known to SEMA, since several of its officials and researchers had participated in the study of this basin conducted during 1977–78 by the Special Committee of Integrated Studies of Hydrographic Basins (CEEIBH). The diagnosis of water and mineral resources in this area that resulted from this study alerted SEMA to the biophysical wealth of the area and gave them a solid base of information for installation of an ecological station there (CPRM 1978). In December 1981, another team was sent to the region to gather additional environmental information about the area to be included in the Jari Ecological Station and to determine the site where the station headquarters and research center were to be installed.

As first established in 1982, the Jari Ecological Station was located on the land between the Jari and Paru Rivers, south of the Carecuru River and north of the Jari Project in the Almeirim municipality of the state of Pará. This area included the magnificent Paredão, a massive rock canyon that is part of the Plateau of Maracanaquara. The rocky terrain of Paredão houses several large, natural clearings interspersed with numerous small niches rich in plant and animal life and many caves and is surrounded by dense tropical forest. The biological, geological, and hydraulic wealth of the region provoked the researchers who wrote the report to claim that "the natural ecosystems of this region have not yet suffered from human interference" (Castro and Elias 1981, 3). This statement attests to the relatively unaltered state of these ecosystems, but it neglected to mention that indigenous peoples have long used this area and that, just a few kilometers north of the Paredão, a small indigenous community of Aparai continued to live along the Jari River (CEDI 1983, 174–81). At no time in the entire process of the creation of the Jari Ecological Station was the presence of this community mentioned or the territorial claims of the Aparai to the area taken into account. Since one of the policies that guided the creation of ecological stations was to avoid indigenous areas, this oversight is glaring. The fact that this community consisted of only ten people allowed SEMA simply to ignore it and in this way avoid the Indian issue.

By the mid-1980s, however, SEMA and other governmental environmental agencies had encountered difficulties as the previous ten-year wave of governmental conservationism began to wane. Brazil suffered from a serious economic crisis spurred by the heavy burden of external debt payments and the world economic recession and was going through the difficult political process of the transition to democracy. This situation provoked a corresponding crisis in the financing and administration of newly established protected areas, of which the remote Jari Ecological Station was one. And while the Jari Project offered logistical support to SEMA for initial scientific studies at the station and partially funded limited research activities—this in spite of the animosity between GEBAM and the Jari Project—the research facilities of Jari Station were never used, and they continue to exist as cement shells, deteriorating because of the ravages of time and lack of upkeep.

The most serious crisis that the Jari Ecological Station faced in its early years was the invasion of the area by wildcat gold miners (*garimpeiros*). The middle and upper Jari River basin had been the site of sporadic gold mining since the 1950s, but with the astronomical rise in gold prices on the London market in 1979–80, "gold mines multiplied in all latitudes, provoking a gold rush without precedents" in the history of Amazonia (Salomão 1984, 62). The center of gold mining along the Jari River was at the mouth of the Carecuru River, the northern border of the Jari Ecological Station, and by 1983 approximately four thousand gold miners had established themselves in the makeshift encampment there. GEBAM was actively monitoring this activity and was responsible for informing SEMA of the invasion of the ecological station (Nogueira-Neto 1991). By this time, GEBAM had turned its attention to the rich mineral potential of the Lower Amazon Basin, but its strategic interest in developing this potential with industrial techniques placed it in opposition to wildcat gold miners who were difficult to control.

In all, an estimated fifty-five hundred gold miners were working in the middle Jari River basin during the peak seasons of the early 1980s (CEDI 1983, 180–81). This number remained constant throughout the 1980s and into the early 1990s, according to estimates made by gold buyers in

The Jari Ecological Station's unused scientific laboratories and housing, 1995

Beiradão, indicating that considerable amounts of gold are still to be found in the area. Most of this mining is done from rafts floating on the river upon which heavy machinery is installed. Using the dangerous system of *mergulho,* skin divers place along the river bottom hoses that suck up alluvial deposits to the raft's machinery, where it is sifted through for gold (see Cleary 1990). This activity is most frequent during the season of low water levels from August to December; during the rest of the year, the river currents are too strong to allow raft mining. In addition to this raft activity, individual miners seek their fortunes along other creeks and rivers scattered throughout the area, many of them within the boundaries of the Jari Station. The station was also the principal land route to the Carecuru mining encampment. This massive invasion of an ecological station by gold miners, combined with the serious environmental impacts that they produced, negated the key function of the station, which was to maintain 90 percent of the area in an unaltered state and free from human intervention. The medieval cathedral that this ecological station was supposed to represent was being blatantly sacked of all its gold.

The reaction of the federal government to this untenable situation was swift, thanks again to GEBAM and its direct access to the military rulers. Given the near impossibility of removing thousands of armed gold miners from the area, the boundaries of the Jari Ecological Station were modified by Presidential Decree 89.440 (13 March 1984) less than two years after their initial establishment. This decree removed from the Jari Station a large chunk of land south of the Carecuru River, the heart of the gold mining operations, and tacked on an even larger portion of land on the other side of the Jari River (in the state of Amapá), giving it a new size of 227,126 hectares. The biophysical criteria that had been used in the original establishment of the station were seriously violated by this second decree, as the station was transformed into an odd-shaped hodgepodge of land that straddled two states. The newly incorporated plot of land in Amapá was not linked to the existing network of trails and scientific outposts and has never been effectively incorporated into the functioning of the Jari Station.

The Jari Station suffered other threats in 1989 from one of its former benefactors, the Jari Project. By this time IBAMA had been created from the fusion of SEMA, IBDF, and two other government agencies and had assumed control of the Jari Station. A burly new agent, José Carlos Carvalho, was stationed in Monte Dourado by IBAMA and commissioned to enforce environmental laws and codes throughout the Jari Region, a task that included guarding the Jari Ecological Station. The Jari Project was in the process of switching all its new plantings to eucalyptus and was clearing native forest to expand this operation. Part of this expansion was to the north, activities that brought it ever closer to the borders of the Jari Ecological Station.

One of Carvalho's first acts as the IBAMA agent was to embargo three Jari Project trucks loaded with freshly cut timber because they lacked the proper authorization for cutting native forest in this area. This move, made in coordination with the federal police and with the consent of IBAMA's president in Brasilia, represented the first time that the Jari Project had experienced governmental pressure for environmental reasons. The Jari Project did not challenge this embargo, choosing instead to halt

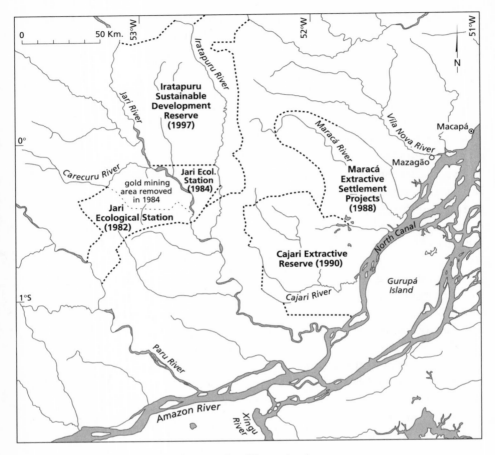

The Jari River Region: Protected and Extractive Areas

its expansion to the north, and the Jari Ecological Station gained an 18-kilometer buffer zone of native rain forest along its southern border (along that part of the station within the state of Pará). Carvalho proudly stated afterward: "The expansion of the Jari Project stopped there and that was that."

The timing of the embargo was important to its success, since the Jari Project was just beginning to remodel its image as a sustainable development enterprise and did not want to make enemies with the main environmental agency in Brazil. In 1991 the Jari Project created an environmental department and hired a specialist in ecology to direct it. This agency was responsible for dealing directly with IBAMA, for the environmental planning of the company as a whole, and for improving the company's tarnished public image. The embargo also established IBAMA as an important new social actor in the Jari Region, one that had considerable legal and enforcement power if and when it decided to use it.

The IBAMA staff then turned their sights on the gold miners still operating on an isolated basis within the redrawn Jari Station boundaries. IBAMA built a gate at the station's main entrance along the only access road to the area and strictly controlled all traffic passing through it, forcing the gold miners to undertake an arduous river journey requiring the fording of several waterfalls to arrive at the mining encampments. This was followed by a blitz operation, once again in coordination with the federal police, that resulted in the confiscation of thirty pieces of machinery used in gold mining, five thousand liters of fuel, and four thousand meters of wire together with the physical expulsion of the gold miners from the Jari Station premises (Carvalho).

The consolidation of environmental cosmographies in Brazil during the ten-year period of 1975–85 helped propel new social actors and territorial claims into the Jari Region. The Jari Ecological Station introduced a distinct territorial presence into the region based on preservationist ideals. The station gained this presence through presidential decrees prepared in Brasilia by bureaucrats who had never visited the area. It reaffirmed this presence through the vigilance of IBAMA, its defender within the governmental conservation bureaucracy. From an operational perspective, the Jari Ecological Station could be considered to be a paper park, since it has never been used for scientific research, the main reason for its existence. From a pragmatic perspective, however, it had an important territorial effect on the Jari Region during the 1980s by introducing and enforcing a preservationist territorial logic. This new presence challenged and, in some cases, halted the expansive dynamics of the development cosmographies that were firmly entrenched in the region.

Cuyabeno Wildlife Production Reserve (Initial Phase)

The establishment in 1959 of Ecuador's first national park in the Galápagos Islands was made not so much in response to local environmental pressure, which barely existed at that time, but out of an implicit ac-

knowledgment of the unique biological treasures contained in these islands and the Ecuadorian government's desire to reaffirm its sovereign
territorial control over this archipelago located more than 1,000 kilometers from the South American mainland. Nine years would pass before
the first park rangers were sent to the islands and minimal conservation
management of the park was undertaken.

By the 1970s civil society preservationist organizations had grown in
strength, environmental studies were conducted, and additional protected areas were created. In 1974–76, an interdisciplinary study, jointly
sponsored by the United Nations Development Programme (UNDP) and
the Food and Agriculture Organization (FAO) of the United Nations, inventoried all of the major ecosystems of Ecuador and designated priority
areas to be granted status as protected areas. This study's recommendations were partially implemented in 1979 in a sweeping interministerial
decree (no. 0322) by the Ministry of Agriculture and Ranching (MAG) and
the Ministry of Industries, Commerce, and Integration (MICI), which
either established or formally delimited ten protected areas, four of which
were located in Amazonia. In the early 1980s environmental legislation
passed in Ecuador gave legal support to these newly created areas and
helped strengthen the environmental movement in the country. The
most important piece of this legislation was the Forestry and Conservation of Natural Areas and Wildlife Law (no. 74) of 1981, which established, for the first time in Ecuador, guidelines for the use of almost all
forestry resources and state-owned land in the country.

The Cuyabeno Wildlife Production Reserve was one of the four Amazonian areas established by the 1979 decree, and its 254,760 hectares
were located in the heart of the Aguarico Region. A brief analysis of
each of the four words of its name—Cuyabeno, Wildlife, Production,
Reserve—will reveal its uniqueness among protected areas in Ecuador.
Cuyabeno refers to the Cuyabeno River, a black-water hydraulic system
whose headwaters lie within the Amazonian lowlands; it drains most of
the area between the San Miguel and the Aguarico Rivers and is the
largest tributary of the latter. The Cuyabeno Reserve was delimited to
include the entire Cuyabeno River basin and, with a few minor excep-
tions, the borders of the reserve are isomorphic with the watershed. The
centerpiece of this area is the Cuyabeno Lakes district, comprising fourteen interconnected lakes and numerous seasonally inundated lands,
making "the area a rare combination of rainforest and wetlands" (Nations and Coello 1989, 141).

The upper Cuyabeno River at the height of the dry season, 2000

While this area houses high levels of floral biodiversity, its most strik-ing biological feature is the wealth of *wildlife,* which provides the princi-pal reason for its establishment as a protected area. Aquatic life includes the rare and endangered pink freshwater dolphin and the manatee, along with more than 250 recorded species of fish, while notable reptiles include the huge anaconda snake and four different species of caimans. Among mammals that live in the area are the capybara, tapir, armadillo, deer, peccaries, and ten species of primates. Birds offer the greatest diversity of faunal life, as nearly five hundred different species, including seventeen species of parrots and macaws, have been sighted in the reserve (Brack Egg and Reck 1991, 48).

Not only was this faunal richness to be protected as a source of scientific research and naturalist observation, but also the reserve was to function as an area of wildlife *production*—both in the wild and in captivity—for human use as a source of food, hides, and sport fishing (Brack Egg and Reck 1991, 37). Through the use of proper scientific management techniques, the reserve was designed to become a model of sustainable development that could generate, according to some estimates, millions of dollars per year (Nations and Coello 1989, 145). From a historical perspective, one could argue that the notion of wildlife production as a sustainable economic activity was established fifty years too late; during 1930–70 uncontrolled and predatory hunting and marketing of animal hides and meat by private traders in collaboration with local indigenous peoples was so extensive that stocks of the most-valued species—caiman and jaguar (for hides), manatee and the *paiche* fish (for meat), *charapa* turtles (for both eggs and meat)—were reduced to the point of local extinction. Ansana estimates that, in the lower Aguarico River basin, some 500,000 animal hides were taken during this period (cited in Coello 1991, 38). Given this history of overexploitation, the recovery of animal stocks to levels that would permit their sustainable harvest was an initial priority of the reserve's management staff.

In spite of these economic goals, the Cuyabeno Reserve's status as a *reserve* places it within the realm of protected areas in Ecuador, which are governed by a single legal code mandating that these lands be conserved in an unaltered state, are inalienable, exist into perpetuity, and cannot house privately owned goods (Aguilar 1992, 8). The establishment of the Cuyabeno Reserve thus added another layer of territorial rules and regulations regarding the use of the land and introduced new social actors into the territorial equation of the Aguarico Region.

Though formally established in 1979, the Cuyabeno Reserve did not receive financial or human resources from the government during the first three years of its existence; it was a paper park that existed only in the bureaucratic paperwork of the government but had no practical on-site manifestations. In 1982 the Division of Natural Areas and Forest Resources (DINAF) of the Ministry of Agriculture and Ranching established a modest presence in the Cuyabeno Reserve and began to realize the scope of the problems it faced in both implementing the goals of the reserve and protecting it from encroachment by a host of sources. Two small buildings—the reserve headquarters in Tarapoa and a reserve checkpoint along the Cuyabeno River—were constructed and housed the reserve superintendent and four park rangers. This small staff was equipped with a short wave radio, providing contact with the DINAF office in Quito, two motorized boats, and a motorcycle and was charged with overseeing and controlling the entire 254,760 hectares of the reserve, a difficult job in the best of conditions and a nearly impossible one given the level of invasions the reserve was experiencing. By the mid-1980s, the petroleum industry was operating throughout the reserve and several thousand colonists had established farms within its established limits.

The social actors directly involved in the implementation of the Cuyabeno Reserve included a mix of government bureaucrats, scientists, and tourist entrepreneurs, a small group of people who, in many cases, knew each other on a personal basis. Most of the government conservation officials responsible for the nation's protected areas were biologists who had studied at the Pontifical Catholic University of Quito, which had a research station situated along the Laguna Grande in the Cuyabeno Lakes district. These biologists-turned-bureaucrats were responsible for authorizing studies of the area, often carried out by their students and colleagues at the university, and for granting approval to tourist companies to operate in the reserve, which in the case of one company was owned by biologists who worked at the research station. This intertwining of interests helped form a tightly knit group of people who served as advocates for the Cuyabeno Reserve within the Ecuadorian political system and who were responsible for shaping its management and protection policies.

The establishment of the Cuyabeno Reserve directly affected two indigenous communities, Puerto Bolívar (Siona) and Playas de Cuyabeno (Quichua), within its limits. Puerto Bolívar was situated in the heart of the reserve, just south of the Cuyabeno Lakes district, near the confluence of the Tarapoa and Cuyabeno Rivers. In August 1979, shortly after the creation of the Cuyabeno Reserve, this community received communal title to 744 hectares of land, an area that included the center of the community but represented only a fraction of their traditional

territory.[5] At the time, this community had a population of approximately sixty people divided into two clans, the Criollo family and the
Piaguaje family. Victoriano Criollo, *cacique* (headman) of Puerto Bolívar
and head of the Criollo clan, gained employment as a biological informant at the Catholic University biological research station on the Laguna Grande. Small groups of tourists began to visit the reserve and
tourism began to be incorporated into the life of the community as other
members of the Criollo family began to work as tour guides and boat
motorists. Gradually, the scientific and tourist activities in and around
the Cuyabeno Lakes district came under the control of the Criollo clan,
to the almost complete exclusion of the Piaguaje clan, a situation that
accentuated traditional kinship rivalries and modern religious tensions
(the Criollos were Catholics and the Piaguajes were evangelicals).

The Playas de Cuyabeno community, located along the Aguarico
River near the mouth of the Cuyabeno River and next to a small Ecuadorian army outpost, was also within the formal boundaries of the
reserve. Since most of the newly introduced scientific and tourist activities were centered at the Cuyabeno Lakes district far from them, this
community was not greatly affected by these activities.

A third indigenous community, the Secoya community of San Pablo,
located along the Aguarico River within the reserve's "buffer zone," was
indirectly affected by the establishment of the reserve. This community
continued to hunt and fish within its boundaries. San Pablo had been
formed in 1973 when members of the Puerto Bolívar community had
split off under the influence of a missionary couple from the Summer
Institute of Linguistics who had been stationed there. In 1978, the San
Pablo community received title to 7,043 hectares of land straddling the
Aguarico River, which again represented only a small part of their area of
territorial occupation (Uquillas 1982). The subsequent splintering of San
Pablo into several smaller communities has left some communities without any legal title to the land they occupy. This area was then invaded on
two fronts: from the west by the expansion of a large African palm plantation and in its middle by non-Indian colonists. The total Siona-Secoya
population in Ecuador is 550 (Ruiz 1991b, 451).

The geographical overlapping of the Cuyabeno Reserve with the petroleum industry is concentrated in the western half of the reserve and
stems from the parallel application of a hydrographic and ecosystemic
territorial logic (the reserve) and a subterranean and geological one (the

oil industry). The first oil development within the Cuyabeno River Basin began in 1970 with the construction of an airport and oil wells in what was soon to become the town of Tarapoa.[6] By 1974 a 78-kilometer road connected Tarapoa to Lago Agrio, the headquarters of oil development in Ecuadorian Amazonia, and an extensive network of oil wells, pipelines, and roads had been established near the headwaters of the Cuyabeno River, giving rise to the oil/colonist towns of Dureno and Pacayacu. Thus, when the Cuyabeno Reserve was formally established in 1979, petroleum development already was occurring within its boundaries. Starting in 1981, the Ecuadorian petroleum industry launched a new phase of expansion that moved them even deeper into the reserve as wells were installed just above the Cuyabeno Lakes district and the Lago Agrio-Tarapoa road was extended northward to the river port of Tipishca along the San Miguel River near the Ecuadorian border with Colombia. The existence of the reserve did nothing to alter this new wave of expansion, since oil companies were operating under the mandate—expressed in a set of hydrocarbon and mining laws—of finding and exploiting all known petroleum reserves (note this other usage of the term) regardless of their geographical location.

Oil development within the reserve created serious environmental consequences for the local ecosystem. Though each phase of oil development—exploration, drilling, production, refining, transportation, and use—causes varied environmental effects, direct oil spills are by far the most damaging to the Amazonian ecosystem. Oil spills are caused by breaks in pipelines, a frequent occurrence, by the overflow of oil well waste pits due to torrential Amazonian rains, or simply the rupture of poorly constructed waste pit walls. The Cuyabeno and Sansahauri wells established along the Tarapoa-Tipishca road in the 1980s were the sites of the most frequent oil spills and waste pit overflows. Topographical and hydraulic factors increased the negative environmental impacts of these spills. Since this oil production was located within the headwaters of the Cuyabeno River, all spills flowed downriver, contaminating the rest of the watershed. The flatness of the land and the existence of extensive swampland areas makes hydraulic flows both slow and expansive, meaning that an oil spill will spread out over extensive areas of the rain forest and stay in place for long periods. The major oil spill of 1989 at the Cuyabeno oil well occurred in November, at the beginning of the three-month dry season, and the oil stagnated in the Cuyabeno Lakes district for months, where it poisoned the soil, fish, birds, land animals, and vegetation and caused a rash of respiratory and skin diseases among the Siona population of Puerto Bolívar downstream.

Ironically, the presence of oil company roads actually helped consolidate the Cuyabeno Reserve. Before the construction of the Tarapoa-Tipishca road, for example, access to the Cuyabeno Lakes district could be made only through an arduous river journey down the Aguarico River to the mouth of the Cuyabeno and then up this river to the Lakes district, a ten- to twelve-hour endeavor with high-speed motorboats. With the new oil road, which crossed the Cuyabeno River just above the Lakes district, this trip could now be made in two hours, and the Tarapoa-Tipishca road quickly turned into the principal entry point for park rangers, scientists, and tourists. The two main pieces of reserve infrastructure—the reserve headquarters in the oil town of Tarapoa and the reserve checkpoint at the Cuyabeno River bridge—were built along this road.

Oil company roads also facilitated the arrival of the colonists. As soon as they were built, colonists from other parts of the country began using them to stake out and settle on 50-hectare plots. The numerous wells and roads in the Dureno and Pacayacu areas, towns located just outside the reserve, made this a prime site for colonization. By the time the reserve was established, as many as eight colonization lines had been established in this area, many of them within the reserve's borders. Meanwhile, the towns of Tarapoa and Bellavista were well within the borders of the reserve, and all of the colonists in this area had plots within its limits. Though many colonists were already living within the boundaries of the reserve when it was established in 1979, the decree that created the reserve made no mention of this problem, nor did it provide guidelines for resolving it. Nonetheless, the majority of colonists settled within the reserve came to the area during the years 1980–85 with the opening of the Tarapoa-Tipishca road, precisely those years when the reserve functioned as a paper park (Trujillo 1986).

During the 1980s the Cuyabeno Reserve experienced another type of colonization, though on a much smaller scale and with minimal environmental effects—colonization by Shuar Indians. The Shuar, together with the Quichua, are the two largest indigenous groups in Ecuadorian Amazonia and were engaged in a process of territorial expansion throughout the twentieth century.[7] The entrance of small groups of

Shuar into the Aguarico River basin takes them far from their traditional homeland to the south and places them among Siona, Secoya, Cofán, and Quichua groups. These Shuar colonists share many of the adaptive strategies of the non-Indian colonists: they stake out family plots of land; they are primarily agriculturalists; they plant corn, coffee, and rice for the market, supplemented by subsistence crops; and they raise cattle on a small scale. They are different from the non-Indian colonists, however, in that their colonization is tied to river travel rather than to roads and their settlements function as kin-based settlements rather than loosely structured communities. These Shuar settlements are organizationally tied more closely to distant Shuar organizations than to the governmental political-administrative units of their place of residence. Two Shuar centers—Tangay and Tayos—were established along the left bank of the Aguarico River above the mouth of the Cuyabeno River, just within the boundaries of the Cuyabeno Reserve, and together house approximately fifty people, making their impact slight when compared to the thousands of non-Indian colonists in the reserve. Furthermore, these two settlements were not part of a nationwide strategy of colonization, but represent the isolated decisions of several Shuar families to strike out on their own far from their traditional homeland.

Just as the notion of wildlife production came fifty years too late, one could argue that the Cuyabeno Reserve was established twenty years too late. If it had been established and rules and regulations for its use enforced before the developmentalist invasions, it would have been in a better position to defend its ecosystems from degradation. In fact, if DINAF had taken the initiative to delimit and control the reserve when it was created, many problems could have been avoided. As it stands, territorial overlap created legal problems founded in the contradictory laws of the Ecuadorian government. Though the legislation used to establish this area and the practices permitted in it are clear—the entire area belongs to the national government and its lands are inalienable and must be protected from environmental alterations—the presence of other social actors and the distinct laws that apply to them make this legislation both confusing and difficult to enforce.

The national government owns all subsurface mineral rights and has divided the entire northern portion of Ecuadorian Amazonia into petroleum concessions. The Cuyabeno Reserve is part of several petroleum concessions ceded to Petroecuador and City Investing Company, a small, privately owned oil firm. Meanwhile, the Sionas of Puerto Bolívar were granted a small plot of land in the midst of the reserve, placing it in legal conflict with the reserve. The Quichuas of Playas de Cuyabeno and the Shuar colonists directly to the west did not have title to their lands, but they were not pressured to move. The non-Indian colonists bore the brunt of the attempts to remove them from the reserve because of the massive scale of their improvisational colonization and its major environmental impacts.

From a geographical perspective, the western portion of the reserve has become the central battleground between two competing cosmographies and the territories they have engendered: a developmentalist front advancing from the west and an environmentalist one resisting this invasion from the east. The developers seek to remove this portion of land from the reserve and put an end to the conflict. The environmentalists are adamantly opposed to this solution. They argue that the reserve was created to include an entire hydrographic basin and that this basin must be protected in its entirety. An argument is also made that giving in to developmentalist forces will set a precedent that will encourage future invasions of this and other protected areas.

While the environmentalist social actors did not possess either the political clout or the financial and human resources to turn the situation around, they were partially successful in slowing the developmentalist invasions and placing the environmental preservation of the area on the agenda. This situation would change dramatically in 1991 with the enlargement of the Cuyabeno Reserve, which initiated a second phase in its existence.

Sustainable Use Territories

The application of the preservationist ideals of wilderness to Amazonia was problematic for indigenous and *caboclo* peoples, since many protected areas were created with these traditional peoples still inhabiting them. Amend and Amend documented that 86 percent of all national parks in South America have people living in them (1992, 463). Preservationist ideals call for the removal of these peoples from the protected areas, since humans are considered to be incompatible with the reigning idea of wilderness.

Traditional peoples openly resisted their forced removal from lands in which they had a long history of continual occupation. The increasing role of Amazonian social movements in political and public policy issues starting in the eighties provoked a rethinking of the relationship between parks and people. As local populations gained a voice in regional and national politics, their protests over the calls for their expulsion from protected areas could not be ignored, and the preservation of natural areas became fraught with conflicts in which the issue of social justice came to the fore. The creation of protected areas effectively cut off access to and use of the many natural resources of these lands upon which local peoples depended for their sustenance.

In addition to the forceful pronouncement of their historical right to their homelands and its resources, these social movements put forth two environmental arguments to justify their continued occupation and use of these lands. First, they asserted that their forms of adaptation were not harmful to the ecosystem and had proved to be sustainable over time, thus placing them within the conservationist framework that guided the establishment of protected areas. Second, they claimed that their very presence in the area served as a deterrent to encroachment by predatory, market-driven social actors, since totally unoccupied lands were the easiest to invade. Traditional populations were well situated to immediately detect and denounce any encroachments and, if necessary, physically defend the area being invaded.

Given the scope of this problem, throughout the late eighties and early nineties new forms of interaction between protected areas and traditional residents were being explored even among the staunchest preservationists. The Fourth World Congress of National Parks in Caracas, Venezuela, in 1992 consecrated these efforts by including as one of the goals of protected areas the protection and conservation of "cultural resources" and adopting measures outlining ways of integrating local populations into the management of protected areas (McNeely et al. 1994).

Yet the direct incorporation of traditional peoples into conservation policies proved to be difficult and was filled with tensions. On the one hand, the environmentalist appropriations of indigenous peoples were often overly romanticized as naturalized and pure peoples who in practice rarely lived up to these ideals (Ramos 1994). Indigenous organizations expressed resentment at being considered as just another part of nature, along with the monkeys and the trees, rather than as human groups with a specific set of peoples' rights. Indigenous movements also complained about the way that environmentalism was being deployed, as this statement by the Coordinating Body of Indigenous Organizations of the Amazon Watershed shows: "The irony of this is that we have been raising this clamor [about environmental destruction] with our own governments for decades, but we had to wait until it was said in English coming from the north, before it was listened to" (COICA n.d., 9). Meanwhile, indigenous peoples have responded to their appropriation by environmentalists in their own ways, creating constantly renewed, cross-cultural dynamics. Recent ethnographic work, for example, has revealed some of the complex ways that indigenous peoples have incorporated and resignified environmentalist discourse and then used this discourse as a political tool (Albert 1995; Conklin and Graham 1995).

A similar process of interaction with environmentalists has been occurring with the rubber tappers and other extractivist populations and is also filled with tensions. After the collapse of the rubber boom and the demise of the rubber barons, local rubber tappers continued to use their *caboclo*-style adaptive techniques, which included supplemental income from extractive activities, though remaining "invisible" inhabitants of Amazonia (Nugent 1993). With the massive invasion of forested lands in the Brazilian states of Rondônia and Acre in the 1970s, however, the local rubber tappers association began to respond with *empates,* or stand-offs, whereby they physically impeded the advance of those hired by ranchers to cut down the forest (Allegretti 1991). This technique caught the attention of environmentalists because of its effectiveness in stopping deforestation, though the rubber tappers were acting in the defense of their homelands and livelihood rather than from an environmentalist stance.

With the formation of the National Rubber Tappers Council (CNS) in 1985, the rubber tappers turned into a political actor in their own right. Under the inspired leadership of Chico Mendes, an informal coalition was formed between the Rubber Tappers Council, which maintained a strong labor-unionist profile, and national and international environmental groups, who were in need of local Amazonian populations to promote their cause. This environmental connection quickly turned Mendes into a type of eco-star—a local, natural-born environmentalist—and the rubber tappers came to symbolize a traditional, environmentally sound lifestyle (Mendes 1989). After Mendes's tragic assassination in 1988, this alliance was difficult to maintain because of both internal disputes with the Rubber Tappers Council and a growing antagonism between its social movement dynamic and the NGO structure of environmental groups.

In the early 1990s, the efforts at rapprochement between environmentalists and Amazonian social movements were buttressed by strengthening of the discourse of sustainable development within the world political movement, particularly due to the 1992 United Nations Conference on Environment and Development (UNCED) in Rio de Janeiro (Little 1995). One result of this discourse was to reevaluate the forms of resource use by traditional peoples. While formerly considered to be backward techniques with little scientific basis, they now gained a place in the vanguard of the search for ways of exploiting the rain forest that did not destroy the biophysical environment nor greatly disrupt ecosystem dynamics. Here again, local social movements responded to this increased interest by environmentalists with proposals of their own geared toward defending their access to and control of natural resources.

The concept of the co-management of territories grew out of these distinct yet interrelated forces, creating a new type of territoriality tied to environmental cosmographical principles. New proposals and practices were established whereby traditional populations would collaborate with government conservation officials in the control and use of protected areas while continuing to live within them. The use of the area, however, would now be structured according to formally established use patterns whose specific content was to be negotiated between the two parties involved.

The notion of *sustainable use territories* emerged from the practice of co-management and posited the dual goals of ecosystem conservation and human use. This use, however, needed to be based on the low-impact, long-term extraction of renewable resources for direct use or sale. In many cases these territories coalesced around the maintenance of existing traditional use systems, though their constant improvement through the incorporation of modern scientific knowledge and new technologies was also proposed. Agroforestry systems based on multiple forms of low-impact production are but one example of how local knowledge systems of traditional peoples are being combined with state-of-the-art Western scientific knowledge to create new, sustainable means of profitably exploiting Amazonian ecosystems (Dubois et al. 1996).

What is essential to the success of these sustainable use territories is the combination of different productive techniques in ways uniquely suited to the ecosystem and its resources, such that productive activities can continue for an indefinite period without depleting resource stocks or irreparably destroying the ecosystem. To achieve this, an intimate knowledge of the ecosystem to be exploited is necessary. This knowledge is precisely what traditional peoples have been developing, using, and refining over centuries. The issue of the intellectual rights that these peoples have over their knowledge systems and technologies also entered into this debate with the advent of biotechnological firms interested in finding, taking, modifying, and then patenting genetic material located on traditional peoples' homelands (Davis and Ebbe 1995).

Anthropologists also entered into this arena as a wealth of new ethnobotanical and ethnozoological information not only began to show the scope of indigenous peoples' historical intervention over rain-forest ecosystems previously thought to be pristine, but further to postulate that these interventions had enhanced levels of biological diversity through the application of finely tuned, indigenous management techniques (Posey and Balée 1990). This line of research has linked biodiversity to sociodiversity (i.e., the existence of a wide array of social organizations and human adaptive practices), since human populations and biophysical environments have developed according to a "complex coevolutionary process" founded in numerous symbiotic relationships (Neves 1992, 39).

The co-management of territories can take on a variety of forms and need not be limited to formally established protected areas, though this is where the notion has most frequently been applied. Furthermore, comanaged, sustainable use territories can be based on vegetal extraction, controlled hunting and fishing, agroforestry systems, some types of mineral extraction, ecotourism, long-term research projects, or any combination of these techniques. The examples presented here—the enlarged Cuyabeno Wildlife Production Reserve, the Cajari Extractive Reserve, the Maracá Extractive Settlement Projects, and the Iratapuru Sustainable Development Reserve—illustrate this variety, while offering only a limited sample of possible forms of the sustainable use of territories within a comanagement framework.

Cuyabeno Wildlife Production Reserve (Second Phase)

On 3 July 1991, Ministry of Agriculture and Ranching (MAG) Ministerial Decree 0328 expanded the Cuyabeno Wildlife Production Reserve to the southeast to include the entire lower Aguarico River basin from the mouth of the Cuyabeno River to the mouth of the Aguarico at the Napo River. This decree enlarged the reserve from 254,760 to 655,781 hectares, nearly tripling its size. The preparatory work for this expansion was conducted with the utmost of secrecy within MAG and became known by the general public only with its publication in the Official Register on 12 July 1991. The newly expanded reserve included large areas of tropical rain forest in an optimal state of preservation, the deepest and most readily navigable portion of the Aguarico River, and two large lakes— Zancudococha and Imuya—and several smaller ones that are part of the Lagartococha River basin. The biophysical justification for this enlargement was that this entire area comprised a "single ecological entity" that "includes wetlands of national and international importance, [and] contains various native and endemic specimens of wildlife and flora of great importance for their conservation and sustainable use" (Registro Oficial 1991, 2). Though the sustainable use of wildlife was formally mentioned here, the lack of any such program during the prior twelve years of existence of the reserve cast doubt on this objective as an adequate justification for its enlargement.

The economic, political, and geopolitical interests in this area are equally, if not more, important in understanding the enlargement of the reserve and the secrecy with which it was accomplished. Economically, national tourist companies sought to set aside a large block of relatively unaltered rain forest to be used to meet the rising market demand of international tourists interested in visiting the Amazon rain forest. Politically, those expanding the reserve sought to preempt oil industry expansion into the area and make any future petroleum development there more difficult, since legally oil could not be exploited in protected areas. Through the maintenance of secrecy, the newly expanded reserve appeared in the Official Register as a *fait accompli* that would be difficult to reverse. From a geopolitical perspective, the Cuyabeno Reserve now bordered Peru, giving Ecuador yet another layer of control designed to protect this area from potential encroachments by this neighboring country.[8]

The enlargement of the reserve brought new social actors into this area, the most important of these being the national tourist industry, which quickly assumed a prominent role. The increase in international demand for rain-forest tourism was directly proportional to the emergence of Amazonia as an international environmental issue during the

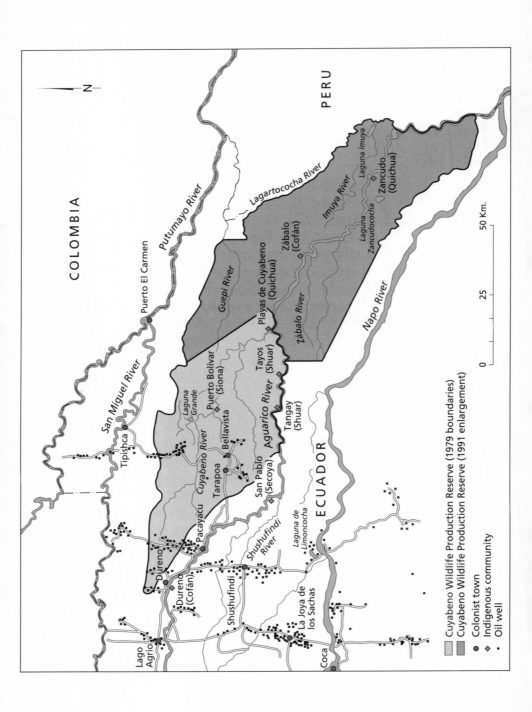

COLOMBIA

PERU

Putumayo River

Lagartococha River

Puerto El Carmen

San Miguel River

Guepi River

Imuya River

Laguna Imuya

Zancudo
(Quichua)

Zábalo
(Cofán)

Laguna
Zancudococha

Playas de Cuyabeno
(Quichua)

Zábalo River

Napo River

Tipishca

Laguna
Grande

Puerto Bolívar
(Siona)

Tayos
(Shuar)

Cuyabeno River

Bellavista

Aguarico River

Tarapoa

Pacayacu

San Pablo
(Secoya)

Tangay
(Shuar)

Dureno

Dureno
(Cofán)

Shushufindi

Shushufindi
River

Laguna de
Limoncocha

La Joya de
los Sachas

ECUADOR

Lago
Agrio

Coca

50 Km.

25

0

Cuyabeno Wildlife Production Reserve (1979 boundaries)

Cuyabeno Wildlife Production Reserve (1991 enlargement)

● Colonist town

◆ Indigenous community

▪ Oil well

1980s, and rain-forest landscapes were transformed into a natural re-source that was commodified by the tourist industry in the form of rain-forest tours.

Metropolitan Touring, Ecuador's largest tourist company, was a prime mover behind the expansion of the reserve. A biologist employed with this company conducted the preparatory study used by MAG to justify the expansion and gave Metropolitan Touring advance and nearly exclusive knowledge of it (Coello 1991). On 25 June 1991, just one week before the decree enlarging the reserve was promulgated, Transturi Inc., the Amazonian operational division of Metropolitan Touring, moved its luxury liner *Flotel Orellana* from its previous base of operations in Limon-cocha on the Napo River to the lower Aguarico River within the new boundaries of the Cuyabeno Reserve. It established two tourist encampments, equipped with cabins, boardwalks, and motor boats, at Zancu-dococha and Imuya Lakes and began selling package tours ranging from high luxury to high adventure, though all offering access to a "remote, virgin, and unexplored system of lakes, each with its own and diverse ecosystem of exuberant vegetation and with the richest faunal life of the Upper Amazon" (Transturi 1992, 2).

Thus, when the reserve was enlarged, it already had a major tourist operation functioning within it in exclusive form. Transturi justified moving its Amazonian tourist operations to the Cuyabeno Reserve on environmental grounds, since in Limoncocha, where the *Flotel Orellana* had been operating, extensive petroleum development had greatly altered the landscape. What Transturi did not publicly state was that years of tourism had turned the local indigenous populations into dependents of the company, rather than the exotic natives that tourists expected and demanded. Metropolitan Touring amplified its presence in the area through the creation in 1990 of the Ecuadorian Foundation for Conservation and Sustainable Development (FECODES), a nongovernmental organization entirely owned and operated by the firm, which would function as its research and environmental policy wing.

Though Transturi dominated tourist operations in the lower Aguarico River basin, numerous smaller tourist firms that had sprouted up in the late 1980s in response to increased demand began to conduct small-scale tours in the reserve. All tourist operators must get approval from the

The Aguarico River Region: Cuyabeno Wildlife Production Reserve (*opposite*)

Ecuadorian Institute of Forestry, Natural Areas, and Wildlife (INEFAN) to operate in the reserve,[9] and by 1991 thirteen different companies had been formally authorized to operate there. By this time, the Ecuadorian Association of Ecotourism had been formed and had enlisted the active participation of many of the firms operating in the Cuyabeno Reserve. During the first twenty years of the reserve's existence, its legal tourism rose dramatically: nonexistent in 1979, it totaled 200 tourists in 1987, jumped to 800 in 1989, surpassed 2,500 in 1992 (PROFORS 1993, Anexo 3), and soared to 10,000 by 1999.[10] This presence turned the tourism industry, together with the tourists who participated in the tours, into key social actors of the Cuyabeno Reserve.

The formal presence of INEFAN increased with expansion of the reserve, as several additional park rangers were hired and a new checkpoint, designed to control the entire lower portion of the Aguarico River, was built at the mouth of the Cuyabeno River. Since the reserve had nearly tripled in size, however, this staff and infrastructure continued to be inadequate for the geographical area to be controlled and the number of problems to be solved. Even with the increase in governmental presence, by 1992 Transturi, which used only one section of the reserve, had built more infrastructure than the government, which was responsible for controlling the entire area.

The enlargement of the reserve also expanded the role of social actors already present in the area, most notably its indigenous inhabitants. The new reserve boundaries encompassed two other indigenous communities: the Cofán community of Zábalo and the Quichua community of Zancudo. With the incorporation of Cofanes, the reserve now had to deal with segments of four different indigenous ethnic groups (Siona, Quichua, Shuar, and Cofán). In spite of the fact that the decree expanding the reserve stated that it should "promote the participation of the local population in the conservation of the area and in the benefit gained from the sustainable management of its renewable natural resources" (Registro Oficial 1991, 2), neither of the two newly included communities was consulted before the reserve's expansion. This provoked an immediate response from the Zábalo community, which sent a delegation to Quito to protest this adjudication of lands, part of which they claimed as theirs.[11] During this visit, the Cofán delegation gained the support of the Fundación Natura, which joined them in negotiating a temporary land agreement to be revised and incorporated into the new management plan for the reserve (Fundación Natura 1992). From this point on, this community would be in the forefront of the struggle of the indigenous communities to gain direct participation in the management of their territories.

Part of the reason for the major role of the Zábalo community in the affairs of the reserve stems from the charisma of its leader, Randy Borman, the blond-haired son of Summer Institute of Linguistic missionaries who was raised in the Cofán community of Dureno, speaks the native language fluently, married a Cofán woman, rose to the presidency of the Zábalo community, and eventually was elected president of the Association of Indigenous Communities of Cofán Nationality (ACOINCO), the principal Cofán political organization within Ecuador. By the early 1980s, the arrival of the oil industry had devastated the Dureno community located along the Aguarico River through contamination of its waters, invasion of its lands by colonists, and deforestation of its hunting areas. During this same period, a group of young Cofanes led by Borman split off from the Dureno community and settled far downriver at the mouth of Zábalo River, an area free from the contaminating influences of the oil industry and the colonists, where game and fish were still abundant and the group could live with traditional adaptive techniques.

This newly established Zábalo community was situated between two Quichua communities—Playas de Cuyabeno and Zancudo—and some members of the former, who had resided there since the 1950s, felt that the Cofán presence was an intrusion into their community territory. The Cofanes responded that the Aguarico River has been a domain of Cofán activity for centuries, since long before the Quichua arrived. In this case, the Quichuas were using a 30-year time frame to argue that they were there first, while the Cofanes were using a 300-year time frame to argue the same thing. The 80 kilometers of (river) distance between them and the small size of the two communities (each had fewer than 120 inhabitants) meant that both were well within the carrying capacity of the region and that they would not be competing for natural resources. The Zancudo Quichua community, located at the extreme southeast corner of the reserve next to an Ecuadorian army outpost of the same name, had been founded in the 1940s by a Quichua soldier stationed in the area. The members of this community were not greatly affected by the Cofán presence, nor did they register an immediate response to the expansion of the reserve. Nonetheless, they were rapidly incorporated into reserve affairs through their involvement with Transturi's tourist operations in the immediate vicinity of their community.

Another social actor who emerged in Ecuador during the 1980s and who would play a role in the affairs of the Cuyabeno Reserve was the activist ecologist current within the nation's environmental movement. The launching of the Amazonía ¡por la vida! international campaign in 1989, led by a coalition of a dozen national ecologist and environmentalist organizations, placed major emphasis on stopping the uncontrolled contamination of Ecuadorian Amazonia by the oil companies (Amazonía ¡por la vida! 1993, 1994). While the creation and preservation of protected areas was never a major goal of this campaign, direct affinities with preservationist goals exist, and the campaign forged alliances with the preservationist wing of the environmental movement, whose chief representative was the Fundación Natura.[12] The Fundación Natura, which had played a brokerage role in the negotiations between the Zábalo community and INEFAN, also controlled $10 million, received as part of Ecuador's first and largest debt-for-nature swaps, to be spent on strengthening the administration of and infrastructure in Ecuador's protected areas. A small part of this money was used in the construction of tourist cabins in the Cuyabeno Lakes district. PROFORS (Programa Forestal-Sucumbíos), financed by the German governmental aid agency GTZ, was another new social actor on the scene; its goal was to assist MAG in the "formulation, planning, and execution of policies designed to use lands in ecologically sound ways" (PROFORS 1993). This program focused on two protected areas in the Sucumbíos province: the Cuyabeno Reserve and the Coca-Cayambe Ecological Reserve, located in the extreme western part of Sucumbíos.

In the midst of this complex, multiactor situation, a scientific research team was formed in 1991 to prepare a new management plan for the entire Cuyabeno Reserve, a job completed with the formal presentation of the plan in May 1993 (MAG 1993). The planning team, which was responsible for drafting the final plan, was formed by two biologists, an agronomist, and an anthropologist. This group was supplemented by five professional assistants—a zoologist, a specialist in protected areas, a specialist in natural resources, and two governmental conservation officials with training in biology—and a team of consultants responsible for undertaking designated research projects and drafting maps. This last group included a forestry botanist, an edaphologist (soil specialist), a hydrologist, an ornithologist, an ichthyologist, a herpetologist, a zoologist, an archeologist, a cartographer, and a petroleum engineer.

The management plan was financed by a grant from FECODES, Metropolitan Touring's private NGO, since MAG did not have funds allotted for this purpose, and the planning core used office space in the company's headquarters in uptown Quito. The national tourist industry's direct involvement in and financial support of the government's conservation bureaucracy expose the latter's inability to adequately fulfill its mandates. This relationship also ingratiates the tourist industry to the very bureaucracy responsible for issuing tourist operator licenses and authorizing the construction of tourist facilities within protected areas.

The preparation of the management plan required both technical and social skills. Technically, the planning team had to review all research reports generated by the team, organize this information in usable form, and draft and revise the final plan. Socially, the preparation of the plan involved on-site observations and investigations, visits to indigenous and colonist communities to discuss the contents of the plan and to receive their comments, suggestions, and criticisms, and meetings with oil company personnel, tourist operators, government conservation officials, and other parties interested in the reserve.

The central territorial innovation contained in the Cuyabeno Management Plan was its call for formal, written agreements (*convenios*) to be established between INEFAN and the indigenous communities within the reserve; these agreements would outline the terms of co-management of specific areas. The co-managed territories proposed by this plan fused collective use principles (i.e., indigenous homelands) with state trust ownership ones (i.e., protected areas), whereby the state would maintain formal ownership of the land but would cede exclusive use rights to indigenous communities according to a set of written conditions negotiated and formally agreed upon by both parties. Each indigenous community would be designated a territory to use and manage in joint collaboration with reserve rangers and other government conservation officials. While this represented a territorial modality that did not exist in Ecuadorian law, moving forward with these agreements established a de facto territorial entity—called *sustainable use territories* here—with its legal status still pending.

Only indigenous communities were allowed to enter into these agreements, a measure tied to recognition of their ancestral rights to these lands, to their history of sustainable use, and to their low demographic density, which minimizes environmental effects. The joint collaboration between the government and indigenous communities, however, tends to hide the fact that two distinct conservation systems are at work here. Though the preservationist approach to protected areas shares some of the same goals of traditional indigenous use—low-impact interactions with the environment, nonpredatory, sustainable use of natural resources, and so forth—the management ideology of preservationists differs radically from indigenous notions of practical and ritual land use. Though both conservation systems rely upon historically constituted knowledge bases, the former uses reductionist science as expressed in highly technical reports, studies, and maps, while the latter is transmitted through oral tradition and practical teaching and is expressed in the daily practices of gaining subsistence, healing, and performing rituals. The co-management agreements represent a hybrid of these two systems, since they incorporate traditional indigenous uses into a technical scientific management plan.

The most technical part of the agreements is the zoning plan for each territory. The informal zoning system used by indigenous peoples, by which they would hunt and fish in particular areas at specific times of the year, gave way to a Western approach to zoning that relied upon highly specialized maps derived from radar and satellite images. In all, seven different zoning categories were used in these agreements: (1) intensive indigenous use; (2) subsistence hunting and fishing; (3) intensive tourism; (4) minimal-impact tourism; (5) maximum protection; (6) administration; and (7) military use. Meetings were held in each of the involved indigenous communities, where members could express their opinions and raise criticisms. At these meetings, traditional and environmental cosmographies sometimes clashed. Abstract Western-style maps used to delimit the different zones, for instance, were not always understood or accepted by indigenous participants. Disagreements also erupted when complicated restrictions were placed on traditional use areas of the community. Nonetheless, the common interests of both parties were strong enough to overcome these obstacles. The final agreements were drawn up by MAG, with assistance from PROFORS, and were signed jointly by the communities and the government.

In all, three indigenous communities entered into these agreements during the early nineties: Zábalo (Cofán), Puerto Bolívar (Siona), and

Playas de Cuyabeno (Quichua).[13] The initial round of negotiations for these agreements at the Neotropic Turis installations on the Laguna Grande in March 1992 involved the leaders of these three indigenous communities, the planning team of the management plan, government conservation officials, and observers from two NGOs (Fundación Natura and PROFORS). During this meeting a conflict developed between the Puerto Bolívar and Playas de Cuyabeno communities over the border to be established between their two communities. Before the meeting, the leaders of the Playas de Cuyabeno community had hammered out a border agreement with the Zábalo community in return for the latter's support in their conflict with Puerto Bolívar. These intraindigenous, interethnic conflicts are often more acute than the conflicts between indigenous communities and government conservation officials. In this particular case, a buffer zone granting common use by the two contending communities was negotiated, momentarily quelling the tensions between them.

At first, the two Shuar communities located within the reserve were deliberately excluded from these agreements, since their adaptive strategies placed them in the category of colonists, relegating their status as indigenous peoples to a secondary role. In this case, being traditional (which as we have seen has ecological as well as historical and cultural dimensions) proved to be more important than being indigenous. The government did not attempt to expel them, but it prohibited the entrance of additional Shuar colonists into the reserve. By the end of the nineties, the attitude of the government had changed and the possibility of both communities entering into co-management agreements was under consideration.

Meanwhile, a Secoya group located just outside the boundaries of the reserve expressed its intention to relocate along the Lagartococha River at the extreme eastern end of the reserve. This move was adamantly opposed by reserve officials, and the soldiers at the Zancudo army outpost were told to intercept and turn back any such advance by the Secoya. By tying them to specific areas indelibly etched in maps, the establishment and expansion of the Cuyabeno Reserve negated the traditional practice of resettlement practiced for centuries by indigenous peoples of the area.

From a geographical perspective, the creation and expansion of the reserve were designed to close the territorial issue of the lower Aguarico River basin once and for all by bringing all of the land under the formal

Part of the Chavez household, Playas de Cuyabeno, 1995

ownership of the state while simultaneously giving it legal protected status that strictly regulated its use. In practice, this move pushed latent territorial disputes into the political arena and, in the process, created a new set of territorial issues. On the one hand, the creation of the reserve benefited six indigenous communities that, at the time of its establish-ment or expansion, happened to be located within its boundaries. The co-management agreements greatly extended the land to which these communities had legal access, even though they were not granted own-ership rights to the land. On the other hand, by dealing only with iso-lated communities and not ethnic groups as a whole, these agreements ignored the territorial claims of those communities located outside of the reserve's boundaries and divided ethnic groups among their different communities.

The three indigenous communities that entered into co-management agreements considered them to be a formal recognition of their territo-ries, and this recognition was used as a bargaining chip in their negotia-tions with tourist firms. Since the three communities now had formal management duties over their respective territories, they claimed that they should also control and participate in the tourism that occurred within them. This created another type of de facto territory—a tourist-indigenous one—in which tourist firms and indigenous communities entered into agreements stipulating the use of particular routes, the building of tourist infrastructure, and the hiring of personnel and re-vealed yet another variant of the notion of sustainable use territories. Though these agreements could not prohibit other tourist firms from using the area, since this control was formally in the hands of INEFAN, they could direct the tourist flow in ways that would directly benefit the agreeing firms and communities. In these agreements, the Indians gained employment income and a ready market for their handicraft goods, while the tourist firms gained cheap labor and the chance to offer encounters with exotic Indian tribes as part of their tourist package.

Individual tourist companies preferred to negotiate directly with com-munities rather than with the ethnic confederations that represented these communities on a regional and national level, since the companies would have a great deal more leverage in the negotiations and would have to give far fewer concessions. These separate community-level ne-gotiations produced a wide array of responses where, once again, the Zábalo community played a key role.

Under the leadership of Borman, nine Zábalo community heads of household established an indigenous tourist corporation that entered into negotiations with Transturi to sell adventure-trekking tours near the Zábalo community. In a 50–50 profit-sharing arrangement, Transturi was responsible for the recruitment of tourists, off-site logistics, and transportation of tourists to the site, while the Cofanes opened the trails, served as guides and nature interpreters, and hauled and cooked the food. Another agreement involved the establishment of a Cofán craft center where tourists from the *Flotel Orellana* would stop to shop. In addition, the Cofán community, using Borman's contacts in the United States, set up a direct-link tourist operation from which all profits would stay in the community. In a different but related plan, the Zábalo community, with material support from the Fundación Natura, initiated a turtle project designed to replenish the depleted populations of two species (*Podocnemis unifilis* and *Podocnemis expansa*), one of the first projects to implement any type of wildlife production within the Cuyabeno Reserve.

The agreements developed between Transturi and the Playas de Cuyabeno and Zancudo Quichua communities were of a quite different nature and functioned according to typical employer-employee relations, whereby indigenous community members gained temporary work on construction crews and maintenance staff, piecework payments for washing the *Flotel Orellana* laundry, and salaried positions as boat motorists and cooks' assistants. Transturi also makes monthly donations of food, pays a schoolteacher's salary, and provides emergency medical and transportation services for these two Quichua communities (Canaday 1994a, 16; Canaday 1994b, 16).

A still different relationship developed between the Siona community of Puerto Bolívar and the Neotropic Turis company operating in the Cuyabeno Lakes district. Neotropic Turis, a small tourist company formed by four biologists who had previously conducted research within the original Cuyabeno Reserve, constructed rustic cabins on the Laguna Grande of the Cuyabeno Lakes district in 1991 and staked out this area as its base of operations. The company entered into a tightly knit relationship with the Sionas of Puerto Bolívar (with whom they had worked previously in biological research activities), who were given hiring preference over all outsiders as part of the company's policy benefiting local indigenous populations. One result of this relationship was the formation of a clan-based capitalist enterprise centered around the Criollo family. This aggravated existing social tensions within the community and produced an economic cleavage between the community's two principal family groups. Other effects of Neotropic's use of Siona labor included the monetarization of economic relations and the unintended devaluation of the Siona language, since young people found it far more prestigious to learn the languages of the tourists (Little 1992, 121–41).

The creation of de facto tourist-indigenous territories led to additional problems between and within indigenous ethnic groups. The members of the Puerto Bolívar and San Pablo communities came from the same linguistic stock, were extensively intermarried, were part of the same political organization (Indigenous Organization of Sionas and Secoyas of Ecuador—OISSE), and, before 1973, lived together in the same community. Their relations became strained over tourism and territorial issues. Members of the San Pablo community resented the significant economic benefits that the Puerto Bolívar Sionas were reaping from tourism because of their strategic location near the Cuyabeno Lakes district. San Pablo asked that a portion of tourist-generated profits be shared with the OISSE, a call rejected by members of the Puerto Bolívar community, whose strategic location within the reserve was an asset they were unwilling to give up or share, even with members of their own ethnic group.

These animosities were aggravated by the effort to create and delimit a unified Siona-Secoya territory. This effort was being financed through a grant by the Danish nongovernmental indigenist organization Solsticio. Since Solsticio was working directly with OISSE and not with individual communities, these funds were administered out of San Pablo, where the OISSE president resided. This created resentment in Puerto Bolívar, where people felt that they were being slighted in the distribution of the funds. The president of the Puerto Bolívar community, on a visit to Quito, sent a fax to Copenhagen asking that the money for delimitation of the Puerto Bolívar community be handled by him. In response to this situation, a representative of Solsticio was sent to Ecuador to defuse the conflict its financing was creating.

The original idea of creating a united and connected territory for all the Siona-Secoyas had to be abandoned. The existence of the Cuyabeno Reserve was an obstacle to realizing this unification, since part of this area was now state trust land. Furthermore, the Sionas of Puerto Bolívar, with their co-managed territorial agreement, had little interest in connecting the two territories because they had gained so much by going it alone as a community. Two separate territories were eventually delimited, one for San Pablo and the other for Puerto Bolívar. Even this process generated problems, since the Sionas delimited the disputed territory with the Playas de Cuyabeno community as being theirs (this occurred in the midst of the co-management agreement negotiations). Even further complicating matters, the land delimited with Danish money did not coincide with the final zoning areas, creating hostility between the head of the management plan team and Solsticio. All of these tensions culminated in the breakup of OISSE into two separate political organizations, one Siona and the other Secoya. In yet another ironic twist, in the midst of these numerous conflicts, the Puerto Bolívar Sionas were able to negotiate the western boundaries of their territory with the colonists, their arch enemies, thus setting a limit to colonist encroachment on their traditional lands.

In summary, the enlargement of the reserve, the protests from indigenous communities, the commissioning of the management plan, and the new mood within the preservationist current all influenced the creation of sustainable use territories. This modality was based in the sale of such resources as rain-forest landscapes and Indian handicrafts. Differentiation between and within the various social actors was made in the process of establishing these agreements, in which some indigenous communities gained a privileged position as long as they were willing to enter into the preservationist logic of the reserve. As the result of these historical processes, the sustainable use territories of the Cuyabeno Reserve became a unique territorial expression within an environmental cosmography that incorporated elements from both indigenous and development cosmographies.

Laguna Grande, Cuyabeno Wildlife Production Reserve

After spending several days in the Siona community of Puerto Bolívar along the Cuyabeno River, my colleague Betty and I were awoken by the *cacique* of the community telling us that R., one of the owners of the tourist firm operating in the Lake District of the Cuyabeno Wildlife Production Reserve, would be at the tourist installations on Laguna Grande and that we could possibly catch a boat ride back to the road with her. We boarded one of several canoes that were heading to Laguna Grande with nearly the entire Puerto Bolívar community aboard. Upon arriving at the tourist accommodations, we were met by R., who immediately asked, "And just who are you?" After telling her of our research in Puerto Bolívar, she continued, "And what may I do for you?" We told her of our need for a ride upriver, and she told us that would be fine; at the end of the day, she would be returning to Lago Agrio.

After a few more canoes arrived, R. gave out presents to the grandchildren of the *cacique* and then called everyone together for a big meeting. Today was payday at the tourist installations. Payday had become one of the few occasions when just about all members of the factionalized Puerto Bolívar community gathered, since nearly everyone had someone in the family who would get paid and whom they would join in heading upriver to town, where they would cash their check, do some shopping, perhaps do some drinking, and in general find numerous ways to spend their money. Before giving out the checks, R. laid down the rules: if you miss three days of work, you'll be fired; if your name is not on the employee register, you can't fill in for somebody else and get paid for it; a new lock has been placed on the warehouse in response to a missing bottle of whiskey; all people who enter the installations must have authorization from the Park Service and from her; mothers who work at the installations will not be allowed to bring their children with them unless they are of nursing age; one bar of soap for every ten sheets washed. She finished by asking, "Everyone agreed?" Silence.

After paying everybody, R. convened a second, private meeting in the guard's shack out back. This meeting (to which I, along with many others, listened from outside the shack) was called to handle two delicate situations: the fact that the amount filled out on a blank check did not coincide with the amount on the corresponding receipt and the settling of a dispute between two Siona brothers over the usurpation of one brother's turn by the other in running the lucrative motorist trade that brought tourists into and out of the reserve. In this sibling battle, R. took on the role of the conciliator. "How can brothers fight when they have a wonderful father and mother [the *cacique* and his wife]? Let's make a pact; in the future brothers who fight will be whipped with nettles and thrown in the lake. Everyone agreed?" Silence.

This glimpse of payday had our heads spinning. In the two short years since the firm had set up operations at Laguna Grande, the social and economic structure of the community had been radically transformed. In the process, R. had become the virtual headwoman of the community, in tacit alliance with the traditional headman, since she controlled the purse strings that financed the newly monetarized Siona life, a situation avidly embraced by the Sionas without really knowing where it would lead them.

At dusk, Betty and I caught a ride up river in R.'s canoe, specially fitted with a large cushioned chair, set in the middle of the launch much like a throne, which she used due to her back troubles. I sat next to R. in the canoe, and we talked of the tourist operation. She explained that one of the tenets of ecotourism used by her company was exclusively to hire local Indian people for on-site work: "The Sionas live in the reserve, they know the reserve, and as such they have the right to work in tourism in this area." This work, however, needed to be strictly controlled. She does not allow the Sionas, for instance, to charge for having their picture taken because she considers that denigrating. "I simply will not permit it because it is the height of exploitation." Silence.

The Cajari, Maracá, and Iratapuru Extractivist Territories

The Cajari, Maracá, and Iratapuru River basins form the heart of the southern tip of the state of Amapá. All three rivers have their headwaters in the Iratapuru highlands of central Amapá, an area rich in natural Brazil nut groves. These groves formed the biophysical basis for extensive Brazil nut extractivism during the first half of the twentieth century. Since the Cajari and Maracá Rivers flow directly into the North Canal of the Amazon River and the Iratapuru River flows in the Jari River, this extractivism had ready fluvial access to the rest of the Lower Amazon Basin, particularly the port city of Belém.

The Cajari and Iratapuru River basins were part of José Júlio's Brazil nut estate and were settled permanently during his reign by *caboclos* from the Amazon Delta islands and peasants from his native state of Ceará. The Maracá River basin was never controlled by José Júlio (though he once attempted to buy it) and historically has been a type of buffer zone between the Jari Region to the southwest and the Macapá urban center to the northeast. It was sparsely settled during most of the twentieth century and only gained a significant permanent population starting in the 1970s because of *caboclo* migrations from the Delta islands.[14] And though these three river basins are geographically contiguous, the fact that river travel requires a long and arduous trip down one river and up the next makes them demographically quite distant from each other. In the case of the Cajari and Maracá Rivers, this distance was greatly shortened with the construction of the BR-156 road, which cut transversely through both basins.

During the 1970s, industrial and individual ranchers began invading this extractive area from two sides. Coming from the southwest, the Jari Project claimed much of the Cajari River basin as its own and placed the bulk of its water buffalo operations in the marshlands of the lower Cajari River. Coming from the northwest, cattle ranchers began an extensive campaign, with technical and financial support from the Amapá territorial government, to supplant beef cattle with water buffalo, an animal readily adaptable to Amapá's numerous marshlands. The expansion of this program onto new lands in the 1970s was so fast that by 1982 the number of water buffalo raised in Amapá Territory had eclipsed that of beef cattle (Raiol 1992, 148). The Igarapé do Lago and Central do Maracá marshlands of the lower Maracá River basin were excellent sites for grazing water buffalo herds, and several extractivist *patrões* who claimed control over these wetlands added ranching to the other economic activities they conducted in the area. The water buffalo ranchers entered into conflict with the local *caboclos,* since the buffalo were rarely fenced in, leaving them to invade the *caboclos'* cultivated plots and eat their agricultural production.

Individual and industrial mining interests also invaded the Maracá River basin. The gold rush that affected all of Brazilian Amazonia starting in 1980 brought hundreds of wildcat miners to the upper Maracá River, where they panned and dug for gold. Industrial mining interests, for their part, began prospecting the middle Maracá River basin for kaolin, stimulated by the favorable finds of the Jari Project in the Jari River basin. The Iratapuru River basin, which lies to the north, was not greatly affected by these development activities of the eighties.

The creation of GEBAM in 1980 installed another social actor into this area. GEBAM's mandate included the search for solutions to the land tenancy problems of the Lower Amazon Basin. Nationalist Admiral Gama e Silva, the head of GEBAM, took this mandate to include the "removal of colonial cysts" from the national territory (1991, 71–92). Upon discovering in 1981 that the Agro-Industrial do Amapá Company, which owned forty-five separate parcels of land in the Maracá River basin, functioned as a front for private British capital (the Eisenberg Group), GEBAM, in collaboration with INCRA, the federal agrarian reform agency, expropriated the entire Maracá River basin, a total of 575,619 hectares, to be used for the public interest (decree 86236). However, since GEBAM's legal mandate did not contain specific measures designed to meet the needs of ex-peons, Brazil nut gatherers, and *caboclos* in general who had longstanding claims to the area, once this expropriation was made, no follow-up activities were conducted and the area existed in a type of territorial limbo, which served to encourage further invasions by water buffalo ranchers.

The *caboclos* were a loosely organized group whose collective identity was often structured around river basins. Rivers have historically been the principal means of transport for *caboclos* and, since most *colocações* are located along rivers, neighborly bonds are established as one travels on the river in fulfilling one's daily chores or as one travels by boat to the city, nearby markets, soccer games, or dances. The river basin also is the main demographic universe for the marriages of young people, thereby adding kinship ties to neighborly ones. In this way group identities have been formed by the people living along the same river, which has resulted in separate social identities for the Maracá, Cajari, and Iratapuru *caboclos*.

These river-based social identities, however, did not translate into strong political organizations in any of these three river basins. The continuing existence of the *aviamento* system, which dates back to the rubber boom years, was a major obstacle to the internal political organization of the *caboclos,* since a local *patrão* controlled many aspects of their public lives and mediated most of their economic and political relationships with the outside world. The high rates of illiteracy among the extractivists also severely limited their ability to fend for themselves within a social and political environment that already had marginalized them. In short, throughout the first ninety years of the twentieth century, the extractivists of the Cajari, Maracá, and Iratapuru River basins did not have their own political organizations capable of protecting their interests and promoting their claims.

By the mid-1980s extractivists throughout Brazilian Amazonia had become an important political force in national politics. After the success of the Acre *empates* in slowing the advance of deforestation by ranchers and land speculators, the rubber tappers, under the leadership of Chico

A *caboclo* family, lower Maracá River, 1992

Mendes, forged strategic alliances with environmental groups and other sectors of Brazilian civil society. With the formation of the National Council of Rubber Tappers at their first national meeting held in Brasilia in 1985, these extractivists burst onto the political scene with a well-developed set of territorial claims and policy initiatives. The most innovative of the proposals to come out of this meeting was the call for the creation of extractive reserves, or contiguous blocks of land historically occupied and used by extractivists, who would be granted collective, rather than individual, titles.

In 1987 a working group within INCRA was set up to consider this proposal within the framework of the agrarian reform goals of this agency, with advisory roles granted to the Rubber Tappers Council and the Institute for Amazonian Studies (IEA), an NGO working in close partnership with the rubber tappers movement. As a result of these efforts, on 30 July 1987 a Ministry of Agrarian Reform and Development Regulation (no. 627) established the territorial modality of extractive settlement projects and placed them under the responsibility of INCRA. During the next two years, ten such settlement projects were established in the states of Acre, Amazonas, and Amapá. This important first step toward the implementation of the extractive reserve concept represented an interim solution for the rubber tappers, since extractive settlement projects were created by a *portaria* (an internal regulation of a government agency) that could easily be revoked and that depended on the adaptation of agrarian reform modalities of land tenancy (hence, the name *settlement projects*) rather than collective modalities founded on sustainable use and conservation goals. Another difficulty with this modality was its requirement that the entire area of the settlement projects be expropriated before being legally delimited and registered by the government.

Extractive reserves were established by law 7804 (18 July 1989) as a new type of governmental protected area, became a formal part of Brazilian environmental policy, and were placed under the responsibility of the IBAMA, which had been created earlier that year (IEA 1993, 123). Decree 98.897 (30 January 1990) provided specific guidelines for the implementation of extractive reserves, defined in article 1 as "territorial spaces designated for the self-sustaining exploitation and conservation of renewable natural resources by an extractivist population." Four large extractive reserves were created in 1990 in traditional rubber and Brazil nut areas, with five smaller ones created in 1992, four in areas of babassu extraction and one in a coastal fishing area. The National Center for the Sustainable Development of Traditional Populations (CNPT) was created within IBAMA in 1992 to give technical assistance to the extractive reserves, and under its leadership this territorial modality was expanded to include all types of extractivism in Brazil (Ruiz and Pinzón 1995). By 1999 there were twelve extractive reserves in ten different Brazilian states.

In spite of the fact that these two modalities—extractive settlement projects and extractive reserves—are under the responsibility of two different government agencies (INCRA and IBAMA) with distinct goals (agrarian reform and environmental protection), their emergence from the same extractivist social base and their effect of granting extractivists formal territorial control over lands that they have historically used in sustainable ways reveals fundamental social and environmental similarities. In both modalities, the land is held in trust by the federal government, which then grants to representative local extractivist associations an exclusive "use-rights concession" (*concessão de direito real de uso*), which formalizes the partnership between the government and the extractivists for the control over the settlement projects and reserves. This control is granted according to what are known as "condominium exploitation" rights, by which individual plots of land are prohibited and local associations, as collective entities, are granted exclusive use and occupancy (Gomes and Felippe 1994). The concessions are granted only after detailed utilization plans (note the emphasis on *use* as opposed to the more preservationist *management* plans of other protected areas) are prepared and approved by the local extractivist population and by the responsible government agencies. These plans then become an integral part of the contract between the government and the association in what represents a co-management agreement. Development plans are then to be drawn up, plans that go beyond resource-use policies to include such items as education, health, and infrastructure designed to improve the quality of life of the extractivists and give the extractive reserves and settlement projects long-term social sustainability.

The three extractive settlement projects Maracá I, II, and III were created in 1988 by INCRA (*Portarias* 1440, 1441, and 1442 of October 27) as three contiguous projects of the lower, middle, and upper Maracá River basin, respectively, covering a total area of 363,500 hectares. During the 1970s and 1980s, the *caboclo* population of the Maracá River basin had grown considerably through migration. These migrants, some with minimal experience in Brazil nut extractivism, would be the beneficiaries of this settlement project. The establishment of the Maracá Extractive Settlement Projects within the area that had been expropriated by GEBAM in 1981 gave these lands a definite public purpose.[15] It also facilitated their formal delimitation, since the costly, time-consuming process of expropriation had already been consummated. During the following five years, however, INCRA did nothing to consolidate these settlement projects, and invasions by buffalo ranchers and gold miners continued unabated.

In addition to INCRA, several social actors in civil society were instrumental in aiding the consolidation of the Maracá Extractive Settlement Projects in their first years of existence. Two environmental NGOs, the Institute for Amazonian and Environmental Studies (IEA) and the World Wildlife Fund–U.S. (WWF), supported studies of the area (Dubois 1989; Allegretti and Little 1993; Vogt et al. 1993), while the Rubber Tappers Council and the Rural Workers' Union of Amapá were instrumental in helping the local extractivist population organize into a functioning association. In 1991, the Association of Agro-Extractivist Workers of the Valley of the Maracá River (hereafter the Maracá Association) was formed as the legal representative of the local population to deal directly with INCRA on all matters concerning the management of the area. In 1992 IEA, with financing from the German Konrad Adenauer Foundation, initiated the Man and Environment in Amazonia Project, designed to strengthen the Maracá Association and to provide technical assistance in the areas of research and development of the Maracá Extractive Settlement Projects. After four years of operation, control of the project passed to another NGO, the Brazilian Agroforestry Network.

By 1993 local environmental NGOs, social movements, and government agencies had formed the Interinstitutional Working Group on Extractivism in Amapá and had begun to exert pressure on INCRA to assume its responsibilities over these settlement projects. In October of that year, INCRA made a census of the local population, in which four hundred families were formally registered, placing the total population of the three Maracá Extractive Settlement Projects at twenty-three hundred people. In coordination with this effort, IEA organized the research and writing of an extensive socioeconomic report of the three Maracá projects (Little and Filocreão 1994). The data from this report were used in preparation of the Maracá Utilization Plan (IEA and INCRA 1995), which, after being discussed in fifteen community meetings, was approved in the general assembly of the Maracá Association in August 1995, making Maracá the first extractive settlement projects in Brazil to meet all requirements for receiving the formal use-rights concession from the government.

Foot-dragging by INCRA, however, delayed this process because of internal resistance from sectors of the agency tied to family-based colonization schemes, which had never approved of the idea of extractive settlement projects in the first place and which did not understand their role within the broader agrarian reform movement. The constant pressure on INCRA from local and state-level organizations, however, proved to be effective, and on 23 April 1997, Raul Jungmann, Brazilian minister of agrarian reform, in a ceremony held at Vila Maracá, formally granted collective use title to the Maracá Association for the three Maracá Extractive Settlement Projects, making them the first such entities to achieve this milestone.

The creation of the Cajari Extractive Reserve in 1990 (decree 99145, 12 March 1990) set aside 481,550 hectares of the Cajari River basin in an area situated to the southeast of and contiguous with the Maracá Extractive Settlement Projects. In 1991 the Association of Workers of the Extractive Reserve of the Valley of the Cajari River (hereafter the Cajari Association) was formed with the assistance of the Rubber Tappers Council, the Rural Workers Union, and WWF. In 1992 a socioeconomic study of the Cajari Extractive Reserve was conducted, and 672 families were registered, setting the total population of the reserve at 3,479 people (Mattoso and Fleischfresser 1994). That same year, IBAMA formally filed for expropriation of the lands enclosed by the Cajari Extractive Reserve, which included more than five hundred separate claims to be settled, many held by the Jari Project,[16] and CNPT launched a training and development program for the local population. A utilization plan for the Cajari Extractive Reserve was prepared and approved by the Cajari Association in 1995.

As in the case of the Maracá Extractive Settlement Projects, several NGOs assisted the Cajari Association in its first years of existence. The Brazilian Agroforestry Network conducted an intensive seminar for extractivists on the latest techniques of agroforestry systems. Another major project funded by several NGOs was the implementation of a program of community-run stores that would offer foodstuffs and household goods to the local population at prices far lower than those charged by itinerant traders who served the area. This program ran into difficulties due to lack of training in accounting, a poor transportation network, lack of adequate storage facilities, and the granting of excessive credit, and it was closed down before it was able to achieve a minimal level of stability.

The Cajari Reserve was one of four such extractive reserves selected to participate in the G-7-funded Pilot Program for the Protection of Brazilian Tropical Forests. In 1995, after three years of negotiations and preparations, a four-year U.S.$9 million project began to be implemented. This project provided funds and technical assistance to both the Cajari Association and the Rubber Tappers Council, began to equip the reserve with production and transportation infrastructure, and furnished much-needed training for local extractivists. At the same time, this project faced numerous difficulties, since it demanded that financial and programmatic reports be presented every two weeks, a near impossibility given the lack of training and infrastructure of the Cajari Association, while it required that monies be spent within allotted time frames or be returned, a policy that sparked major buying sprees of equipment that then lay idle because of the lack of preparation. In spite of these many difficulties, by 1997, with financing from WWF and technical assistance from the Pilot Program, a palm heart factory had been constructed within the reserve and was operating under the direct control of the Cajari Association.

From a territorial perspective, the Maracá Extractive Settlement Projects and the Cajari Extractive Reserve jointly encompassed 845,050 contiguous hectares that had been formally placed under the control of a new type of social and political organization—the local extractivist associations. These associations were qualitatively different from any other organizations that had existed among the *caboclos*. The creation of the Maracá Extractive Settlement Projects and the Cajari Extractive Reserve proved to be an important external stimulus for the political organization of extractivists, since only through a formally established representative organization would they be able to receive use-rights concession from the government. Though the formation of the Maracá and Cajari Associations was nominally based on the previous social identity of these two groups of *caboclos* with their respective rivers, these new organizations represented far more than the mere transference of a social identity to political goals.

These two associations were totally new organizations that now had greatly expanded economic, political, social, cultural, and territorial attributes. Economically, they are responsible for the development and implementation of a utilization plan for their respective areas geared to turn them into profitable, productive entities. Politically, they are imbued with the responsibility of negotiating directly with the government on matters of mutual concern and preparing a long-range development plan geared to meet their collective needs. Socially, they are responsible for the conservation and protection of the varied ecosystems that these areas contain. Culturally, they are charged with the maintenance and strengthening of *caboclo* extractivist culture. Finally, these associations are territorial entities with specific parcels of land for which they share responsibility, with the federal government, for sustainable use and defense from outside forces.

These extractivist populations, which had historically been marginal to regional political structures, now had this wide scope of powers formally recognized by the federal government. Such a drastic change in such a short time left these associations ill prepared to adequately fulfill these new responsibilities, since most of the adult population lacked formal education, had little experience in democratic forms of organization, and knew little of the mechanisms demanded of them by the outside world. Herein lies a partial explanation of the failure of early efforts at economic development, such as community stores, and the difficulty in preparing detailed biweekly reports for the Pilot Program's Extractive Reserve Project.

The most pressing challenge to these two extractivist associations, however, arose from the multiple economic forces that sought access to these 845,050 hectares of protected land to exploit its many natural resources for private economic gain. In addition to the invasion of these areas by water buffalo ranchers and gold miners, commercial fishing boats enter the two rivers and, through the use of predatory fishing techniques, take large amounts of fish, which are then processed, frozen, packaged, and shipped to regional and national markets. The local extractivists do not gain any economic benefit from this activity, while the rivers' fishing stocks are depleted, destroying one of the main sources of protein for local residents. The predatory cutting of assai palm trees for palm hearts, another activity controlled by external commercial interests, devastates natural palm tree groves and provides little economic benefit for the local population. Illegal logging and clandestine sawmills are still another type of invasion that these two associations must confront. Finally, the invasion of lands within these areas by small-scale farmers who squat on lands next to the recently constructed state road represents a major threat to the territorial and biophysical integrity of these areas (Little and Filocreão 1994, 101–13).

The defense of the Maracá Extractive Settlement Projects and the Cajari Extractive Reserve against these many economic interests became an urgent task of the extractivist associations. This defense could be effective only with the wholehearted cooperation of those government agencies responsible for co-managing these territories, a collaboration that throughout the 1990s was notably lacking. In 1995 an important precedent was set at the Cajari Extractive Reserve when a land speculator who was planning a colonization scheme within the reserve was forcibly removed from the area by IBAMA with the aid of the federal police. In the Maracá Extractive Settlement Projects, INCRA has been far less willing to engage in conflicts and in one case actually encouraged illegal logging. In 1995 INCRA gave a water buffalo rancher a ninety-day deadline to leave the Maracá I Settlement Project; after this time elapsed, he was still there, and they did nothing to enforce their expulsion order.

Given the tenuousness of the co-management partnership between the government and the extractivist associations, the latter looked for and gained help from sectors of the civil society. Social movements such as the Rubber Tappers Council and the Rural Workers Union and environmental NGOs such as IEA and WWF have provided crucial assistance to both the Maracá and Cajari Associations. The Interinstitutional Working Group on Extractivism in Amapá also has helped in publicizing illegal invasions of the two areas and in placing formal complaints with government agencies responsible for controlling them.

With the inauguration of João Capiberibe as governor of Amapá in 1995, the extractivists gained formal support at the state level, which historically had been tied to economic interests benefiting from the invasion of these lands. Among the changes in policy implemented by the Capiberibe government were the construction of infrastructural works in these two neglected areas, the ceding of productive and transportation equipment to the associations, and the commitment by the state government to purchase the Brazil nut production of these areas for use in its school lunch program.

The most ambitious project of the Capiberibe government with regard to extractivism was the creation in 1997 of a *state-level* extractivist territory that encompassed the entire Iratapuru River basin in the western part of the Amapá, just north of the Cajari Reserve, which was placed under the joint control of the local extractivist population and the state government. In all, 806,184 hectares were set aside and christened as the Iratapuru River Sustainable Development Reserve. The Extractivist Producers Cooperative of the Iratapuru River, founded in 1992, was the local association responsible for managing and protecting this immense area. Since this area has been less affected by invasions, its extractivist potential was more easily implemented. By 1999, just two years after its creation, the Iratapuru Reserve had two small Brazil nut processing plants operating within it.

In the span of a decade (1988–97), extractivist populations had made enormous gains in consolidating their political power and establishing territorial claims to the lands they occupied. This represented a dramatic change of course from the development cosmographies that had been installed in the area by other social groups since the 1940s. Both the Maracá Extractive Settlement Projects and the Cajari Extractive Reserve are legally established federal sustainable use territories in an incipient state of becoming economically profitable, socially viable, and biophysically sustainable. The Iratapuru Sustainable Development Reserve builds on these two previous experiences and serves to strengthen the goals of sustainable use extractivism at a state government administrative level. In all, a total of 1.65 million hectares of land in southern Amapá has been formally designated for extractivist sustainable use, thus reaffirming the extractivist vocation of the area. This large area represents a partial reconstitution of José Júlio de Andrade's immense Brazil nut estate, only this time the vast tract of land was placed under the control of the people who do the actual extraction, accompanied by explicit conservationist goals.

Central do Maracá, Maracá Extractive Settlement Projects

The special meeting of the Association of Agro-Extractivist Workers of the Valley of the Maracá River was in its second day of deliberations over the Utilization Plan for the Maracá Settlement Projects when the debate over biotechnology erupted. The local *caboclo* extractivists were analyzing the plan point by point in small groups, and their comments would then be brought to the plenary session, where they would be discussed and a final version approved. After sailing through the first seven points, point 8 caused a snag. It declared: "The rights acquired over discoveries within the area of the Maracá Settlement Projects should be formalized through agreements between the Association and the researchers and/or companies responsible for the discovery, setting a royalty fee which the Association will receive with the marketing of the biotechnological processes derived from the discovery."

This point had been introduced into the text several months earlier by a committee under my leadership at a workshop for government and civil society professional staff who worked with extractivism to make suggestions on the plan. Our committee drafted point 8—at the behest of the state coordinator of the Rubber Tappers Council—as a kind of insurance policy against possible future exploitation by unscrupulous biotechnology firms coming into the settlement projects.

Returning to the plenary session, one group reported that they didn't know what this point meant and suggested it be struck from the plan. In the ensuing discussion, several examples of medicines that could be derived from plants were mentioned as possible types of biotechnological applications. At this point, the official representative of the state governor chimed in. He argued forcefully that it would be a grave mistake to remove this point and supported his claim with the example of taking a single cell from the arm of a person and from that cell creating an entire human being. If the confusion over biotechnology had been high to begin with, after this wild example confusion reigned supreme. The assembly agreed to reconsider the issue in the small group sessions that afternoon.

In the succeeding plenary session at the end of the day, point 8 was raised again. This time, however, a different group took the stance that royalties weren't enough and that the association should be the sole owner of all biotechnological processes developed from plants discovered in the Maracá Settlement Projects. This led to a discussion of the feasibility of the association engaging in biotechnological work and its necessity to collaborate with high-tech firms that operated sophisticated scientific laboratories and equipment in developing these products. Point 8 was once again sent back to small groups to be decided on the next day.

In the final plenary session, the assembly voted to strike the point from the plan, since it was just too damn confusing. The governor's representative took the floor once again to say that they were making a mistake and once again gave his example of a human cell used to create a human clone. Supposedly, the issue was put to rest. But the secretary responsible for officially recording the events of the assembly did not register this decision (for whatever reason). In the final text that was edited and approved by the federal government, point 8 remained just as it had appeared in the draft version.

All this maneuvering would probably not have a direct effect on the settlement projects and could be chalked up as an academic debate. Yet it is significant, not only for revealing the existing gap between complex scientific issues and the possibility of local control of them, but as a harbinger of debates to come.

CHAPTER FOUR

Disputing Territorial Claims

*Contemporary Frontiers in Amazonia
during the 1990s*

Continuing Struggles over the Jari Region

The Territorial "Taming" of the Jari Industrial Complex

During the first fifteen years of operation of Ludwig's Jari Project, conflicts over the creation of the towns of Beiradão and Beiradinho, the adequate treatment of workers, and the titling of the land severely strained
the relationships among this project, the federal government, and the
Amapá territorial government. With the purchase of the Jari Complex by
Brazilian industrial interests, some of these conflicts intensified. During
the 1990s three new territorial conflicts emerged: (1) the legal dispute
over the lands of the Cajari Extractive Reserve, (2) the environmental
dispute over the expansion of Jari eucalyptus plantations into Amapá,
and (3) the political dispute over the adjudication of squatter lands.

The establishment of the Cajari Extractive Reserve in 1990 by the
federal government created a serious situation of territorial overlap,
since well over half of the 481,550 hectares of the Cajari Reserve were
claimed by the Jari Complex as part of its 1,632,121 contiguous hectares.
Brazilian law requires that any newly established protected area resolve
its land tenancy situation through the mechanism of expropriation for
public use of all private lands contained in it within two years of its
establishment. This requirement is rarely fulfilled, given the slow working of the federal bureaucracy and the intricate and time-consuming
process of revision and authentication of all land titles within the area,
pricing of the land and all improvements made upon it, and authorization and final payment of the private land holders.[1]

As the two-year time limit was drawing near, Maria Benigna Jucá, a
lawyer within IBAMA stationed in Amapá, realized that the federal government had made no effort to expropriate the lands within the Cajari
Reserve, and she hastily put together an expropriation order and filed it

with the government. The Jari Complex, in an effort to protect its lands within the reserve, sought to nullify the order, claiming that the government had formally passed the deadline. After a lower court ruled in favor of the Jari Complex, IBAMA appealed the decision to a higher court, which overturned the lower court's ruling and authorized IBAMA to continue the expropriation process.

More than five hundred separate claims to the land were filed seeking indemnification, with the bulk of these titles belonging to the Jari Complex. At this stage of the conflict, the government found itself in a dilemma because its own records of the land titles were in complete disarray, a situation aggravated when a past administrator had simply thrown away certain documents in what was most likely a case of either outright corruption or *grilagem*. This made it difficult for the government legally to prove which lands belonged to it and which lands were legitimately in the hands of private owners. Since the Jari Complex had over the years kept minute care of its land titles, given the constant disputes over its territoriality, they were in a far better position to prove their control over the lands than was the government, creating the rather absurd situation in which the government would indemnify the Jari Complex for some lands that belonged to the government, since it could not prove ownership because of its own history of bureaucratic incompetence and corruption.

Brazilian law stipulates that, in addition to the value of the land per se, all improvements made upon the land must also be included in indemnification. The Jari Complex had a eucalyptus plantation within the Cajari Reserve (which, in the economic logic of the law, is considered as an improvement on the land), along with several corrals and other ranching infrastructure used in managing the thousands of head of water buffalo that graze on the marshlands of the lower Cajari River. The issue of pricing the value of the land and the improvements made on it turned into a separate, but related, legal battle, suggesting that a definitive indemnification settlement could be very expensive and take years. In the meantime, the local extractivists continued with the process of consolidating their control over the Cajari Reserve and implementing programs designed to make it economically viable and ecologically sustainable.

Brazilian environmental regulations stipulate that every protected area should have a 10-kilometer-wide buffer zone around its circumference. Special rules apply to this buffer zone; while less stringent than those for the protected area, these rules nonetheless stipulate that any major changes in the landscape be formally approved by competent environmental authorities. The existence of the buffer zone affected the Jari Complex, since two of its expansions of eucalyptus plantations in Amapá, named Felipe I and Felipe II, were contained within it.[2] Felipe I was established by the company without prior concern for the reserve. By the time Felipe II was planted, environmentalist pressures had resulted in the development of a formal Environmental Impact Study (EIS). This eighty-four-page report prepared by the C.R. Almeida consulting firm in Curitiba, thousands of kilometers from the Jari Region, concluded that "the implementation of the [Felipe II] project will be positive for the environment in question," since the "planting of a new forest, with greater *productivity* [than that of the old, native forest] would provide for greater *efficiency* in the use of raw materials and energy" as well as for "an improvement in the social and economic conditions of the population directly or indirectly involved in the project" (Siqueira 1992, 82, emphasis added). In the mandatory public hearing about this project, this report was questioned as being far too concerned with economic issues and giving short shrift to the serious effects to be caused by the felling of five thousand hectares of native rain forest. Though the Jari Complex eventually implemented the project, its continued expansion onto native forestlands in this area became more difficult because of having to comply with the many environmental and legal requirements stemming from the existence of the buffer zone.

The third conflict involving the Jari Complex's territoriality was over lands along the left bank of the Jari River (i.e., the Amapá side), which were occupied either by *caboclos* with a long history of presence in the area or by squatters who had come into the region during the past two or three decades. From the point of view of the Amapá government, these lands were *terras devolutas* (unused lands returned to the public domain) that were under the control of the state government. Since the municipality of Mazagão (from whose western edge the municipalities of Laranjal do Jari and Vitória do Jari were later created) had long been neglected by the territorial government of Amapá, this area became a type of no man's land, which *caboclos,* squatters, and the Jari Complex all used for their respective purposes without direct concern for the question of legal tenancy.

With the installation of the Capiberibe government in Amapá in 1995, this situation changed dramatically, since the governor was committed to protecting the rights of small landowners and traditional extractivists in the face of an assault by the Jari Complex. Capiberibe named Maria Benigna Jucá (who took leave from her position as IBAMA lawyer) to head the Amapá Land Institute (TERRAP). Upon assuming this position, Jucá launched a major effort to review (*discriminação de terras*) the effective occupation and legal tenancy of all lands along the left bank of the Jari River, with the goal of adjudicating lands to all local residents who could prove legitimate occupation and use under Brazil's laws of possession.[3] In the words of Governor Capiberibe, "Over the past thirty years no administration has had the courage to review [*discriminar*] the lands claimed by the Jari Project."

Initial visits by the TERRAP team revealed more than three hundred separate claims to parcels of land along the Jari River for which the Amapá government, according to Jucá, "will give out legal titles to all those claims which are found to be legitimate." This was a solid blow to the Jari Complex that would further diminish its presence in Amapá, a presence that had already been weakened by the emergence of the towns of Beiradão and Beiradinho and the creation of the Laranjal and Vitória do Jari municipalities. In an eventual negotiated settlement, the Jari Complex ceded its claims to approximately 100,000 hectares of land in Amapá to the state government. As part of this process, several hundred *caboclos* or long-term squatters gained legal title to the lands that they occupied.

The situation on the other side of the river, in the state of Pará, where 70 percent of the Jari Complex's claimed 1,632,121 hectares lie, is markedly different. Most of the complex's tree plantations and its key infrastructure—including its Munguba industrial sector, its Monte Dourado headquarters, its bauxite mine and processing plant, its two forestry villages, its railroad line, and most of its roads—are located in Pará. (On the Amapá side lies its kaolin mine, the Felipe tree plantations, and most of its water buffalo herd.) Those areas where the Jari Complex effectively occupies the land have served to consolidate its possession. The main dispute over the boundaries of the complex in Pará was over the buffer zone of the Jari Ecological Station, and this dispute was with IBAMA, a *federal* government agency, not a state one. The state of Pará is reluctant to antagonize the Jari Complex, since it generates a great deal of tax and

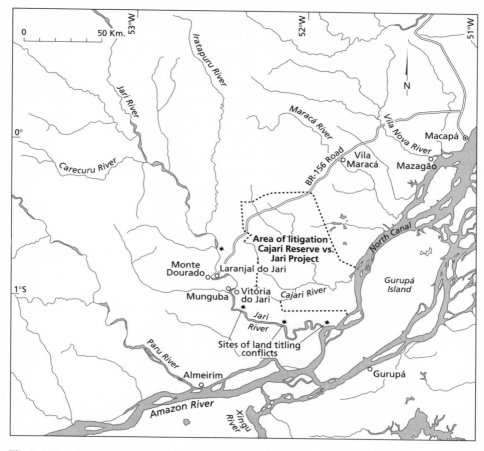

The Jari River Region: Territorial Disputes of the 1990s

royalty revenue for state and municipal coffers, especially those of the Almeirim municipality, where the complex is located. Within the Pará Land Institute (ITERPA), the counterpart to TERRAP in Amapá, several bureaucrats have sought to declare some of the Jari Complex's lands as *terras devolutas* in apparent deference to logging companies interested in cutting timber, but these efforts were not supported at higher levels of the state government because of fear of alienating the Jari Complex administration.

Another key difference between Pará and Amapá has been that the Almeirim municipality has not been subdivided into smaller municipalities, as occurred in Amapá, in spite of the rapid increase in population of Monte Dourado and Munguba and the enormous size of the municipality, which stretches from the Amazon River in the south to the Suriname border in the north. If a Monte Dourado municipality were created, Almeirim would lose most of its current revenue. This marriage of convenience, whereby the Almeirim municipality receives financial benefits in return for not questioning the Jari Complex's territorial claims and not encouraging squatting or illegal logging on this land, has proved to be stable over the past three decades.

In summary, the territoriality of the Jari Complex is being "tamed" by a host of forces. Its partial encirclement by preservationist (Jari Ecological Station) and sustainable use (Cajari Reserve) territories tied to environmental cosmographies gave it firm northern and eastern limits. The actions of the Amapá government to take effective control of its lands and attend to the needs of its citizens in the Jari Region diminished its claim to numerous lands in Amapá. The notion of exclusive use of private property based on legal titles is clearly important and is the mainstay of the Jari Complex's presence in the region. Yet having legal title to unused land in this region (and Brazilian Amazonia as a whole) is not always sufficient to maintain ownership claims to these parcels. This can best be done by effective occupation and use of the land on a regular basis for specific economic or environmental purposes.

Beiradão and the Construction of the BR-156 Road

The construction of new roads is one of the most polemical issues on contemporary frontiers in Amazonia. Road construction is part of a broader trend in the transition from river-based communities, which have long been the mainstay of traditional peoples' homelands, to road-based ones, which form the core of development cosmographies. Roads are an integral part of development cosmographies not only because of their link to modern types of land transport, such as trucks, cars, and buses and the economic integration they produce, but also because they represent key arteries of entrance (and exit) by development-led social actors, particularly rural and urban migrants.

By the late 1980s, the population of Beiradão had reached twenty-five thousand people, making it the third largest city in the state of Amapá, but it still lacked a road connection to the rest of the state (or to anywhere, for that matter). Its only access to the rest of the country was by slow rides on old, overworked boats; fluvial passage to or from Santana took anywhere from eighteen to twenty-six hours, to or from Belém thirty to forty hours, and to cities up the Amazon River, such as Santarém or Óbidos, several days.[4] As the population and commercial activity grew in the city, anti-enclave forces began pushing for the construction of a federal road connecting them to the rest of Amapá. Appointed governor Aníbal Barcellos who, since Amapá had gained statehood in 1988, would have to be freely elected to maintain his post, made the construction of this road and more development for Laranjal do Jari into two of his campaign promises. After his election in 1990, he began the process of road construction.

The road to be built would complete the federal BR-156 road running the entire length of Amapá from Oiapoque in the northeast along the French Guiana border to Laranjal do Jari in the extreme southwestern portion of the state, a stretch of road that would be nearly 1,000 kilometers long. The part that needed to be constructed had an extension of 172 kilometers and would require the construction of eight large and thirty small bridges. The completion of this road had been under consideration as part of the Territory of Amapá's development plan since the 1970s.

Opposition to the construction of this road came from two longtime rivals within the region: the Jari Complex and the extractivists of the Cajari Reserve and the Maracá Settlement Projects. The proposed road would slice through the middle of Maracá Extractive Settlement II, the Cajari Extractive Reserve, and the Amapá portion of the Jari Complex. The fear of these groups was that the construction of a road would facilitate the invasion of their lands by agricultural migrants, land speculators, and logging crews. This, in turn, would provoke a new wave of social conflicts, increase environmental destruction of the area, and diminish the effective control that they exercised over their territories. Though the Jari Complex and the Cajari extractivists were involved in a separate territorial dispute, this did not prevent them from forming a tacit alliance to repulse a common threat to these lands, regardless of whose claims would eventually be recognized. Once again, tactical alliances among contradictory forces are made out of strategic necessity, since the ever-changing circumstances of the regional frontier demand flexibility to maintain or strengthen one's territorial base.

The residents of Beiradão, for their part, were incensed by this opposition to the road. For them, the road represented an important lifeline to the rest of the state that would facilitate the flow of goods both in and out of the region, pushing them ever closer to their goal of becoming a regional development pole in Amazonia. It would also cut their travel time to Macapá to only eight hours, less than half the time it took by boat. Their main source of strength lay in their demographic/voting power, which had helped elect a governor, and now they demanded that he fulfill his promises.

The law required that, before the construction of the road, an environmental impact study had to be made and then discussed in a public hearing. This report was prepared by C.R. Almeida, the same Curitiba-based consulting firm that had conducted the EIS for the Jari Complex's Felipe II project. The same pro-development arguments used to justify the implementation of that project were repeated in this report. After noting numerous negative social and environmental impacts, the report went to great lengths to present a conclusion favorable to the construction of the road: "When analyzed individually and in isolation, the negative effects appear to be greater than the positive ones; but when interrelations are established between effects (positive-negative), phases of implementation (construction-operation), and the different areas of impact (socioeconomic, biological, and physical), then they produce satisfactory conclusions at a regional level" (C.R. Almeida 1991, 30).

The many tensions over the construction of the road came to a head in 1991 at the public hearing held in Beiradão to review the results of the EIS and tentatively to establish an agreement between opposing forces. Several hundred people showed up at the meeting. The interests of Beiradão were represented by local businessmen and townspeople, who expressed their sentiments that the road would provide direct benefits to their daily lives and was a clear sign of progress for the region as a whole. On the other side were extractivists, rural union leaders, and environmentalists,[5] who expressed their fears that the road would encourage invasions and provoke a new round of environmental destruction. The extractivist-environmental alliance, while not opposing the construction of the road per se, sought guarantees that their claims to land would be recognized and respected and that ranchers who were using these lands for grazing would be removed.[6] Straddling the fence in this debate were a host of federal and state government officials, since some were tied to the construction of the road (which after all was a government endeavor) and others were responsible for the environmental protection of the area.

A compromise was reached, whereby Governor Barcellos set up a commission to supervise the demarcation of areas reserved for extractivism, promised to remove persons conducting illegal activities in these areas (including ranchers and gold miners), and offered to finance economic extractive projects. By 1992 the gravel road connecting Beiradão to Macapá had begun operation. Maintenance of the road by the government, however, was minimal; during the six-month rainy season, the road filled with potholes and gullies that made it impassable for all but the most rugged vehicles. In effect, the stalemate at the public hearing was reflected in a type of empirical stalemate, since the road that eventually was built functioned only half the time. This greatly reduced, but by no means prevented, the arrival of colonists, land speculators, and loggers. If the road eventually is paved, these flows will certainly increase.

The main new town that resulted from the building of the road was Vila Maracá, situated on the left bank of the Maracá River where the new bridge crossed it, in the heart of Maracá Extractive Settlement Project II. The mayor of the Mazagão municipality, as part of a larger strategy to settle its sparsely populated interior, unilaterally decided to establish Vila Maracá as a new settlement and began construction of seventy houses there. The location of Vila Maracá within an extractive settlement project that had its own set of use rules was not taken into consideration by the mayor; he wanted development for his municipality and was determined to take maximum advantage of the new road built by the government. Municipal funds for the project were in short supply, however, and only half of the projected houses were eventually built.

Most of these houses were occupied by extractivists who had *colocações* along the Maracá River and who used the town as a type of second home that was conducive for sending their children to the school established there, for utilizing the small health clinic that operated intermittently, and for making trips to the towns of Mazagão, Santana, and Macapá. The state government operated a truck between Macapá and Vila Maracá every fifteen days to haul agricultural and extractive produce for the local residents. This trip took three hours, instead of ten for the boat trip. Because of these changes, Vila Maracá became the most important nucleated settlement of the three Maracá Extractive Settlement Projects and rapidly began transforming the extractivists there from a river-based people to a road-based one.

Four years after its founding in 1991, Vila Maracá had a population of only 280 people. Although this number was high for the area, Vila Maracá did not show signs of the uncontrolled growth that Beiradão and Beiradinho had experienced (Westerman 1995, 17). Nonetheless, members of the Maracá Association have lodged several complaints of illegal logging in the area of the Preto River to the east of the Vila and of land speculation in Laranjal do Maracá to the west, indicating that the potential for conflict and uncontrolled invasions remains high.

The existence of a new town has also sparked nonlocal interest in the creation of new municipalities by state political leaders who seek to extend their power by placing their party's people in positions of power at the municipal level. Paulo Leite, of the conservative PFL political party, has been a prime mover of this trend and visited the Maracá Extractive Settlement Projects, where he extolled the advantages of creating a Maracá municipality, indicating that it automatically would receive state funds for administrative purposes. This effort was greeted with some apprehension by the leaders of the Maracá Association, who were in the process of establishing their legitimacy as representatives of the Maracá Extractive Settlement Projects and felt that the installation of a municipal government, which almost invariably is tied to developmentalist ideologies, might pose a challenge to their authority and create conflicts with the environmental and economic goals of the Maracá Projects.

The construction of the BR-156 road also served as a stimulus for the opening of feeder roads. Those extractivist communities located farthest from the road continue to depend on the slow and unreliable river transport system available to them. The direct access to urban markets and services of their road-based neighbors, which from their perspective represents the wave of the future, has led them to petition for the construction of feeder roads to connect them with this transportation network. Of course, any new road built would also facilitate the invasion of their *colocações* and the cutting down of the jungle, a risk that many extractivists are willing to take.

The most important feeder road to the new stretch of the BR-156 road connects Beiradinho, the new municipal seat of Vitória do Jari, with Beiradão. This road caused consternation among the Jari Complex management because it cut through one of their eucalyptus plantations. It also sparked a wave of illegal deforestation facilitated by the road's closeness to the town of Beiradão, where several sawmills and the services of a river port permit rapid cutting, planing, and sale of the timber. The Jari

Complex was in no condition to stop the construction of this feeder road, since the expansive dynamic of municipalities had been fully installed in Amapá and any interference in it would have provoked confrontations with the government, which the Jari Complex sought to avoid. Luis Cláudio Castro, environmental director for the Jari Complex, admits that "beginning in 1988 [when the new Brazilian Constitution was ratified] the Company no longer has the capacity to intervene in these decisions . . . since the municipalities have a large degree of autonomy guaranteed by the Federal Constitution. All we can do is attempt to manage these new situations to the best of our abilities."

The new strategy adopted by the Jari management is to promote a process of regionalization of the complex, which seeks to establish partnerships between the company and other social actors in the fulfillment of mutual goals. The complex seeks to minimize past tensions and establish working relations with potential adversaries. The Jari Complex has an enormous advantage in this field, since it is by far the richest of the social actors of the Jari Region, as seen in the new wave of capital investments that began in the 1990s.

Big Capital Returns to the Lower Amazon Basin

In 1996, the Jari Cellulose Company (Companhia Florestal Monte Dourado) turned a profit for the first time since its installation in 1967 due primarily to a dramatic rise in the world price of wood pulp.[7] With a production of nearly 300,000 tons per year, Jari Cellulose is Brazil's fifth largest producer of wood pulp. A subsequent drop in prices once again put the company in the red and led to a sustained search for new capital investments as part of a concerted effort by the Jari management to shed its "development project" mentality and establish an efficient, profitable capitalist enterprise. Important parts of these changes included turning over Jari-constructed educational and health infrastructure and service operations to local and state governments, thereby freeing the company from many of its social expenditures, and continued mechanization of its tree plantations, which reduced its overall labor force and cut expenditures.

The biggest impulse for change, however, was to come from a projected influx of nearly U.S.$200 million in new investments over the coming years. The first round of new investments began in 1996, when

U.S.$30 million was pumped into the modernization of the wood pulp factory whose twenty-year-old technology had been surpassed by new techniques. This capital has come in almost equal parts from the opening of new shares on the Rio de Janeiro and São Paulo stock markets, from investments by the Azevedo Antunes family group, and from debt relief by the Brazilian National Development Bank and the Bank of Brazil, which have had a stake in the operation ever since the Figueiredo administration engineered its nationalization by private capital in 1982.

Part of this investment was used to install a whitening technology that is oxygen, rather than chlorine, based, producing a significant reduction in pollution generated by the processing plant. The implementation of industrial processes that are less polluting has come in direct response to market demand, particularly that of Europe, for "green" products that have been internationally certified as having been produced and packaged in ways that minimize environmental damage. Fulfilling this requirement is important for the Jari Cellulose operation, since they bear the additional environmental onus of producing wood pulp on Amazonian lands.[8]

This wave of new investments is not limited to Jari's industrial facilities. By 1997 plans had been completed for the construction of the first phase of a hydroelectric generating station to be located on the Jari River just above the Santo Antonio waterfalls. This station is the first of three modules to be implemented over a span of fifteen years, with each module designed to generate 33.3 megawatts of electric power per hour. Ten percent of the capacity of the first module is reserved for use by Beiradão, with the rest to be used by various sectors of the Jari Complex. When this first module comes on-line, it gradually will replace the three generating plants currently in operation in Munguba (two fueled by biomass and one by fossil fuels). Thirty percent of the cost of the first phase is being put up by the Jari Cellulose and Caulim da Amazônia companies, with the remaining 70 percent coming from external financing (Jari Energética 1996). The second and third phases of this project will supply electric power to areas outside the Jari Region and are designed to furnish energy for economic expansion throughout all of Amapá (especially the free trade zone of Macapá/Santana) and northern Pará.

The construction of this hydroelectric station revived an old dream of Ludwig's, whose initial request to build a hydroelectric dam was turned down by federal government officials, which was one of the reasons behind his disenchantment with the Jari Project and subsequent sale of

The Santo Antonio waterfalls, the site of a proposed hydroelectric plant, 1995

it. The new ownership decided on a much smaller generating plant, which would not create a large reservoir but would apply advanced technologies that take advantage of current flows within the Jari River. This would limit (though not eliminate) the environmental and social effects of this hydroelectric project. The implementation of this technology is a direct result of years of struggle by local populations and environmental groups against large Amazonian dams that flood thousands of hectares of fertile *várzea* lands and displace scores of local communities (see Sigaud 1988; Castro and Andrade 1988; Castro 1989; Bartolomé 1992; Baines 1994). Without the adoption of this technology, the project most certainly would not have been authorized by the state and federal environmental agencies responsible for its oversight. Nonetheless, six years after formal approval, construction of the first phase remained stalled because of problems in financing the endeavor.

On 31 May 1997, a fire destroyed the control panel of the Jari power-generating plants, causing complete paralysis of wood pulp production for six months because no other source of electric energy is available in this part of the Lower Amazon region. This caused even deeper financial losses for Jari Cellulose and put its very existence in danger. This led the CAEMI group to float the idea of selling the operation outright. After two years on the market, in late 1999 CAEMI finally sold Jari Cellulose for the symbolic price of U.S.$1 to the Grupo Orsa, a paper and cellulose company controlled by São Paulo businessman Sérgio Amoroso. With its purchase, the Grupo Orsa also assumed the U.S.$410 million outstanding debt of Jari Cellulose, most of this with the Brazilian National Development Bank and the Bank of Brazil. As part of the purchase package, the new owners received an eleven-year U.S.$100 million loan guarantee in exchange for a fixed percentage of future wood pulp sales. The Grupo Orsa immediately announced that it would invest U.S.$54 million in the modernization of the cellulose plant and, at the same time, began looking for investors for the hydroelectric project, now estimated to cost U.S.$150 million.

All these events have created the paradoxical situation whereby, after thirty years of operation and as much as U.S.$1 billion in investments, the large amount of land controlled by the Jari Cellulose Company has not been sufficient to guarantee its profitable operation. The capital-intensive nature of the enterprise turns the land into a mere commodity necessary for the massive production of trees to be industrially processed by its factory. The key territorial considerations for the company continue to be the existence of large tracts of land capable of producing eucalyptus trees and ready fluvial access to the site. The issue of raw material self-sufficiency also enters the economic and territorial considerations of the Jari Cellulose operation. Throughout the early years of the 1990s, the Jari cellulose plant imported as much as 25 percent of its raw material from the northeastern state of Bahia (eucalyptus grown on lands previously forested by native Atlantic rain forest), since most of Jari's tree plantations, which in the 1980s began to be completely changed over to eucalyptus, were still in the process of maturation. During these years the production of Jari wood pulp was responsible for environmental effects both in the Amazon rain forest, where its own trees were located, and in the Atlantic rain forest, from where it imported wood. The goal of the company was to be completely self-sufficient in eucalyptus wood production by the turn of the century.

This goal, however, houses hidden environmental consequences. Starting in the late 1980s, eucalyptus trees planted on Jari plantations were genetic clones of high-yielding species (Lins 1991, 212–14). These species raise the productivity of plantations, which for Jari had been well below average when compared with other eucalyptus plantations in Brazil (Belo 1996), thus requiring less territorial expansion and, hence, less deforestation of native rain forest. At the same time, planting these clones virtually eliminates species diversity and greatly increases the risk of devastation of all the plantations by diseases or plagues. When viewed in the time frame of natural history, the Jari Cellulose operation represents the rapid transformation of highly diverse, native rain forest into highly uniform, exotic plantations, setting the stage for a future environmental disaster. Since the company operates on a short to middle-range economic time frame, completely removed from the much longer time frames of natural history, these environmental factors are not taken into consideration. They provide an important perspective, nonetheless, from which to question the company's claim that it is a "sustainable development model in the Amazon" (Companhia Florestal Monte Dourado 1994).

A wave of capital expansion is also affecting other parts of the Lower Amazon mesoregion. Within the state of Amapá, AMCEL (Amapá Celulose Ltda.), another company within the CAEMI group, operates a large pine tree plantation in northern Amapá, which supplies the raw material for its wood chip processing plant in Santana. In 1995, AMCEL began seeking U.S.$100 million in foreign investments to develop new biotechnology in seed manipulation as a means of intensifying production within its plantations, though with the same environmental risks just mentioned (Scofield 1996).

One of the largest and most ambitious of the projects involving new capital investments in the Lower Amazon is that of the Champion Paper Corporation, a U.S. firm with several subsidiaries operating in Brazil, which in 1995 began planting a 250,000-hectare eucalyptus tree plantation in the open grasslands (*cerrado*) of Amapá just to the north of the AMCEL plantations. Champion quietly began buying up large tracts of land in three northern municipalities, principally through the use of proxies. By the time that state officials learned of their plans, the company had already purchased 90,000 hectares and had installed a pilot plantation. All of this was done before any environmental impact study had been made and before approval had been granted by any of the corresponding state governmental agencies. Once the story came to public notice (Martins 1996), Champion offered to inform the government of its plans and jointly negotiated the establishment of a high-profile environmental commission to review the implementation of the project (Gonçalves 1995).

By late 1996, when Champion had completed the purchase of 250,000 hectares, environmental concerns about the project began to be raised within sectors of the state government and within the state's civil society, and formal public hearings were called for. By this time, some of Champion's land purchases were being questioned because of the existence of multiple titles to the same plot of land and the general confusion of the land titling process so common throughout Amazonia (Comissão Especial de Investigação 1995, 1997). Champion's short-term solution to these difficulties was to buy out AMCEL, which gave it immediate control of an existing pine tree plantation and an operating wood chip factory. The investments that AMCEL was planning to make would now be made by Champion. This purchase gave Champion control of more than 400,000 hectares of partially contiguous land and provided it with ample room for expansion in years to come.

This example illustrates how large-scale development projects, and the development cosmographies that undergird them, continue to advance into Amazonia. Just as with Ludwig's Jari Project of three decades earlier, the Champion/AMCEL industrial forestry project operates according to an enclave territoriality that requires large tracts of land for homogeneous plantations, made its site selection based on the existence of large tracts of cheap land, and was strategically placed in an isolated region of the country where local political institutions are weak and open to manipulation.[9] In other words, Champion represents a new generation of large-scale development projects that pay lip service to environmental concerns, but whose bottom line is to become profit-making enterprises.

Champion's version of a development cosmography varies from that of its immediate ancestor in several important ways and pushes it toward a fusion with a revitalized mercantilist cosmography. First, the current development discourse has eliminated most tinges of nationalism, in both its nation-building and national security varieties. National sovereignty, as it was conceived and debated in the 1970s and 1980s, is no longer part of the development agenda, which is now dominated by the unabashed search for new capital investments at almost any cost. The new development goal is to enter the global economy on its terms, and this means making whatever internal changes are necessary so that products sold on the market are able to compete in the so-called free market of world trade. The key structuring guidelines of this new era are the GATT agreements signed by more than a hundred nations in 1994 and watched over by the newly established World Commerce Organization. The battle to expel Daniel Ludwig and his capital from Jari for its threats to national sovereignty seems to be an anachronistic episode in recent Amazonian history in light of the worldwide neoliberal assault on Latin American economies.

Second, this updated version of a development cosmography has learned to deal with competing environmental cosmographies in novel ways. Managers of large-scale projects are well aware that at their core these projects do not fit into the vision that environmentalists hold for Amazonia. Sustainable development efforts in Amazonia almost invariably seek to maintain genetic diversity, minimize environmental impacts, and involve traditional populations by learning from and adopting their traditional adaptive techniques. Large-scale development projects are based on diametrically opposed principles: homogeneity instead of diversity, large scale instead of small scale, and transformation of traditional peoples into wage-scale workers. In spite of this basic contradiction, development actors have partially incorporated an environmental discourse and seek to use it for their benefit. According to the new wisdom, the market is the best guide for making environmental decisions, since the market simply expresses the wishes of the populace who want what is best for them in the very short term. The continued treatment of environmental effects by economists as external costs precludes any serious encounter with the main tenets of the environmental movement.

Finally, traditional peoples and their territorial claims also get shuffled to the side in this neoliberal version of the development cosmography. Since historical claims to land do not have a market logic, they have no space in this ideology and for that reason are not considered legitimate. As capital pushes the bottom line, it highlights the wide gap between it and all other cosmographies, thereby promoting the establishment of alliances between traditional peoples and environmental social actors.

Continuing Struggles over the Aguarico Region
The Expansion of Petroecuador onto Sustainable Use Territories

In 1991 Petroecuador published a report detailing the expansion of its operations into the lower Aguarico and middle Napo River basins involving the establishment of new wells at seven widely dispersed sites (Petroproducción 1991). It also contemplated the construction of roads connecting these wells to each other and to the rest of the oil road network, which would open up a vast section of the jungle for colonization. Nationalist and technical criteria were used to justify this expansion, with the argument that, since the known petroleum reserves of the country would last only another twenty years, Petroecuador was *"obligated* to explore new fields both in the Cretaceous and the Precretaceous (primarily Santiago Formation) and discover additional reserves at least equal to the current annual production so as to *assure the oil future of Ecuador"* (Petroproducción 1992, 4, emphasis added). Since this area had not previously been auctioned off to foreign firms in the form of petroleum concessions, the task of oil development automatically passed to Petroecuador, who took on this responsibility with unbridled enthusiasm.

The area where this proposed expansion was to take place was covered with dense tropical forest containing extremely high levels of floral and faunal diversity. Three of the proposed well sites would be located within the enlarged portion of the Cuyabeno Wildlife Production Reserve, two well sites were to be established within the neighboring Yasuni National Park (which in 1990 had its border redrawn to exclude another area of potential oil development), with the remaining two sites being within the buffer zones of these two protected areas. None of these facts was mentioned in the Petroecuador reports. Their mandate was to discover oil fields, build wells, and pump oil, and the existence of "external" environmental factors was not considered to be a problem. This attitude was reflected in the press conference given in 1991 by Luis Román, then president of Petroecuador. He outlined the four criteria that Petroecuador was using to decide whether to exploit a petroleum reserve: quantity of the reserve, quality of the oil, difficulties in access to the site, and problems in the transport of the oil. In a later interview, Román stated that the previous existence of indigenous territories, protected areas, or environmental factors was taken into consideration only to the degree that it would present legal or social problems for the company. The mandate of Petroecuador, he further stated, was to find and exploit oil *any-where* in the country.

Petroecuador established an elaborate timetable for this expansion, indicating the precise dates when perforations would be made at each well site, when each connecting feeder road would be built, how much oil would be pumped out of each well, and how many years each well was to last. Initial seismic reports estimated that as many as 250 million barrels of oil lay under the ground, a figure that could be confirmed only by direct perforation at each site, an operation that also would determine the quality of the oil. By 1995, several perforations had been conducted and estimates of reserves had risen to 800 million barrels, provoking Julio Prado, subdirector of the Pacayacu Petroproducción compound, to state proudly, "Our gold mine lies in those reserves. Although much of the oil is heavy crude that is difficult to transport, we must invent ways to pipe it out because demand for oil is rising throughout the world."

As the news of the expansionary plans of Petroecuador reached the Aguarico Region, it provoked a variety of responses. Colonists and land speculators, for example, began staking out claims in the area where the road was supposed to pass in order to gain access to the most valued plots of land, which could then be sold to colonists who would enter the area as soon as the road was opened. Environmentalists, for their part, immediately opposed the Petroecuador plan on several grounds. First, they claimed that new petroleum development on formally established protected areas required authorization that Petroecuador had not been granted. In this respect, the enlargement of the Cuyabeno Reserve had come just in time to provide legal support for halting petroleum expansion. Second, they opposed the general expansion of the oil industry into rain-forest areas because of the disruption of natural cycles and the contamination of pristine ecosystems that it would cause. Finally, the construction of new roads was seen by environmentalists as an open invitation for the invasion and deforestation of the rain forest by colonists, just as had occurred with every other example of oil road construction in Ecuadorian Amazonia.

The tourist industry also was alarmed by this proposed expansion, since several firms had invested heavily in the Cuyabeno Reserve, thinking that its rain forest would be left intact. The steadily increasing tourist trade into the area gave the industry hope that the Cuyabeno Reserve would be a booming jungle tourist site for years to come. The arrival of

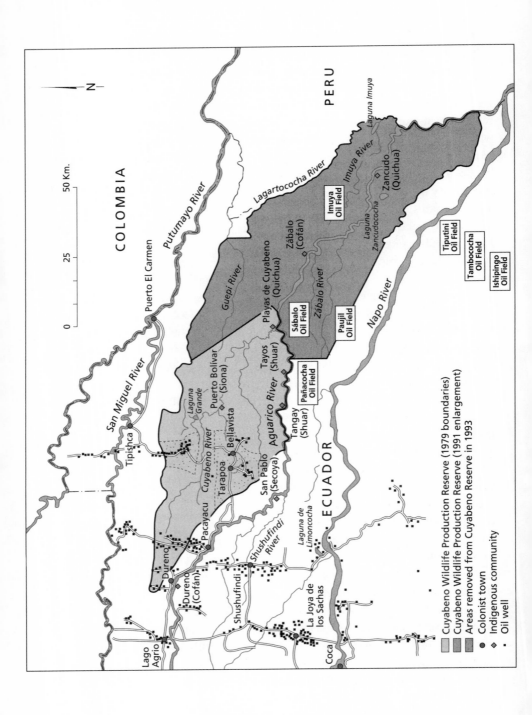

heavy oil machinery, the construction of oil pipelines and roads, and the colonization and deforestation of the area would all severely damage the investments of tourist companies. They argued that tourists traveled long distances and were spending thousands of dollars to see pristine jungle landscapes, not the inner workings of the oil industry.

Meanwhile, the response of indigenous peoples came with the physical presence of seismic crews on their lands. Seismic exploration usually is conducted by small, highly specialized foreign firms that open trails and conduct tests on a contract basis. As these crews entered the area, opened trails, and did exploratory work with dynamite, local indigenous communities were given a firsthand glimpse of the specific sites where the oil industry would be installed on their lands. Each affected community would develop a unique response to this expansion.

Petroecuador's proposed expansion stimulated the formation of an ad hoc group called the Association for the Defense of Cuyabeno, comprising environmental NGOs, scientists, journalists, ecotourism companies, and indigenous communities, whose goal was to protect this swath of Amazonian jungle from the destructive effects of petroleum development. The underlying fear that motivated this association was that, if areas of great natural beauty and traditional indigenous occupation that had been formally set aside by the national government for protection were not off limits to oil expansion, then nothing would stop the oil industry as it advanced onto new areas throughout the jungle. A critical mass of opposition had been formed around shared tenets of an environmental cosmography, and the moment for action seemed to be at hand.

This vehement and organized response was handled by the environmental division of Petroecuador, established in 1991. This office assured those opposed to oil expansion that strict controls would be placed on road traffic, thereby limiting the amount of colonization (though colonist activity before the road's construction made a mockery of this claim) and that new, clean technologies would be used in the exploration for and exploitation of oil. These clean technologies would cause minimal damage to the environment. The technical division of Petroecuador, for their part, had strict timelines to fulfill in both the installation of the wells and the construction of the roads and were determined to accomplish them.

The Aguarico River Region: Territorial Disputes of the 1990s *(opposite)*

International tourists and Siona women and child, Cuyabeno River port, 2000

During the two-year period encompassing 1992–93, a series of confrontations between these many social actors at these new well sites strengthened environmentalist forces within the Aguarico frontier power field. The first set of confrontations came early in 1992, during seismic explorations at the Zábalo well site. After several visits to the area, members of the Zábalo Cofán community, under the leadership of Randy Borman, "arrested" twenty-three technicians of the seismic team for working in the area without the proper authorization of the Forestry Subsecretary (SUFOREN). The Cofanes were using the existence of the reserve (whose establishment they had previously protested because it prevented them from gaining clear title to their lands) to protect their lands and, in fact, were voluntarily fulfilling the role of park rangers. Borman then radioed Pedro Proaño, the manager of Transturi Inc. with whom the Zábalo community was involved in joint tourist ventures, who provided support by informing journalists and transporting them to the area. After expelling the technicians from the site of seismic explorations, the Cofanes sent a delegation to the military post in Lago Agrio to inform the commanding officer of the operation and explain its motives. Meetings were then held with the head of the SUFOREN, who reluctantly committed his agency to expulsion of the technicians, even though SUFOREN had not initially intended to do so. Afterward, the superintendent of the Cuyabeno Reserve, now with support from his superiors, visited the area and made the technicians' expulsion official. The Zábalo community was rewarded for these efforts by signing the first co-management agreement for the reserve in 1992 while the Management Plan was still in the formulation process.

A second set of confrontations in early 1993 took place at the Imuya well site, located near beautiful Lake Imuya, where Transturi had set up one of its tourist installations. Petroecuador invited journalists to the area to demonstrate the cleanliness of its operation. One journalist, who was a member of the Association for the Defense of Cuyabeno, tipped off the Zábalo community and the Acción Ecológica group, which promptly organized a protest to greet the journalists, surprising Petroecuador. After this fiasco, the head of INEFAN (previously SUFOREN) visited the area, was moved by its luxurious beauty, and then denied authorization for Petroecuador to perforate a well there, making this the first time since petroleum development had begun over twenty years earlier that a state environmental agency had denied a request for authorization to explore for oil by the state petroleum company.

Petroecuador appealed the decision, and President Sixto Durán set up a special interministerial commission to review the process. This body voted 5 to 1 to uphold INEFAN's decision, while making the suggestion that technologies less damaging to the environment be used by Petroecuador (Amend). One such technology considered at this point was the so-called ecological drilling well available from the French firm Forasol, which can be transported by helicopter to the site, requires less deforested space for its installation than do traditional wells, and reinjects water used in the drilling process (Saenz 1994). The possibility of installing an oil pipeline without the construction of roads was also brought under consideration.

A third moment of confrontation came after President Durán's whirlwind visit to several of Petroecuador's sites, when he wrote and signed a letter authorizing the company's continued exploration in the area, ostensibly overriding the decision handed down by the interinstitutional commission. In Quito, environmental groups filed a suit in the country's Tribunal of Constitutional Guarantees, contesting this authorization by claiming that the president had illegally usurped INEFAN's authority in writing the letter. Though this suit never prospered, the very fact that it was filed, along with the publicity it generated, infuriated the president and the management of Petroecuador.

All of these events culminated in the takeover of the Paujil I well site on 28 October 1993. The bulletin sent out by the Ecuanet electronic news service serves as a good introduction to the Paujil confrontation:

> The installations of the Paujil I oil well, located in the Cuyabeno Ecological [*sic*] Reserve, fell last Thursday in the hands of *50 Cofanes*, in protest against the exploratory activities that *Petroecuador* is conducting in the area and which has been questioned by diverse sectors of *public opinion*.
>
> The Cofanes, armed with lances and hunting rifles, entered the Paujil well installations and forced the *oil workers* to suspend their perforation activities, according to a report to the *Hoy newspaper* by *Andy Drumm*, representative and photographer for the *Association for the Defense of Cuyabeno.* . . .
>
> Shortly afterwards, the *Superintendent of Petroproducción* arrived accompanied by a *petroleum engineer* and *two high-ranking military officers* of the *Coca Jungle Brigade,* with whom an initial agreement was reached that allowed the perforation activities to continue. However, this agreement was annulled by [*authorities from*] *Quito,* at which time the Cofanes demanded the presence of the *President of Petroecuador* in Zábalo on Monday (Ecuanet 1993, emphasis added).

The italics added to this bulletin highlight the large number of separate social actors involved in this single event. The joint arrival of top-level petroleum industry management and high-ranking military officials reveals the operational alliance between Petroecuador and the armed forces and how the notion of threats to national security continues to be used to justify the major presence of the military in the Aguarico Region.

By looking beyond the directly observable aspects of this confrontation to the tactics and strategies used by each social actor, one discovers the dynamics of the power equation. Since the only access to the well was supposedly by helicopter, the Cofanes decided on a surprise land approach (Borman). After marching for two days from their community through dense jungle and extensive swamplands, they arrived near the well site, stopped, washed themselves, changed into clean, traditional tunics (*cushmas*), painted their faces (though this is typically done for festive occasions, the Cofanes knew that it would be viewed by the oil workers as war paint), and emerged out of the jungle at the well site with lances drawn. The Cofanes brought with them an environmental lawyer, who filmed the entire event for later use in fundraising and consciousness raising efforts (it eventually made its way to CBS News), and a photographer of the Association for the Defense of Cuyabeno, who wrote the Ecuanet report quoted above. It was hoped that the presence of an environmentalist and a journalist would not only guarantee publicity for the takeover but also offer a certain level of personal protection for all those participating in it.

The Cofanes then physically occupied the site and demanded the cessation of all activities until they could negotiate with the president of Petroecuador. After on-site oil workers radioed to headquarters, the petroleum and military contingent arrived to negotiate. At the initial encounter the head military officer refused to negotiate with Borman, arguing that he was an American and had no business interfering in Ecuadorian affairs. The vice president of the Cofán delegation informed the officer that Borman was an Ecuadorian citizen and the president of their community; thus, any negotiations toward ending the takeover would have to be with him. The superintendent of Petroproducción then stepped in to take over the negotiations.

Nightfall arrived, and the negotiations were suspended until the following day. The Cofanes then put forward three basic demands: (1) Petroecuador should receive authorization from the Zábalo community for all activities in their territory, (2) the community should receive all documentation about the operation, and (3) the company should provide solar panels for all houses in the community. As the day advanced without any notable progress, the negotiations were broken off and scheduled to resume in the Zábalo community several days later. The Cofanes were then flown back to their community by Petroecuador in two helicopter trips.

In subsequent negotiations, Petroecuador rejected outright the demand for community authorization for oil exploration, claiming that this was INEFAN's responsibility, though they offered the community copies of all documents that they gave to this agency. The company did agree to donate $10,000 worth of solar panels and batteries to the Zábalo community. A written, unofficial document signed by Petroecuador and the community formally put an end to the confrontation. Activities at the Paujil well site were suspended shortly thereafter, and Petroecuador announced that the perforations there had come up dry. One of the Petroecuador engineers present at the well site during the takeover later gave this reading of the event: "I was one of the 'kidnapped' technicians. At no time did I feel that my life was in danger. We actually have good relations with the community. The takeover was nothing more than a tactic to get the company to negotiate."

A different situation developed at the Pañacocha II well site, which lay within the buffer zone of the Cuyabeno Reserve and the claimed territory of the Playas de Cuyabeno Quichua community. This community immediately entered into direct negotiations with the company, receiving a host of community benefits in return for their tacit approval (their agreement not to make trouble) and also hoping to gain employment at the site. In an ironic twist of events, the Quichuas were somewhat dismayed when activity at this well was halted by Petroecuador because only heavy crude was found there, and this would need to be mixed with light crude to make the well economically viable. Petroecuador hoped that light crude would be found in other wells downriver, particularly the well at Imuya, where they had been refused authorization to perforate.

The markedly different responses to oil expansion by two neighboring indigenous communities can be explained partially by historical, ethnic, and personal factors. The Zábalo community was formed by a breakaway faction of Cofanes fleeing from the negative effects of oil development on their original Dureno community. They knew what oil development brought, and they were adamant in not letting it happen to them. Also, the fact that Zábalo is a young community (in terms of both its years in existence and the age of its members) gives its members a heightened sense of cohesion. Community members are at Zábalo because they consciously chose to settle and establish a new life there. Finally, Borman's leadership, honed as it is by his knowledge of the invading world, is a key factor behind this community's leadership role.

The Playas de Cuyabeno Quichua community is different in each of these respects. The long history of Quichua participation in oil development in Ecuadorian Amazonia, which dates back to the first explorations in the 1920s, was simply continued by the negotiations that this community sought with Petroecuador. The Quichua have long shown a willingness to integrate themselves into the new economic forces that come into the area, a fact embedded in their very emergence as an ethnic group. Furthermore, the Playas de Cuyabeno community maintained cordial relations with its neighboring military post, and many of its members have served in the armed forces, making outright rebellion against the established order something that is not part of the community's life. Playas de Cuyabeno also lacks the cohesiveness of a young community and does not have a dynamic leader to push it into new initiatives.

The historical moment when the confrontations occurred is a crucial factor in understanding their influence on internal power relations within this regional frontier. The high profile of environmental factors in world political discourse, together with the attention given the destruction of the Amazon jungle, has become powerful enough to make even oil companies take notice and respond. These companies, which just two generations ago in the age of the Seven Sisters were the predominant economic force in the world, are now required to show that they are in tune with current trends. As Borman himself admits: "Twenty years ago it would have been impossible for us to take over an oil well. We would have either been shot or ignored." In fact, they might have suffered both fates, being shot and then ignored.

But the oil industry insisted on its expansionary efforts, and the conflicts continued unabated throughout the nineties. The Ecuadorian government proceeded to parcel up the entire Amazonian area into oil blocks to be auctioned off to international petroleum companies in new rounds of bidding. With the establishment of the Environmental Ministry in 1996, a new strategy was developed within the national government to prevent the exploitation of oil within protected areas. A new legal category—untouchable zones (*áreas intangibles*)—was applied to parts of the Cuyabeno Reserve and the Yasuni National Park. In all, 72 percent of the Cuyabeno Reserve was designated as untouchable by presidential decree 551, signed into law on 29 January 1999 by Ecuadorian President Mahuad. Decree 551 included the signatures of the minister of energy and mines and the minister of the environment. This decree had the effect of removing the entire northern portion of a petroleum block from the bidding process, thereby saving the isolated Imuya area from further rounds of petroleum expansion.[10] The category of untouchable zones thus represents yet another layer of territorial control established in the midst of the multiple territorial disputes of the region and placed on top of the other, already existent forms.

Colonists versus the Cuyabeno Reserve

While the phrase *sustainable development* has become a panacea for social and environmental problems in Amazonia at a discursive level, the two-decade-long dispute between colonists and the administration of the Cuyabeno Reserve shows just how difficult it is to reconcile development and environmental cosmographies in practice. This dispute has its origin in the 1979 establishment of the Cuyabeno Reserve in an area that already had petroleum development and colonization. Garcés notes that the creation of the reserve "did not alter the internal dynamic of the social actors in the area: neither that of petroleum development nor the increasing entrance of colonists" (1994, 10). The government began to realize the scope of this problem in 1982, when it named a superintendent for the reserve and began to assume its management responsibilities. The initial approach of DINAF to this problem was to inform the surprised colonists that they were illegally settled on reserve land, that their presence was destructive to the reserve and its fragile ecosystem, and that for this reason they must move out immediately. On several occasions, DINAF's attempts to solve the problem amounted to little more than "scaring the colonists through campaigns using mobile loudspeakers through which they demanded that all deforestation cease and proclaimed that the forced removal of the colonists was imminent" (Trujillo 1986, 62).

In response, the colonists proclaimed that they would fight rather than leave and on one occasion expelled at gunpoint a researcher who was conducting interviews for the government. The colonists claim that they are victims of the incompetence of the government and are only doing what colonists in other parts of Ecuadorian Amazonia are doing: turning the jungle into farmland just as the government had encouraged them to do for decades. Those who had settled in the area before 1979

claim rights based on being there first, while those who arrived in succeeding years affirm that there were absolutely no indications that this
was a reserve. The colonists claim that, although they are not as destructive to the area as is oil production, they are being asked to leave while
the oil companies are not, which adds weight to their argument that
they are the victims of unfair treatment. The colonists also point out that
the same government that supposedly wants to remove them from the
area has built schools, clinics, and community centers for them within
the reserve's boundaries.

In 1985, in yet another intragovernmental contradiction, Tarapoa
became a parish, further legitimizing colonist presence and integrating
colonists into the political-administrative structure of the state. The demographic strategy that colonists employ to increase their power within
the governmental structure is also being used to prevent their removal
from the reserve, since they know that the larger their population, the
more difficult it will be to remove them physically from the area. This
encourages, rather than discourages, further colonization of the area.
This problem quickly arrived at an impasse as the two sides shouted at
each other without ever finding a common solution.

Within this dispute over lands, three separate but interrelated issues
can be identified: social, legal, and environmental (Aguilar et al. 1990).
The social issue centered on the needs of the colonists, who were, for the
most part, marginal farmers seeking to make an honest living by culti-
vating the land and whose livelihood was now being threatened by a
governmental action. The legal issue grew out of contradictory regulations within the governmental apparatus, whereby IERAC was charged
with granting titles to colonists who had established farms on previously
forested lands but was prevented from fulfilling these obligations by the
prohibition (contained in the Forestry Law) against ceding individual
titles within nationally established protected areas. The environmental
issue focused on the high rate of deforestation by colonists, who were
cutting down the rain forest to expand the country's agricultural frontier. Any lasting solution to this land conflict would have to address, in a
comprehensive form, these three issues.

Negotiations designed to resolve this dispute got off to a difficult start
at a meeting between DINAF and the colonists on 6 October 1983, when
two irreconcilable positions were put forth. DINAF officials demanded
immediate expulsion of the colonists from all lands within the limits of

the reserve. This demand was mitigated by their offer to provide the colonists with parcels of land in other parts of Amazonia. On the other side, the colonists demanded that legal title be granted to the land they occupied. They mitigated this demand with the suggestion that additional unoccupied lands be added to the reserve to make up for those that would be removed.

The negotiation process, which has continued for nearly two decades, generated a new political space characteristic of regional frontier situations. New social actors were constituted and immediately expanded the political process through the formation of alliances with other social actors. The colonists arrived in the area through individual initiative or via family ties from all parts of Ecuador. Their first organizational initiative was the formation of pre-cooperatives, which are used to gain titles to the land. However, the dispute over the Cuyabeno Reserve's lands presented special problems that required new types of political organizing.

In 1983, with the help of the Carmelite Catholic mission, which had developed an extensive pastoral relationship with the colonists using the tenets of liberation theology, the Committee for the Defense of the Land in Cuyabeno was formed. This was followed in 1984 by the establishment of two second-level associations that grouped together existing pre-cooperatives and represented those colonists directly involved in the dispute: the Association of Pre-cooperatives of Pacayacu and the Association of Pre-cooperatives February 12th. These colonists also received support from peasant unions in the Sucumbíos province that were organizing around the land issue, as well as a host of other economic and social issues such as the need for schools, potable water, health care, jobs, and public transportation, all tied to what they saw as a severe lack of governmental attention. These unions gradually gave way to an even broader coalition known as the Sucumbíos Strike Committee, which conducted a provincewide strike in 1993 over the lack of attention Sucumbíos had received from the national government. Another source of support, both technical and political, for the colonists came from FEPP (Ecuadorian Populorum Progressio Fund), a progressive, Catholic Church–based development agency.

Negotiations on the side of the government were handled by the agency responsible for protected areas and forested lands within MAG. With each new national administration, this agency was restructured and renamed; the negotiations started out with DINAF, were continued

Pacayacu, colonist and petroleum town, 2000

by SUFOREN in 1989, and passed on to INEFAN in 1993. Each administrative change provoked policy changes, which produced highly erratic sways in the terms of negotiation, causing this dispute to drag on for years. The Fundación Natura, Ecuador's largest conservation organization, has been an ally of all three of these government agencies and has provided consistency (and intransigence) to the government position through its conservationist counsel, its studies of the reserve, and its financing of reserve infrastructure. By the early 1990s, the environmental NGO, Cordavi, and German government–funded PROFORS program had also become involved in the negotiating process.

In the mid-1980s, the Ecuadorian government embarked on a nationwide project formally to delimit all protected areas in the country, an activity that would have negatively affected the colonists' interests. This mobilized colonist and peasant organizations and resulted in an informal agreement between DINAF and the Cuyabeno colonists in 1986 (which would never be implemented), stipulating that their lands would be excluded from the delimitation of the reserve. An earthquake in 1987, whose epicenter was in the Sucumbíos province, cut off road contact with the rest of the country for several months and restructured the interests of the colonists toward the pressing needs of obtaining food, gaining access to health care, and rebuilding destroyed infrastructure. Meanwhile, the government was involved in the preparation of the first Management Plan for Cuyabeno (Coello and Nations 1987), and by 1988 it had postponed indefinitely the delimitation effort of the Cuyabeno Reserve.

The dispute was reactivated in 1989, this time under the administration of newly elected President Rodrigo Borja. An interinstitutional committee was established by MAG to study the issue and make recommendations. After a series of negotiations, the colonists and this committee signed a formal agreement on 22 June 1989, in which the colonists' farms within the reserve would be demarcated and legalized in return for colonist guarantees of preventing future colonization of the area. The following month MAG nullified this agreement, stating that the committee was not authorized to negotiate formal agreements and that the agreement was contrary to current ministry policy.

Over the next three years, the conflict became a hot political issue within the Sucumbíos province. In 1992 Eliceo Azuero, national congressional deputy from Sucumbíos,[11] introduced the cause of the colonists in the Congressional Committee for the Defense of the Environment over which he presided. The commission appointed by this committee to study the issue recommended "the legalization of all currently occupied lands" within the reserve (Espin and Guerrero 1992, 8). This provoked a vehement denouncement from the Fundación Natura accusing Azuero of crass electioneering while claiming that this measure was "completely illegal" and would cause the "irreversible destruction of an enormous expanse of tropical rainforest" ("Elecciones" 1992, 4). The colonists gained additional political support when the January 1993 provincewide strike included within its list of demands to the national government the granting of legal title to the colonists settled within the reserve.

By this time, the environmentalists involved in managing the reserve had developed a counterproposal that they offered to the colonists, whereby pre-cooperatives, rather than individual families, would be granted collective titles to the land, titles with environmental constraints built into them. This category of ownership does not exist in Ecuadorian law, and the colonists adamantly rejected the proposal, since this would make it extremely difficult to sell their land, an important aspect in their overall adaptive strategies. This rejection emphasizes the point made earlier that pre-cooperatives and cooperatives are not considered by the colonists to be collective territorialities, but only a means to the ends of gaining free title to the land and facilitating the marketing of their agricultural production.

In 1993, when the new INEFAN agency was established under the administration of President Sixto Durán, Jorge Barba, its director, held a meeting with the colonists where he proposed that the colonized area be removed from the Cuyabeno Reserve and placed under the title of Forestry Patrimony, a modality similar to that proposed earlier by environmentalists, but with two key differences: pre-cooperatives would be granted collective *use* titles rather than formal collective titles, and this modality was a functioning part of Ecuadorian law. Still another idea suggested as a compromise solution to the conflict was that of Family Patrimony, whereby an individual family would receive exclusive use rights over a parcel of land that could be passed on to future generations of the family through inheritance but that could not be sold to another person on the open market. Both proposals were rejected by the colonists, who maintained their demand for individual, free title to the land. This issue encompassed the core territorial dimension of this dispute and placed in relief the differences between development and environmental criteria.

From the environmentalist perspective, biocentric criteria are ascendant as the conservation of the biophysical environment is what must be maintained above all other considerations. The social dimension of this view is that some social groups, indigenous communities, for example, are seen as being capable of occupying, using, and at the same time conserving a tropical rain-forest area in ways that agricultural colonists are not. This idea is reflected in the co-management agreements negotiated between the government and indigenous communities. The environmentalists were to be offering a similar type of agreement to the colonists and saw their refusal as proof that they are not interested in or capable of maintaining collective control over the land. They further assert that the colonists' desire for individual titles shows that land speculation is at the heart of the colonist enterprise.

The colonists and their allies offer a markedly different reading of this situation. First, the transposition of indigenous values to family-based migrants is criticized for its lack of cultural understanding. In the words of Xabier Villaverde, the director of the Lago Agrio branch of FEPP, collective titling is "culturally incompatible" with the colonist endeavor, since it "does not correspond to their specific roots." He also affirms that this modality opens up the titling process to outright political manipulation by the heads of pre-cooperatives. Thus, when one pre-cooperative in the Pacayacu area decided to negotiate a collective title agreement through the intermediary role of the environmental NGO Cordavi (Real), it was criticized by other colonist organizations and by FEPP for breaking ranks and introducing division within the colonists, who for over a decade had remained steadfast in calling for individual titles.

FEPP has taken the lead in presenting alternatives to the collective title proposal by outlining a program of Integral Farm Management (Villaverde). This program recognizes that colonist farms contain a wide diversity of soils and argues that, with proper orientation, those lands apt for agriculture can be cultivated. This program also contemplates small-scale ranching, the reforestation of pasture land, the implementation of vegetal (principally yucca) fences, and the introduction of coffee and rice strains adapted to Amazonian soils and climatic conditions. Another argument used to support colonist permanence in the reserve is that, after twenty years of colonization, only 25–30 percent of the colonized area has been deforested, meaning that 70–75 percent of the area can be managed by colonists as family forest reserves. Finally, the colonists assert that, due to the expansion of the reserve in 1991, the lands they occupy represent only a small part of the new total and could be removed without harming the biophysical basis of the reserve.

The negotiations between INEFAN and the colonists deteriorated again in July 1993, when INEFAN unilaterally removed 52,000 hectares of colonized land from the western part of the Cuyabeno Reserve, but instead of giving out individual titles to the land, placed it under the domain of Forestry Patrimony.[12] The colonists criticized this move on two fronts. First, its legality was challenged, since the enlargement or reduction of a protected area could not technically be done through simple agency decree. Second, they argued that this move actually increased the potential for deforestation, since logging firms could sign contracts for the exploitation of timber located on forestry patrimony lands, while it prevented small-scale individual ownership. INEFAN director Barba's former position as manager of a large Ecuadorian timber company also was brought out as evidence of his favoritism toward logging activities.

Another round of negotiations was held between INEFAN and the colonists, and in 1994 an informal agreement was made in which INEFAN would seek to introduce reforms in the Forestry Law that would permit the granting of individual titles on Forest Patrimony lands, titles that would require the recipients to abide by a management plan that would guarantee adequate use of natural resources (Garcés 1994, 14). The fact that action on these reforms was stalled in Congress for the ensuing six years meant that by the year 2000 the colonists were still without a solution to their land titling problem.

In summary, two decades of negotiations witnessed marked shifts in their scope and content without ever definitively resolving the dispute. What started out as a shouting match evolved into a complex negotiating process involving newly established colonist organizations, provincewide peasant organizations, local politicians, the National Congress, a Catholic mission, and a church-sponsored development agency on one side and an ever-changing government forestry agency, a new Environmental Ministry, and several environmental NGOs on the other.

The colonists, who began as a disorganized group of migrants, gradually turned into a politically aware social group capable of defending its interests and asserting its rights as Ecuadorian citizens, even though they were at a clear disadvantage from both legal and environmental standpoints. A strong demographic factor also operated in their favor: they were more than eight thousand people who refused to be removed from their farms. The colonists also came to adopt a softer attitude toward the environmental discourse and its conservationist aims. In fact, they were never against integral management of their farms as long as two conditions were met: that these techniques be economically viable and that they include individual titles to the land.

The environmental side of the negotiations resisted giving in to the colonists and broke several agreements, which contaminated the entire negotiating process. The formal removal of the colonized area from the Cuyabeno Reserve represented a Pyrrhic victory in the struggle of the colonists, since they did not receive clear titles to their farms. The entire process reveals the many practical difficulties in implementing sustainable development policies in the midst of social conflict, legal confusion, and environmental constraints.

Hotel Real, Quito

It was eight o'clock in the morning when I was awoken by the high-pitched sound of chanting voices. I was sleeping in one of the back rooms on the fourth floor of the Hotel Real in central Quito, and for the life of me I could not figure out what could possibly be making that sound. I hurriedly got dressed and descended to the street. There I was greeted by hundreds of kindergartners marching down the main street chanting war slogans in support of the Ecuadorian troops that were fighting Peruvian forces in the Amazon jungle. The children were heading to the central plaza in Colonial Quito where, led by their teachers, they would join thousands of kindergarten, elementary, and secondary school students in a signal to aging President Sixto Durán that the war he was commanding must be won by the Ecuadorians for the dignity of the nation.

This massive participation by schoolchildren was an expression of the Ecuadorian education system, which for decades had played a key role in instilling an anti-Peruvian sentiment among the populace. Children are taught as a matter of historical fact that Peru not only has repeatedly stolen Ecuadorian land, but also is a ruthless aggressor intent upon dominating the peace-loving Ecuadorian people. Some of the strongest propagators of this ideology are state schoolteachers, whose union provided the bulwark of support for the pro-Albanian Ecuadorian Communist Party.

As I watched the marchers file by, my mind wandered back to the time, several years earlier, when I had led a workshop for schoolteachers. During one session I had been openly accused by a teachers' union leader of sowing divisions in the Ecuadorian educational system because I had asked the teachers to brainstorm ways of overcoming tensions with Peru and suggested ways that citizens of the two countries could collaborate in joint projects. My mind then returned to the kindergartners marching in front of me. In another thirty years, when they would be adults holding positions of power and influence, would they seek to reproduce this ideology? Or would they be able to put this training behind them and establish a lasting peace with their Peruvian neighbors?

War in the Upper Amazon Basin

Though the precise moment of the eruption of wars is often difficult to predict, certain situations give clear indications that sooner or later war will break out. Such is the case with the 1995 war between Ecuador and Peru over an isolated stretch of their common Amazonian border. Though the actual military encounters of this war did not take place in the Aguarico Region under study here, the war had many direct effects on that region. Furthermore, this war can tell us much about Amazonian territorial conflict per se, as well as about the continuing territorial dynamic of the Upper Amazon Basin.

After the humiliating defeat of Ecuador by Peru in 1941–42, the Rio de Janeiro Protocol established new borders for both countries that consolidated Peru's territorial expansion. In 1947, U.S. planes equipped with aerial photographic technologies began mapping the newly established border and discovered an entire hydrographic basin—later named the Cenepa River—unknown to the leaders of either Peru or Ecuador. The existence of this watershed made a 78-kilometer stretch of border described in the Rio Protocol nonexecutable, since the language in that document did not correspond with geographical reality. Once again, a hydrographic basin entered the Amazonian territorial drama as an important biophysical component.

Ecuadorian nationalism intensified during the 1960s as the country's national leaders sought to integrate their Amazonia into the national economy. This unresolved border area became an ideal site for ritually reaffirming Ecuador's Amazonian-based nationalism while creating an enemy, Peru, that could be a foil for covering up past failures. This disputed border could also be seen as a festering political wound in Ecuadorian-Peruvian relations, which neither side allowed to heal precisely because it could be used so effectively for political and military ends.

The four-day 1981 Ecuador-Peru war in this area (called the Paquisha War in Ecuador after the key site of struggle) mobilized Ecuadorian nationalism shortly after President Jaime Roldós had introduced draconian economic measures in the country. It also led to a wave of military spending just two years after the generals had handed over state power to civilians. The historic 1991 visit of Peruvian President Alberto Fujimori to Quito seemed to herald a new age in relations between these two nations.

By late 1994 the internal situation in both countries had deteriorated, making the strategic eruption of another border war a viable option for both political and military reasons. Politically, Ecuadorian President Sixto Durán's popularity ratings had plummeted to 10 percent, while Fujimori was in the middle of a hotly contested reelection campaign.

Militarily, the Ecuadorian armed forces were concerned about congressional renewal of a law that guaranteed them 30 percent of all oil revenues, and a military-run bank owned stock in a gold mine located in the disputed area, which was in the initial phase of exploitation. Meanwhile, in Peru high-ranking military officers were involved in a drug trafficking scandal (which soon disappeared after the war erupted).

Throughout January 1995 there were several skirmishes between Ecuadorian and Peruvian troops along the undrawn border; both sides blamed the other for starting the clashes. Since no independent sources could confirm the reports and since no one knows just where the border lies, the start of the war will remain shrouded in doubt. On January 26 an intense land battle took place, and air power was sent into the area. By January 29, the forty-third anniversary of the signing of the Rio Protocol, all-out war had erupted. Over the next two months, heated battles would be waged over control of Ecuadorian and Peruvian military posts that had been recently established along a 6-kilometer-wide swath of no man's land.[13] Ecuador's armed forces were logistically better prepared for the war (causing one to speculate that they were the key instigators of the conflict), and the superiority of their Israeli-made Kfir and United States–made A-37 warplanes helped them down three Peruvian planes (Russian-made Sukoi and French-made Mirage) and two helicopters. By early March, the intensity of the conflict had declined as the four guarantor nations of the Rio Protocol—Argentina, Brazil, Chile, and the United States—mediated a series of negotiations that culminated in a signed cease-fire and the placement of an international force between the warring troops.

Within Ecuador the war produced, once again, an outpouring of nationalist fervor so strong that any hint of opposition was treated as the equivalent to treason. Durán's popularity skyrocketed (only to plummet again after the war), the military got a fifteen-year extension on its guaranteed take of oil revenues, newspapers increased their sales, and the populace mobilized on all fronts. Young men from all parts of the country enlisted in the army to help defend their country and its Amazonian lands from the "Peruvian aggressor." Student rallies and parades in support of the troops included all ages from kindergartners to university students. The right and the left marched hand in hand in unified display of Ecuadorian patriotism.

The active role of Amazonian Indian soldiers in the battle was noteworthy. The disputed border divides Shuar society in half, and over the past several decades the armed forces of both countries have been actively recruiting the Shuar. In Ecuador an all-Shuar special forces unit was formed to conduct dangerous reconnaissance and infiltration missions. This unit was a key element in the Ecuadorian success on the front and garnered the support of the populace as a whole, thereby embellishing their nearly mythic reputation as fierce and hostile headshrinkers.[14]

Though actual combat was limited to the specific area of dispute, the entire Ecuadorian-Peruvian Amazonian border was fortified with fresh troops, thus directly affecting the Aguarico Region, which has an extensive border with Peru. Here a similar level of indigenous participation in the military was evident, with the Quichua, who have a long history of participation in the armed forces, providing the bulk of the troops. Both the Zancudo and Playas de Cuyabeno Quichua communities are located next to Ecuadorian military outposts, and in both communities most of the able-bodied men immediately (re)enlisted in the army and were sent to the front. The Zábalo Cofán community also organized a local indigenous contingent, which performed reconnaissance work along the Peruvian border. A small contingent of Ecuadorian soldiers was placed alongside the community to collaborate with the Cofán troops, who were under the leadership of Borman.[15] All of these efforts meant that the principal defenders of Amazonia for the Ecuadorian nation (and for the Peruvian nation as well) were indigenous peoples.

The participation of indigenous peoples in wars between other groups has a long history; in Amazonia, it dates back to sixteenth-century battles between Portuguese, French, Spanish, English, and Dutch invaders. In each case, the specific political and cultural elements that underlie the agency of these groups must be analyzed. A common argument used against indigenous territorial claims in Ecuadorian Amazonia, particularly strong among certain segments of the armed forces, is that indigenous territories represent a threat to the sovereignty of the Ecuadorian nation by giving indigenous peoples nearly exclusive control (subsoil rights are always excluded) over large tracts of land. By fighting in the Ecuadorian army and defending the national territory, indigenous peoples seek to destroy the bases of that argument by demonstrating their loyalty to the Ecuadorian nation, for which they put their lives on the line. In such a situation, they are clearly patriots who do not represent a separatist movement within the structure of the nation-state. This political strategy also allies them to the military, an important force in Amazonia, thereby broadening their power base in negotiations over issues of concern to them. Amazonian indigenous peoples thus use participation in the armed forces as a space of power and as a structural modality designed to strengthen their society in relation to the national one.

Other forces operate at a cultural level. Without buying into the stereotypical image of the fierce headhunter, one can note that warfare retains an important function within Shuar society and gains a contemporary expression through Shuar participation in the armed forces.

Another important insight from this war is gained by analyzing territorial disputes at a mesoregional level within the context of microregional disputes. During the war, the existing disputes over territory between indigenous communities, colonists, the petroleum industry, tourist companies, and environmentalists were temporarily put aside while this larger conflict was waged. This in no way diminishes the intensity of the disputes on the microregional level, but rather shows that at each level of analysis specific factors and issues tend to predominate, which are not necessarily evident at other levels. At a mesoregional level, the issues of nationalism and formal international boundaries between nation-states are highlighted. At a microregional level, on the other hand, social groups and their struggles over collective territories are the principal issues of concern.

This leads us to other insights regarding the notion of the frontier. The historical analysis of Amazonia presented in chapter 1 showed how frontiers are opened, closed, and reopened within different regional contexts depending on the unique set of biophysical and social characteristics present in the region. The imposition of national territorial claims and identities emerged in the early nineteenth century as an important, but by no means the only, element in the historical development of these multiple frontiers. What the Ecuador-Peru Amazonian war of 1995 demonstrates is that the nation-building process within Ecuador (and to a lesser extent within Peru) is not yet complete. The national trauma of the 1941–42 war in the Ecuadorian collective identity has not yet been overcome, as seen in the decades-long refusal to accept their defeat, a refusal fueled by opportunistic political leaders.

The waging of this war in Amazonia, a site of historic ambivalence for Ecuadorian leaders, forces the nation to come to grips with the tenuousness of its presence in the area and at the same time places indigenous peoples and their millenary presence in this region in a role of greater importance. In other words, Ecuadorian Amazonia can now perhaps be better integrated into the nation-state as a whole, but not exclusively on the terms of the nationalist development project of the nation's military leaders. Recent events have compelled leaders to view Amazonia as more than a site of valuable natural resources to be extracted as fast as possible. This vision must now include the presence of indigenous peoples' homelands,[16] the existence of high levels of biodiversity, and the need to preserve beautiful rain-forest landscapes. These elements have become an integral part of the Ecuadorian Amazonian territorial equation when seen from national and mesoregional perspectives.

Over the next three years, intense negotiations between Ecuador and Peru were held, though with little progress, as both sides were unwilling to make significant concessions. The congresses of the two countries finally voted for the four guarantor nations to conduct binding arbitration, which quickly led to a formal peace agreement. On 26 October 1998, Ecuadorian President Jamil Mahuad and Peruvian President Alberto Fujimori signed a peace treaty in Brasilia, thus formally putting an end this fifty-seven-year-old border dispute. At first, the agreement was greeted with reticence within the general Ecuadorian populace, since Ecuador was not granted any of the land it claimed except the 100-hectare Tiwintza hill area, which Ecuadorian soldiers had successfully defended in 1995 (granted by the guarantor nations in a symbolic gesture of goodwill). Nonetheless, the peace treaty generated a simultaneous feeling of relief that the long process of conflict had finally ended, and a host of bilateral agreements have emerged as a means of consolidating friendly neighborly relations (Alvarez 1998; Klein 1998).

Pousada Equinox, Macapá

Though I had spent the entire two months of the 1995 Ecuador-Peru War in Ecuador, I had been unable to substantiate rumors concerning a rich gold mine located near the disputed border that was reputedly owned by top officials in the Ecuadorian military. It was only several months later, while lodged at the Pousada Equinox in Macapá, Amapá, at the other extreme of the Amazon River Basin, that I was able to uncover some hard facts about the case. Staying at the same hotel was a Brazilian engineer who worked for the Canadian TBX mining company, which was in the process of closing down its gold-mining operations in Amapá and starting a major new operation in Ecuador, just 60 kilometers from the disputed border area with Peru.

Over several bottles of cold Cerpa beer, he informed me of many things that I had been unable to ascertain in Ecuador. First, he told me that the mine had twelve confirmed veins of gold, some of which were believed to be a kilometer long. If this length was confirmed, it would be one of the richest gold mines in the world. Second, he explained that the Andean escarpment that faced Amazonia, due to the uplifting and over-lapping of geological layers, had produced a great deal of quartz along with a host of heavy metals such as mercury, gold, lead, and silver. For this reason, the entire eastern slope of the Andes was being targeted by private mining firms as the site of major mining operations in the decades to come. Finally, he gave me the details of the mine's ownership. TBX was the controlling partner in the operation, with the Ecuadorian military retaining 32 percent of the mine.

Here was yet another example of the connectedness of Amazonian activities in distant, seemingly unconnected, parts of the jungle. One could roam from one end of the basin to the other and find people and companies that were involved in making these connections. Of course, the engineer could have had the same sense of this connectedness. He was in the process of moving to Ecuador, where he would be responsible for the logistics of setting up the new operation, equipping the mine, and maintaining it with supplies. Having found in Amapá an anthropologist who knew about the area where he was going to be working, he took the opportunity to ask me about some of the challenges and difficulties of living in Ecuador. I, too, was a small part of these connections.

CONCLUSION

Amazonian Territoriality Today

Comparative Territorial Dynamics

This chronicle of Jari and Aguarico regional frontiers started from the premise that human territorialization is rarely based in a single, immemorial foundational act of a social group, but rather is an ongoing process that can include migrations, conflicts, and changes over long periods. By looking at territorial behavior from the various points of view and sites of action of specific social groups, the distinct means of claiming, appropriating, and defending territories in Amazonia came into direct view.

The indigenous homelands of the Siona, Secoya, Cofán, and Quichua peoples in the Aguarico Region and the *caboclo* homelands in the Jari Region have the longest territorial continuity of all those groups studied here and have suffered from the greatest number of changes. These peoples have adapted to the territorial intrusions of European conquerors and explorers, to the nucleated settlement patterns imposed by the various orders of Catholic missions, to the decimation of their numbers provoked by the Indian slave traders, to the miscegenation resulting from continual waves of migrants, and to the debt peonage of rubber barons. Their cosmographies have been succeeded and overlapped by the installation of other cosmographies, but they have been neither temporally superseded nor spatially supplanted by them. Five hundred years of assaults involving torturous processes of ethnocide and ethnogenesis have resulted in very different indigenous and *caboclo* homelands in the two regions, which nonetheless continue to express vital cosmographies with their own set of territorial claims.

Today, these groups are presenting historical claims to territory based on their prior presence in the area as an essential point of legitimizing their formal control over their homelands. These homelands are not adequately classified as either public or private lands but are more aptly conceived as social territories founded in collective access to and use of resources under the socially established norms of that group. As these groups become incorporated into larger political structures such as the nation-state and develop contacts with social actors tied to worldwide organizations, they gain powerful links that strengthen their historical claims to territory. In addition, as they forge links with other traditional groups, creating national federations and confederations, continent-wide organizations, and worldwide levels of interaction, new cross-levels of territoriality are established.

The arrival of the developmentalist frontier wave in Amazonia was tied to a specific moment in world and Latin American history (the 1950–60s) and to the ideological and utopian attributes that social groups brought with them. The incorporation of the key tenets of development cosmographies by different social groups, each with its own territorial and political interests, generated specific enclave and migrant territories. The Jari Project, under both Ludwig and subsequent Brazilian owners, is a manifestation of this cosmography in a way that José Júlio de Andrade's Brazil nut estate is not, even though they both functioned within the same geographical space. The installation and nationalization of the petroleum industry in Ecuadorian Amazonia during the country's "revolutionary nationalist" military dictatorship also places it squarely within a developmentalist framework.

These large-scale development projects created new territories and wielded enormous power because of the physical energy at their disposal based on the use of advanced technological systems. The global, continental, and national cross-level ties of these projects (and the accumulation of power they imply) catapulted them into a position of hegemony within their respective regions almost immediately upon their installation there. Meanwhile, the presence of innumerable local factors invariably made this installation irregular and unpredictable, particularly in regard to Amazonia's specific biophysical characteristics.

The rural and urban migrants who entered the Aguarico and Jari Regions with these large-scale projects are distinguishable from previous migrants, since they operated within this particular developmentalist wave. The sheer numbers of these migrants gave them a powerful demographic presence in their respective regions that strengthened their migrant territories. This power equation produced major changes in existing social territories of the traditional peoples of these regions, greatly reducing the amount of land over which they had effective control. The rural and urban migrant territories that were installed alongside the enclave ones are founded in demographic movements within a nation-state giving migrants cross-level power connections as citizens within county/municipal, provincial/state, and national administrative units. They are also part of a broader change at an infrastructural level from river-based societies to road-based ones.

Development-led social groups do not recognize the length of occupation as a legitimate claim to territory and instead promote presentist claims based on the immediate fulfillment of human needs and desires. These needs and desires can be of a household scope, as seen in poor peasant families that squat on jungle lands as part of a survival strategy and that appeal to their rights as national citizens; of a national scope, as seen in Petroecuador's claim that oil exploitation is the foundation of Ecuador's development as a nation; or of a global scope, whereby the world demand for paper spawned the Jari eucalyptus plantations.

The environmentalist frontier wave came directly on the heels of the developmentalist wave and represents perhaps the most significant change in the past twenty years in the way Amazonia has been understood and territorially appropriated. The fundamental change in perspective encompassed in environmental cosmographies is the rise of a Western, science-based biocentric viewpoint that challenges the hegemony of anthropocentric perspectives based on immediate human need fulfillment. In the biocentric perspective, the biophysical environment is valued in and of itself as a defining dimension of Amazonia, while the concept of ecosystems offers a potent new way of categorizing and understanding this geographical space. The territorial implications of the biocentric view can be seen in the installation of preservationist territories, a process that reached its high point during the late 1970s and throughout the 1980s in almost all Amazonian countries.

In Ecuador, the physical assault on the Cuyabeno Wildlife Production Reserve quickly became an important political issue within the country, garnered the support of many different social sectors, and slowed (but by no means stopped) the expansion of oil development onto its lands. In Brazil, state-of-the-art scientific criteria were used to establish protected areas, something sorely lacking in Ecuador. Nonetheless, the large number of new protected areas created and the high cost of maintaining them generated a crisis within the national protected areas system. The Jari Ecological Station is but one example of this crisis: its significant physical infrastructure has never been used, it has never had a full-time professional ranger working at the site, and very few research activities have been carried out there.

The claims to territory by many environmental social actors, particularly those with a strong preservationist viewpoint, are justified not according to the length of past occupations nor the immediate needs of present populations but rather according to the future needs of the earth and humanity in its attempt to survive as a species. By placing Amazonia in the much longer time frame of natural history, preservationists argue that certain areas must exist in perpetuity to maintain both the essential natural cycles that regulate the global environment and those wild areas and genetic stocks that are necessary for the spiritual and economic benefit of future generations.

The power of environmental social actors stems from the growing social and discursive force of the worldwide environmental movement, which has presented a compelling claim for conservation of the Amazonian biome. This claim is backed by Western scientific knowledge and the wealth of information that it has revealed about Amazonia, giving the claim a legitimacy respected even by development social actors (who depend on a similar knowledge base), which was one of the factors that allowed environmental cosmographies to challenge development ones with such force.

A key outcome of the environmental frontier wave in Amazonia has been the meeting and partial union of the historical claims to territory by traditional groups and the future claims of environmentalists under the banner of sustainability. The creation of sustainable use territories, for example, has directly incorporated the needs and interests of traditional groups into environmental cosmographies while maintaining many biocentric criteria used to identify, delimit, and justify the existence of these territories. At the same time, these territories have often incorporated the interests of the tourist industry, government agencies, and environmental NGOs.

In Ecuador, the notion of sustainable use territories emerged by default rather than as part of a specific demand by an Amazonian social movement. The Cuyabeno Reserve was a pioneer in this regard by creating a territorial modality that did not have any legal precedent within Ecuadorian law. This development, however, was possible only because of the political strength of indigenous peoples within the national political structure. The formation of the Shuar federation in 1964, the Confederation of Indigenous Nationalities of Ecuadorian Amazonia (CONFENIAE) in 1980, and the Confederation of Indigenous Nationalities of Ecuador (CONAIE) in 1986 contributed to the growing presence of indigenous peoples within the political arena (though not within the formal structures of government), facilitated the incorporation of indigenous demands within the national protected areas system, and led to the creation of a separate legal category of "indigenous territories" first applied in 1990 with the Huaorani. Throughout the 1990s, after a series of nationwide indigenous uprisings (*levantamientos*), indigenous peoples gained certain guarantees of their rights in the new Constitution promulgated in 1998.

In Brazil, the emergence of the rubber tappers' movement and the subsequent implementation of extractive settlement projects and reserves created an entirely new territorial entity that is formally recognized by the government and also a result of direct social group action at a national level. Sustainable use territories have a distinct advantage over strictly preservationist ones with regard to environmental protection in areas of strong developmentalist pressures, since extractivist populations live on the site and are directly involved in protecting the area, which is also their homeland. The formally sanctioned Maracá, Cajari, and Iratapuru Extractive Areas in Amapá, administered under three different government agencies, have become functioning units because of the active participation of these populations along with the support they have received from social movements, environmental NGOs, and other sectors of civil society.

Pan-Amazonian Trends and Policy Options

The existence of what have been called here *perennial frontiers* represents a key pan-Amazonian trend over the past centuries. The repeated emergence of frontier waves has been a powerful force in the long-term process of globalization of Amazonian social groups. The historical epoch in which each wave of frontier expansion took place oriented the struggle for hegemony between cosmographies at a regional level. Within regional frontiers, some cosmographies became partially hegemonic during a particular historical moment only to lose strength as new ones were superimposed. Some cosmographies have come and gone (e.g., mission ones); others (e.g., national and mercantile ones) have been incorporated, in varying degrees, by indigenous groups into their own cosmographies; while still others (e.g., development and environmental ones) are recent arrivals. Thus, frontier history is not a process of linear historical succession; rather, it is marked by coexisting temporalities, cultural interpenetration, and recurrent territorial disputes. When the numerous historical epochs that have been fused into these frontiers are taken into account, along with the specific biophysical characteristics of Amazonia, the uniqueness of this long-term frontier expansion becomes evident, particularly when compared with other frontier expansions, such as those of the U.S. West, the Russian steppes, or the Australian outback.

Mercantile cosmographies were the first to introduce global power dynamics into Amazonia in a significant form and, over the past four centuries, have functioned as a type of joker within Amazonia because of their ability to enter the region, stimulate the emergence of new social groups, fuse with existing cosmographies, and then change again as a different demand for resources develops. From gold to quinine, to rubber and Brazil nuts, on to petroleum and kaolin, back again to gold, and on to ecotours and rain-forest landscapes, mercantile territories based in the exploitation of specific resources have long generated connections that span regional, national, continental, and global levels of social articulation.

The implementation of mercantile cosmographies, though clearly tied to the expansion of the world capitalist system, did not always produce a subsequent expansion of the capitalist principle of private property based in exclusive ownership and control of land. What was sought was unrestricted access to resources that could be marketed, and this has historically occurred through a host of land tenure systems. What makes Amazonia unique, when compared with other more densely populated parts of the continent, is that it has not been thoroughly parceled into private properties. Though isolated, privately owned parcels of land have existed in Amazonia for centuries, it was only with the arrival of development cosmographies, particularly in the forms of large-scale development projects and colonization programs, that privately controlled lands began to be massively installed in these two regions, radically altering their territorial dynamic. Today, a new generation of mercantile cosmographies fueled by a powerful neoliberal ideology has incorporated certain elements of development cosmographies and is rapidly assuming a position of hegemony that is eclipsing all existing cosmographies.

The enormous social, cultural, biological, geological, and hydraulic wealth housed in Amazonia makes it a source of ever-new resources that emerge as technologies and social needs change. The intense international debate over the biodiversity convention—in which Amazonia is a key site of struggle—is a harbinger of the opening of still other regional frontiers, where the search for genetic material may create a type of genetic front. The exploitation of biodiversity depends on highly sophisticated biotechnological and genetic manipulations that are still in an incipient stage of development, making the issue of the precise use and value of biodiversity an uncertain one. The growing demand for unique genetic strains and chemical compounds, along with the possibility of developing numerous new commodities ranging from pharmaceuticals to foodstuffs, places biodiversity within a mercantilist framework. The jobs and profits generated by exploiting biodiversity make it a decidedly developmentalist endeavor. The need for the preservation of ecosystems that house biodiversity ties this issue to environmental cosmographies. The role of traditional peoples in the care, development, and control of these resources places the genetic front in contact—and often conflict— with traditional cosmographies; a host of social and political questions concerning the intellectual rights of these peoples to past modifications of existing genetic material and their current control over and access to these resources will need to be resolved.

The related issue of territorial control over Amazonian lands has— during the past two centuries—been invariably linked to the nation-state. The consolidation of national cosmographies starting in the early nineteenth century changed the territorial dynamics of Amazonia by introducing the notion of exclusive sovereign control over territory within the domain of the state. Given the political hegemony of nation-states in the contemporary world, public domains have become one of the principal means of conceiving the issue of ownership and control over territory. Large tracts of state-held lands continue to exist throughout Amazonia in each of the seven nations that have lands in this biome.

In recent years, certain sectors of national governments have intensified their efforts to maintain firm territorial control over Amazonia, under the banner of responding to what are considered as threats to state sovereignty. This notion is particularly strong in military circles. In Brazil, for example, the 1990s witnessed efforts to zone its entire Amazon region according to the technical land use criteria used in its Ecological-Economic Zoning Program (ZEE). Meanwhile, the installation of the U.S.$2 billion System of Vigilance for the Amazon (SIVAM) is an effort to have top-down control over everything that moves in Amazonia. The national security zone in Ecuador's Sucumbíos province and its recent extension to the newly created Orellana province also indicate that the military seeks to maintain tight control over the area rich in oil reserves.

The territorial dynamics inside nation-states reveal how other cosmographies continue to exist within a broad national cosmography and how social groups have partially or wholly incorporated its tenets into their territorial claims. Thus, national cosmographies may be uniform when viewed from the perspective of state leaders, but when seen from the perspective of the distinct social groups that live within national boundaries, their diversity and complexity become evident. This has led to new calls for a ground-up approach to territorial control and policy formation, calls that start not from the notion of national sovereignty but from the empirical fact of the local and regional presence of different social groups housing divergent claims to territory. This view argues that only by directly incorporating these groups, and their claims, into the planning and management process can sustainable control over territory be achieved. Within this framework, the negotiation and resolution of territorial disputes become increasingly viable. New forms of implementing policies that directly involve local populations, such as co-management agreements, present policy options that have only just begun to be explored. Essential to the success of these efforts is the joint participation of local populations and the state, the partial cession of state control over public lands to social groups, and the mutual recognition of differing roles and responsibilities based in the strategic place of each social actor in the territorial equation of the region.

In addition, different agencies of the state maintain diverse relations with each of the social actors involved in territorial conflicts as part of their responsibility of representing (however minimally) their interests while also promoting their own institutional agendas. While the interests of large capital are powerful forces in the play for hegemony within certain sectors of the state, other sectors have direct links to weaker social actors and provide counterforces to this attempt at hegemony. This places the state in the contradictory role of promoting and defending antagonistic interests, making it an integral part of these territorial conflicts. Thus, one agency of the state can encourage colonization of lands that another agency has designated as a protected area, while still another agency may hand out fiscal incentives for ranchers to enter into these same lands.

In spite of these divergent roles of the state, a common effect of national cosmographies throughout Amazonia has been the increasing institutionalization of all territorialities based in clearly defined boundaries and explicit use restrictions. This formalizing trend occurs within the legal structures of the state, thereby reinforcing the notion of state sovereignty over these territories and apparently heralding the official closing of the territorial issue in Amazonia. The notion of the definitive closing of the territorial issue, however, is not supported by the historical record described here and, in fact, harbors a contemporary bias: Given the turbulent history of the region, there is little reason to believe that laws, parks, or even countries are eternal. The lesson of perennial frontiers seems to lead to the conclusion that all territorial claims can be contested as historical situations change and as new social groups, with new interests and power, emerge and migrate.

A further lesson seems to be that the natural and social effects of past, present, and future frontier dynamics on Amazonia will continue to generate intense debate and struggle well into the twenty-first century. While deforestation is hardly a new phenomenon, the scale and rapidity of rain-forest destruction has reached unprecedented levels with full effects that can only be known in the future, when there may not be time to reverse negative consequences. And while the destruction of indigenous peoples, either through ethnocide or genocide, is also not a new phenomena, today the emergence of indigenous organizations capable of defending their rights has radically altered frontier dynamics. In sum, the combination of natural and social factors, together with the complexity of their interaction, unites technical and scientific issues with political ones and requires that policy options develop new analytical and methodological instruments for meeting these challenges.

The regional analysis used in this study, which has served as a key means of understanding human/biophysical dynamics, can also be applied to policy issues. One such policy approach is to use the watershed as a central planning unit, whereby the topographical and hydrological features of a river basin are placed within the framework of the specific uses of diverse social groups. Though this approach shares some tenets with bioregional approaches (see Sale 1985), this study has introduced several concepts that make a strictly bioregional perspective problematic.

Watersheds are not immutable natural settings in which a single, best set of uses can be scientifically ascertained. On the one hand, watersheds can house multiple, long-term disputes over what resources are and how they should be used, in what have been called here *regional frontiers*. In these scenarios, regional planning approaches are faced with the challenge of incorporating techniques of conflict resolution and political power-sharing mechanisms that are tied, either directly or indirectly, to world economic and geopolitical conditions. On the other hand, the biophysical dynamics within each watershed, which operate according to their own type of natural agency that scientific research is only beginning to understand, add a constant and unpredictable dimension to policy planning. These dynamics become even more difficult to predict when the magnitude and intensity of biophysical alterations are high.

Another problem with a strict bioregional approach is that watersheds cannot be adequately conceived as self-contained units. Though watersheds are clearly a major force in maintaining a certain degree of regionalism, as we have seen in the cases of the Jari and Aguarico Regions, the fractal scaling analysis developed here reveals how social forces and groups beyond the regional level can be important actors in how regional frontier dynamics are played out. Fractal power emanates from the conjunctures of local autonomy and global interdependence, whereby the exercise of power requires that different levels of social articulation be identified by social groups and that they be strategically employed in their daily struggles. Fractal power is also exercised through the creative empowerment of unforeseen relationships. Disjunctures can create ever-new possibilities of social action that can be utilized by social actors situated at all levels.

One consequence of this situation is that, for policies to be effective, they must incorporate diverse social actors operating at different levels of social articulation—both larger and smaller than that of the nation-state—into the policy planning and implementation process. The innovative Pilot Program for the Protection of Brazilian Tropical Forests, for example, which is financed by the Group of Seven industrialized countries and the Brazilian federal government, is being implemented in Brazil at national, regional, and local levels and shows how social actors operating at distinct levels of social articulation can share responsibilities for the use and management of this biome. At the same time, the conflicts and tensions that have arisen from the varied interests and practices of these diverse actors indicate that sharing responsibility in policy planning and implementation is a highly difficult endeavor.

Finally, the narration of these two long and complex regional histories can offer insights into the widely divergent visions of Amazonia that were mentioned in the preface. These many visions—earthly paradise or counterfeit paradise, green cathedral or green hell, the last chapter of Genesis or a coming red desert—have an essential reality (regardless of their empirical grounding) to the degree that they provide a motivating force for human actions. Each vision depends upon the social group that is appropriating territories, the historical epoch in which this appropriation takes place, and the symbolic systems and adaptive technologies available. On the one hand, Amazonia's biophysical diversity has allowed it to be many things to many people; on the other, its sociocultural diversity has modified and molded its many ecosystems in highly contrasting ways. The unpredictable nature of these social/biophysical interactions leaves many questions unanswered. Certainly, a key factor in the way these issues are approached lies in the global environmental and geopolitical consciousness about Amazonia that has emerged in recent decades. Only time will tell whether this consciousness will be translated into actions that will make Amazonia look more like the last chapter of Genesis or the first chapter of the Apocalypse.

Glossary

aldeia (Port.) village

andiroba (Port.) Amazonian tree (*Carapa guianensis*) used for its wood and oils

áreas intangibles (Sp.) untouchable zones

aviador (Port.) creditors of the aviamento system

aviamento (Port.) commercial debt peonage system commonly used in extractivism

balata (Port.) rubberlike gum obtained from the sap of the balata tree (*Manilkara bidentata*)

branco (Port.) white person

caboclo (Port.) autochthonous, mixed-blooded Amazonian peasant

cacique (Sp.) headman

cafusos (Port.) Indian-black mixed-blooded person

Calha Norte (Port.) North Corridor (Brazilian borderlands national security program)

câmara (Port.) settler town council in colonial Brazil

campos alagados (Port.) marshlands and semiflooded palm groves

casa de farinha (Port.) shed where manioc flour is made

castanhal (Port.) Brazil nut grove

castanha (Port.) nut

castanheira (Port.) Brazil nut tree (*Bertholletia excelsa*)

cauchero (Sp.) rubber trader

caucho (Sp.) rubber from *Castilloa elastica* tree

charapa (Sp.) Amazonian turtle (*Podecmemis unifis/expansa*) used for its edible meat and eggs

choladas (Sp.) "detribalized, acculturated, but unassimilated Indians" (Stocks 1978)

colocação (Port.) a family-run, agroextractive productive unit

concessão de direto real de uso (Port.) use-rights concession

convenio (Sp.) written agreement or contract

copaíba (Port.) Amazonian tree (*Copaifera guyanensis*) exploited for its oils

criollo (Sp.) American-born children of Spanish colonial elite

cushma (Cofán) traditional tunic of the Cofán people

descimento (Port.) process of forcibly settling Indians into mission villages

Diretório dos Índios (Port.) a Portuguese colonial decree promulagated by Pombal

discriminação de terras (Port.) official review of land titles

El Dorado (Sp.) Land of Gold

empate (Port.) political confrontation that ends in a standoff

empreiteira (Port.) private contracting firm

encomendero (Sp.) owner of Spanish colonial land grant

encomienda (Sp.) Spanish colonial land grant

entrada (Sp.) Jesuit reconnaissance trip

garimpeiro (Port.) wildcat gold miner

gato (Port.) subcontracted labor recruiter

grilagem (Port.) fraudulent land titling

huasipungo (Quichua) semifeudal land tenure system formerly used in Ecuador's highlands

índio (Port.) Indian person

latifundiário (Port.) estate boss

latifúndio (Port.) large estate or ranch

levantamiento (Sp.) (indigenous) uprising in Ecuador

língua geral (Port.) indigenous creole tongue derived from the Tupi language family

Lojano (Sp.) person from Ecuador's Loja Province

mameluco (Port.) European-Indian mixed-blooded person

Maranhense (Port.) person from Brazil's Maranhão State

mergulho (Port.) gold mining conducted by skin divers

mestiço (Port.) mixed-blooded person

mestizo (Sp.) mixed-blooded person

minifundización (Sp.) acute land parcelization

mulato (Port.) black-white mixed-blooded person

muntun (Quichua) Amazonian Quichua social and territorial structure

mutirão (Port.) voluntary, collective work sessions

naranjilla (Sp.) edible fruit (*Solanum quitoense*) native to Ecuador

Oriente (Sp.) the East (Ecuadorian Amazonia)

ouriço (Port.) hard shell of the Brazil nut tree, which houses numerous Brazil nuts

paiche (Sp.) large, edible, freshwater fish (*Arapaima gigas*) native to Amazonia

País de la Canela (Sp.) Land of Cinnamon

pardo (Port.) brown-skinned person

paredão (Port.) canyon wall

patrão (Port.) estate boss or owner

patria (Sp.) national homeland

patrón (Sp.) estate boss or owner

peão (Port.) low-paid worker; peon

pita (Sp.) agave cord

portaria (Port.) an internal regulation of a Brazilian government agency

posse (Port.) effective possession

posseiro (Port.) squatter

preto (Port.) black person

quilombola (Port.) individual member of a maroon society

quilombo (Port.) maroon society (fugitive slave community)

reducción (Sp.) mission town

regimento (Port.) legal disposition of the colonial Portuguese Crown

resgates (Port.) so-called rescue expeditions used to capture Indian slaves

ribereño (Sp.) traditional Amazonian riverside dweller

seringa (Port.) rubber from the *Hevea brasiliensis* tree

seringalista (Port.) see *aviador*

seringal (Port.) rubber tree stand

seringueira (Port.) rubber tree (*Hevea brasiliensis*)

seringueiro (Port.) rubber tapper

sesmaria (Port.) Portuguese colonial land grant in Brazil

silvícolas (Port.) wild forest peoples; Indians

silvi-vila (Port.) forest town

tapuios (Port.) "detribalized and deculturated Indians" (Moreira Neto 1988)

terra firme (Port.) upland (nonflooding) areas

terras devolutas (Port.) unused lands returned to the public domain; also vacant lands

terras indígenas (Port.) Indian lands or territories

tierra firme (Sp.) upland (nonflooding) areas

tropas de resgate (Port.) slave-capturing troops

uhu (Makuna) "owner" of a parcel of land

várzea (Port.) floodplains

vila (Port.) small town

Notes

Preface and Acknowledgments

1. For Amazonia as green cathedral, see Hudson 1904; as green hell, see Rivera 1935; as the last chapter of Genesis, see da Cunha 1909; as counterfeit paradise, see Meggers 1971; as red desert, see Goodland and Howard 1975. On the process of the "invention of Amazonia," see Gondim 1994; on Amazonia as a "landscape of the imagination," see Taussig 1987.

Introduction

1. For some recent studies in environmental history, see Worster (1979, 1993), Cronon (1983), Dean (1987, 1995), Merchant (1989), and Radding (1997).

2. Schwoch (1995, 460) pushes this issue a bit farther by observing that, in the Amazonian city of Manaus, "one simultaneously experiences the modern and the post-modern world-systems." This, too, does not go far enough, since, with little difficulty, one could easily find in contemporary Manaus many premodern systems still operating.

3. This theme is echoed by a host of other scholars of Latin America in general and Amazonia in particular in such phrases as the "interweaving of historical temporalities" (Vovelle 1987, 280), "complex articulations of traditions and (diverse, unequal) modernities" (García Canclini 1989, 23), "conflicts of temporalities" (Oliveira 1994, 91), and "mixed temporalities" (Calderón 1995).

4. The term *socionatural region* is defined by Smith and Reeves as "a system in which diverse human groups have adapted in patterned ways to plant, animal and environmental resources, to one another, to hierarchical market and administrative forces, and to pressure groups and other forms of quasi-organized social and political interest" (1989, 14).

5. For some important studies in political ecology, both ethnographic and theoretical, see Schmink and Wood (1987, 1992), Sheridan (1988), Little (1992), Stonich (1993), Peet and Watts (1996), and Bryant and Bailey (1997).

6. The rather futile debates over whether human territoriality is an "instinct"

(Ardrey 1966) have not greatly advanced our understanding because of both the vagueness of the term *instinct* and the high level of generality offered by ethological comparisons. If we want to understand *human* territoriality in depth, we must look primarily to human beings and not to birds or orangutans, thus making this understanding an essentially anthropological endeavor. Within anthropology, however, the study of human territoriality has been heavily focused upon small-scale traditional or nomadic societies whose territoriality is understood as an adaptive response to the constraints of the biophysical environment (see Dyson-Hudson and Smith 1978). This limited approach developed models that are not widely applicable to contemporary complex societies that have the biosphere as their adaptive framework.

7. This definition of human territoriality is adapted from that of Sack (1986, 19): "the attempt by an individual or group to affect, influence, or control people, phenomena, and relationships, by delimiting and asserting control over a geographic area."

8. For the sake of terminological clarity, a *region* is a delimited sphere of interaction, and a *territory* refers to the appropriation of a specific portion of a region by a social group according to their respective cosmographical tenets. This distinction between region and territory roughly corresponds to that between space and place made by Tuan (1977), to that between space and territory made by Raffestin (1993), and to that between functional spaces ("created through connectedness") and formal spaces ("created through relatedness") presented by Lewis (1991).

9. A distinction needs to be made between territorially based social *groups* and social *actors* in general. A social actor is any human entity (e.g., an individual, a government agency, a private corporation, a church group, a research institution) that exhibits a purposeful agency upon a social space, an agency based on the exercise of power (Giddens 1984).

10. When a photographic image is superimposed upon another, for example, this superimposition is made in a temporal moment that succeeds the impression of the first image and is achieved through the spatial overlap of one image upon another within the same physical space. By analogy, cosmographies can exhibit successive overlaps through which one comes after another in historical time and occurs in the same space. This successive character, however, does not imply an improvement upon the previous one. Cosmographies *succeed* but do not necessarily *supersede* each other in time. Spatially, there is a horizontal overlapping in which one group's territoriality is placed over part or all of the territoriality of another group without necessarily extinguishing it. Cosmographies *overlap* but do not always *supplant* each other in space. For some other uses of the concept of superimposition in social analysis, see Bachelard (1988), Hurtado (1969), and Darnton (1995). My thinking here has benefited from many dialogues with Carlos Rojas, who develops similar notions elsewhere (Rojas 1995).

11. Bourdieu defines a field of power as "a space of relations of force between

different kinds of capital or, more precisely, between agents who possess a suffi-cient amount of one of the different kinds of capital to be in a position to domi-nate the corresponding field, whose struggles intensify whenever the relative value of different kinds of capital is questioned . . . , that is especially when the established equilibrium in the field of instances specifically charged with the reproduction of the field of power is threatened" (1998, 34).

12. In frontier situations as in Amazonia, the force of *habitus* among the social actors is generally weak (Bourdieu 1977), since social rules, norms, and conven-tions that guide human interaction either have not yet been firmly established within the frontier field of power or must be constantly modified to attend to new circumstances. In such a situation, not only the reproduction of the social space of certain groups is being contested but also the production of a new frontier space that incorporates new social groups.

13. In one case, a frontier created in the Lacandona jungle of Chiapas, Mexico, by indigenous peoples fleeing persecution and land expulsion produced a revolu-tionary situation that jelled into the Zapatista National Liberation Army (Barabas 1996). Though revolution is hardly a common outcome of frontier situations, this example shows the wide range of possible responses that can be generated by a partially structured frontier dynamic.

14. Fractal analysis was first developed in the work of mathematician Benoit Mandelbrot (1977), who created a novel type of geometry based on nonlinear means of examining irregular shapes; this geometry sought to move beyond the centuries-old Euclidean geometry of regular shapes. The term *fractal* was derived from the Latin *fractua* (irregular) but was also invoked by Mandelbrot to suggest "fractured," "fragmented," and "fractional" (Briggs 1992, 22). The development of a new mathematical method of scaling shapes provided a means of drawing relationships between different scales of the same entity.

The introduction of fractals into social theory is hazardous, since one runs a risk when directly transposing a mathematical concept to social realities that operate according to social criteria. However, fractal analysis represents a potent spatial conceptual tool that can be useful—in both its functions as methodologi-cal analogy and as theoretical construct—in intellectually confronting an increas-ingly complex and globalized world noted for its new types of time-space inter-relations across multiple levels of social articulation. Fractal analysis also offers the advantage of moving beyond functional, integrative models and gets us thinking in terms of irregular, complex dynamics.

15. By analyzing historical processes in two regions, certain spatial and demo-graphic momentums, both convergent and divergent, can be identified, based on what Evans and Stephens call "historic causes" (as opposed to "constant causes"), in which "events and institutional arrangements of the past are an essential part of the explanation of current arrangements and dynamics" (1988, 730).

16. The subversive power of the cartographic effort is evident in the study

conducted by Almeida (1994), who mapped the conflictive Cajarás region of Brazilian Amazonia. Almeida gave the claims of actors from civil society a cartographic representation, in many cases for the first time ever.

Chapter One: Invading Indigenous Homelands

1. Other movements into the area have been postulated, ranging from Steward's hypothesis of a northern Atlantic coastal entry into the Amazon Delta (1948, 885) to Evans's suggestion of an inland route from the Caribbean to the northern Amazon (1950, 125–27) and Salzano and Callegari-Jacques's mention of a southern entry to the Amazon River Basin from the São Francisco River valley (1988, 23).

2. Though a 1500 letter by Américo Vespucio seems to indicate that he had entered into the waters of the Amazon River three months earlier, in October 1499 (1985, 11–27), this claim has been contested by historians (see Hemming 1978, 529).

3. On 22 April 1500, Pedro Álvares Cabral, commonly considered by Brazilians to be the discoverer of Brazil, landed on the Atlantic Coast at what is today Porto Seguro, far from Amazonia, and laid claim to this unknown land for the Portuguese Crown. He promptly continued on to Asia to conduct trade, the major concern of his voyage.

4. This trip was put together as a response to the arrival in Belém, from Quito in early 1637, of two Spanish Franciscan friars and a dozen Spanish soldiers. These Spaniards, who had sailed all the way down the Amazon River, were fleeing from an attack on their expeditionary crew by the Encabellados of the Napo River. The Portuguese were alarmed by this unanticipated Spanish incursion into territory that they had just spent the previous two decades conquering (Golob 1982, 175–76).

5. This process has been characterized as one of "Tupinization" of the Lower and Middle Amazon Basins (Galvão 1976; see also Parker 1985a, xxvi), though Wagley suggests that this term should be used in conjunction with "Jesuitization." (1967, 44). The *língua geral* was by far the predominant language throughout the Lower and Middle Amazon Valleys (and, for that matter, throughout colonial Brazil) from the seventeenth century to well into the nineteenth century.

6. The Jari Region is bordered on the south by the Western Delta Island Region, dominated by Gurupá Island, with the North Canal serving as the border between these two regions. To the east lies the Macapá Region, with the Preto River serving as the border between them.

7. The Portuguese and their indigenous allies proceeded to destroy the English forts of Tilletite and Uarimuacá on the Cajari River in 1623, the Irish-Dutch fort of Torrego on the Manacapuru (now Vila Nova) River in 1629, the English forts of Felipe and Camaú near present-day Macapá in 1631–32, and several smaller

Dutch and English forts located on Tucujus (now Gurupá) Island (Hemming 1978, 223–28, 580–86; Santos 1993, 10–11).

8. The Ucayali and Marañón Rivers, which drain most of the central Peruvian highlands, converge in the Peruvian lowlands to form the Solimões River, another name for the Amazon River until its union in Brazil with the Negro River.

9. Other notable early expeditions from other entry points into the Amazon include those of Mercadillo and Nunes (1538–39, Huallaga and Marañón Rivers, respectively); Salinas de Loyola (1557, Santiago and Marañón Rivers); and Ursua and Aguirre (1560–61, Huallaga, Marañón, and Amazon Rivers) (Golob 1982, 130–44).

10. The bitter disputes among the Jesuits, the Dominicans, and the Franciscans over the rights to specific indigenous groups and the mission territories they enclosed are not our concern here (see Moya 1992, 23–26; Naranjo 1977, 148–50). The historical analysis in this section will focus on the Jesuits, since they were in control of most of the area under study.

11. Quechua, the language of the Incas, was imposed on the northern Andean highlands with the Inca conquest of this area just seventy years before the Spanish conquest of this same highland area. Catholic missionaries helped consolidate Quichua, a dialect of Quechua, as the principal indigenous language in both the northern Andean highlands and the Amazonian lowlands through their use of it as their principal evangelizing language. The use of Quichua by the Jesuits in Amazonia was also dictated by the plethora of languages spoken by the numerous indigenous groups of the Upper Amazon, making the use of a lingua franca necessary.

12. When an author is cited without the subsequent bibliographic reference, the citation refers to information contained in field interviews conducted by the author. These names are cross-referenced with the list of field interviews that appears at the back of the book.

13. The Záparo, who resided along the lower portions of the Napo, Bobonaza, Curaray, Pastaza, and Tigre Rivers, precisely those areas of peak rubber exploitation, were divided among those who resisted the rubber traders and those who became laborers. The former were almost completely wiped out, while the latter gradually merged into the more numerous Quichua populations who participated along with them. Thus, both options led to ethnic dissolution.

14. The term *Seven Sisters* refers to the seven large oil companies that dominated world petroleum production during the middle decades of the twentieth century.

15. Other researchers suggest that the Cofán language is of independent origin or not classified (Narvaez 1982, 23; Telban 1988).

16. In 1973 SIL missionaries encouraged the splitting of the Siona-Secoya Puerto Bolívar community and accompanied one (predominantly Secoya) group to the San Pablo settlement along the Aguarico River, where it could expand its

agricultural base. The center of SIL missionizing among the Siona-Secoya was thus transferred to the San Pablo community, where a group directly allied to the mission and its work was established. As with the Jesuit missions of two centuries earlier, SIL's desire to establish spiritual dominance over sedentary villages produced changes in the territorial structure of indigenous villages.

17. While estimates of indigenous populations at the time of European contact vary widely (see Wilbert 1994), Denevan calculates that the Amazon River Basin had a population of approximately 5 million people at the time of the first European contacts (1976, 229), while Beckerman affirms that the indigenous population was growing steadily at this time (1991). Meanwhile, estimates of depopulation rates during early decades of contact range from 10:1 to 50:1 (Denevan 1976). In spite of these discrepancies, all observers agree that European contacts resulted in not only the death of millions of native individuals, but also the extinction of hundreds of indigenous societies.

18. Villarejo, in his study of the Upper Amazon, lists 131 tribes that have disappeared in the Putumayo River basin alone (1959, 234–37). For the Ucayali and Apurimac River basins, his figure is 93 tribes; for the Napo River Basin, he lists 59 tribes; for the Huallaga River Basin, his number is 53 tribes. While some of these groups may represent duplicates because of the existence of more than one name for the same group and others may be subgroups of larger entities—both of which would reduce these figures—other groups never known or described by Europeans are left out of this list but nevertheless became extinct because of epidemics or warfare that resulted from the European presence in the area. Whatever the precise figures, the evidence of massive demographic destruction of entire peoples (i.e., genocide) is overwhelming.

19. The term *traditional* needs some clarification. *Traditional* conjures up notions of an immutable past and is often used as an antonym for *modern*. This chapter clearly indicates that these peoples have experienced constant changes over the past several centuries and have incorporated many elements of so-called modern culture. Furthermore, the term *traditional peoples,* as used here, does not seek to eliminate internal distinctions between indigenous, *cholada, ribereño,* and *caboclo* peoples. Rather, it serves to distinguish them as a general grouping from recent arrivals, such as colonists, oil workers, gold miners, and environmentalists, who are entering and creating regional Amazonian frontiers. At the same time, the term leaves open the possibility of future mixtures among current traditional groups and recent arrivals on Amazonian soil. Other possible substitutes for the term *traditional peoples* are "ecosystem people" (Dasmann 1988) and "ethnological ethnicities" (Parajuli 1998).

20. Throughout its fifty-seven-year existence (1910–67), the principal activity of the SPI was the "attraction" and "pacification" (euphemisms for conquest) of isolated Indian groups (see Ramos 1995). During this period indigenous societies were sometimes allowed to stay on their lands of traditional occupation and at

other times forcibly removed and placed in Indian parks. The concept of "indigenous lands" (*terras indígenas*) became a formal legal category with the Indian Statute of 1973 (law 6001) (Oliveira Filho 1983, 4).

Chapter Two: Taming the Jungle

1. The notion of conquest was not limited to Brazilian Amazonia. Two-time Peruvian President Belaúnde Terry advocated, in *Peru's Own Conquest* (1965), massive colonization of Peruvian Amazonia designed to turn it into a major agricultural center. This would be accompanied by the construction of a pan-Amazonian highway that would connect Colombia with Brazil, passing through Ecuador, Peru, Bolivia, and Paraguay (see Kandell 1984).

2. The Portuguese-controlled firm Empresa de Comércio e Navegação Jari Ltda. bought José Júlio de Andrade's Brazil nut estate in 1948 and by 1967 had three registered firms operating in the region: Jari Indústria e Comércio, Companhia Industrial do Amapá, and the Navegação Jari S/A. Ludwig bought all three firms and the land they controlled.

3. Hereafter, references to the company will be used interchangeably with the terms *Jari Project* or simply the *project*.

4. Kaolin, also known as China clay, is a white clay first used by the Chinese in making porcelain but now also used as a filler, whitener, and coating for high-quality paper products.

5. A thousand-megawatt hydroelectric plant that Ludwig sought to construct near the Santo Antonio waterfalls would have guaranteed the energy needs of the project for years to come but met strong resistance from the Brazilian government, which maintained near-monopoly control over hydroelectric generation in the country. Plans to set up a paper factory were also aborted when the government refused to authorize the importation of the prebuilt factory and was unwilling to authorize loans for its installation.

6. The District of Monte Dourado within the Almeirim municipality was finally created in 1983, a year after Ludwig sold out to national companies.

7. The title to the Saracura Ranch, now held by the Jari Project, was issued in 1894 and is a good example of this confusion, since the estimates of its size range from a high of 2,640,000 hectares to a low of 4,356 hectares (Sautchuk et al. 1979, 63; Silveira 1980, 92–93). Part of the problem stems from an apparent error in the drafting of the title, whereby the term *million* (*milhão*) was perhaps (we really cannot know) used instead of *thousand* (*mil*). However, since it was common at the time to grant titles to immense tracts of land in this area, which was little known by the people making the award, the use of "a million meters deep" is plausible. The legal acknowledgment of the title by Brazil would cause an international scandal, since it would encompass a large part of Surinam and French Guiana.

8. Estimates of Ludwig's total capital investments in the Jari Project range from $500 million to $1 billion, while he sold the project for less than $200 million. Since much of the money he invested came from loans to himself and relied upon Brazilian government concessions, it is hard to know precisely how much Ludwig actually lost.

9. The only other efforts at an ecological analysis of the Jari Project tended either to praise its "rational use [of land] on a scale unknown in Amazonia" (Paiva 1979, 9) or its "thoughtful and scientific approach" to plantation forestry, which "is greatly preferred over the two development models now prevailing in Amazonia-forest conversion to annuals crops and cattle pasture" (Goodland 1980, 11). McIntyre, in a laudatory piece about Ludwig, dismissed environmental concerns about the Jari Project with the argument that one should "blame Johann Gutenberg," since "the disappearance of broad belts of the age-old Jari jungle and the hurried life cycle of the new pulp forest are consequences of the information explosion, of today's world demand for paper, and of one man's scheme for meeting that demand on into the 21st century" (1980, 711).

10. Of the eleven international oil companies conducting explorations in the Ecuadorian Oriente in the early 1970s, most pulled out of the country after these nationalist measures. CEPE subsequently entered into the Texaco-Gulf Consortium, bought out the Gulf shares, and by 1976 owned 62.5% of the shares of the CEPE-Texaco Consortium. By this time only one other private firm, the City Investing Corporation, had stayed on and was producing small quantities of oil in its fields near Tarapoa within the newly formed consortium CEPE-CEPCO. This private operation formed a private oil enclave within the much larger state-dominated CEPE-Texaco enclave, which was responsible for 97.5% of total Amazonian production in the Oriente.

11. These concessions required the introduction of risk capital, since the costs of exploration would be reimbursed by the Ecuadorian government only if oil was found, in which case the company also would get a percentage of the revenues from the oil produced from these deposits. This arrangement allowed the state to maintain formal ownership of the oil while infusing the industry with new technologies and private capital.

12. In 1998, the province of Orellana was created out of the eastern portion of the Napo province as a result of the discovery of new oil deposits there, thus establishing yet another Amazonian petroleum province.

13. The close ties between the armed forces and the oil industry in Ecuador, forming what I have called a "military-petroleum development complex" (Little 1992), are important but do not preclude their functioning as distinct social actors in the Amazonian milieu.

14. Though territoriality is usually understood as pertaining to the surface area of land, the notions of use rights and occupation have also been applied to parcels of the sea and the fish beneath its surface (see Maldonado 1993). Vertical ter-

ritorialities from the surface upward—generally referred to as *air space*—tend to be the domain of the state, though it is not always clear where the verticality starts (the tops of the trees?) and where it ends (the stratosphere?).

15. These housing sites also harbor striking similarities to the PICOP tree plantation and paper factory located on Mindanao Island in the Philippines, as described by Caufield (1991, 183): "There is a huge gulf between the laborers and the managerial staff, who live in Bay View Hills, the residential section of the fenced-off PICOP compound. Their ranch-style houses, set in large, well-manicured gardens, contrast sharply with the shacks of Mangagoy, the nearby shantytown where most of the laborers live."

16. I use the term *improvisational migration* rather than the more common *spontaneous migration,* since it more closely reflects the strategies and actions of the migrants as they respond to multiple contingent factors.

17. Since initial colonization is almost wholly conducted by men, I use the masculine pronoun when referring to these colonists.

18. Only a small number of the colonists who settled the Aguarico Region came from urban areas, with the rest having been involved in agricultural activities immediately before migrating. In fact, some of the urban migrants were former peasants who had gone to the city to find work only to leave the city for the jungle to go back to agriculture.

19. When Lago Agrio became a provincial capital with the creation of the Sucumbíos province in 1989, it was renamed Nueva Loja in recognition of the many Lojanos who had migrated there. Since virtually no one uses this name, I continue to use the name Lago Agrio.

20. These figures refer to permanent residents. At any given time, the actual number of people in Lago Agrio is generally much higher than the permanent population because of the presence of thousands of temporary workers, who come and go according to their work schedules.

21. The process of creating new administrative units continued when in 1998 the Cuyabeno Canton was carved out of the southeastern portion of the Lago Agrio Canton, with Tarapoa being designated as the new canton seat. One of the reasons used to justify the creation of this new canton was that the richness of its biodiversity would establish it as a model "ecological canton." Yet this biological wealth stood in stark contrast to the poverty of its human inhabitants: upon its creation, the Cuyabeno Canton immediately became the poorest canton in all of Ecuador, with 98.8% of its population living in conditions of poverty (Guzmán 2000, 12).

22. The Grande Carajás project was the largest of these. The construction of a railroad line and numerous roads together with the creation of new jobs turned the region into a major site of population migrations, and it is now a densely populated, highly conflictive area marked by the rapidly growing urban areas of Marabá, Carajás, Redenção, and Conceição do Araguaia (see Hall 1989).

23. This bad luck continued when, in April 2000, two floods during consecutive weeks inundated the town of Laranjal do Jari and left thousands of people homeless.

24. The remaining five thousand people live in dry, upland areas.

25. Prostitution has been a constant in the town since its founding and has distorted another aspect of *caboclo* life. *Caboclo* women tend to marry and begin establishing a family at a young age, often as teenagers. Historically, they have also been subjected to forced acquiescence as concubines for plantation owners, ranch bosses, and other powerful men of the region. The tendency to become sexually active at a young age has been transposed to the activity of prostitution, and many of the prostitutes of Beiradão are teenagers and, in some cases, preteenagers. In his illuminating report on teenage prostitutes, which includes a chapter on Beiradão, Dimenstein narrates cases in which young teenage girls are subjected to a life of near slavery in their work as prostitutes (1992, 37–58). They are often moved to other Amazonian towns by their pimps, since their clients have a constant demand for "fresh meat."

Chapter Three: Saving the Rain Forest

1. Brazil was a leader in the effort to expand the governmental environmental sector, as seen in the formation of the Brazilian Institute for the Environment and Renewable Natural Resources (IBAMA) in 1989 from the fusion of four lesser agencies and the creation of an Environmental Ministry in 1993. On a programmatic plane, Brazil launched the U.S.$100 million nationally financed "Our Nature" program in 1989, the U.S.$166 million internationally financed PNMA program in 1990, and the U.S.$250 million Pilot Program for the Protection of Brazilian Tropical Forests financed by the Group of Seven industrialized countries in 1992.

2. Though the demarcation of Indian lands has become an integral part of some Amazonian environmental programs, governmentally sanctioned Indian territories—lands set aside by national governments for the exclusive use and control of indigenous groups—will not be dealt with here under the rubric of environmental cosmographies, since they have their own set of historical and cultural conditions that makes them distinct from those directly linked to environmentalism. Only the territoriality of those indigenous communities that participate in the control over and management of protected areas will be addressed directly here under "Sustainable Use Territories."

3. During the 1960s and 1970s, important advances in the scientific understanding of Amazonia added urgency to the need to preserve the vast biological wealth contained in this tropical rain forest and provided guidelines for determining how this could best be done. Pioneering phytogeographic analyses of Amazonia by Ghillean Prance led him to postulate the existence of eight different regions within Amazonia (1976). The coalescing of Pleistocene Refuge Theory

sought to decipher the complex biological history of Amazonia through its claim that during the drier epoch of the late Pleistocene, which created large savannas and dry woodlands, tropical plant and animal species were concentrated in refuge areas; when the region became increasingly moist, these fragmented forest areas maintained the highest levels of biological diversity. Island Biogeographic Theory was another influential trend in Amazonian research at this time and applied knowledge of the evolution of island ecosystems to Amazonian ecosystem dynamics. This theory sought to define with great precision the equilibrium point between rates of species extinction and species colonization within a specific ecosystem, data that could be used to determine the size of a protected area needed to maintain existing levels of biological diversity (Foresta 1991).

4. Even though Suriname does not have lands in the Amazon River Basin, it was a signatory of the Treaty for Amazonian Cooperation.

5. The existence of titled lands—both individual and communal—within protected areas is prohibited by Ecuadorian law, since all protected area lands are inalienable and belong to the state. However, given the small size of the Siona allotment, this overlap was minimal and did not become a legal issue at the time.

6. A sister town of Bellavista, also known as Aguas Negras, just 8 kilometers to the east of Tarapoa, also sprouted up shortly after the drilling of new oil wells in the area.

7. Ruiz places the Amazonian Quichua and Shuar populations at sixty thousand and forty thousand, respectively (1991b).

8. The expansion of the reserve had little effect on the Ecuadorian military, and the soldiers stationed at distant outposts continued to hunt and fish illegally in the area. The military's lack of interest in protected areas is illustrated by an interview with a top official of Ecuadorian Army Battalion 55 located in Puerto El Carmen, just 10 kilometers from the northern border of the reserve, who did not know of the existence of the Cuyabeno Reserve in either its original or its expanded form.

9. In a major restructuring of the Ministry of Agriculture and Ranching in 1992, control over protected areas was given to INEFAN, which replaced the Forestry and Renewable Resources Subsecretary (SUFOREN), which several years earlier had replaced DINAF.

10. These figures refer only to those tourists who formally registered to enter the park or who participated in authorized tours. Luis Borbor, superintendent of the reserve, estimates that another 20–30% of tourists enter the reserve illegally, thus raising these figures substantially.

11. On two occasions the Zábalo community has attempted to gain from IERAC, the government land titling agency, legal title to 36,700 hectares of land around their community, without success. With the enlargement of the reserve, these efforts were nullified, since IERAC could not adjudicate land within protected areas.

12. There have been numerous discrepancies between these two currents, one

of which led to the expulsion of the Fundación Natura from the campaign in 1992, when they secretly negotiated an agreement with Texaco in the midst of an international boycott against this oil company.

13. The Zancudo Quichua community was slated to enter into these agreements as well; because of internal legal and financial problems, however, the negotiations with the reserve administration have not been carried to fruition.

14. The extractive vocation of the Cajari, Maracá, and Iratapuru basins can be seen in data from 1949 showing that the Mazagão municipality, which at the time encompassed the entire southern and western portion of the Federal Territory of Amapá, was responsible for 100% of this territory's Brazil nut production (e.g., 903,680 kilograms), 99% of its timber extraction (e.g., 722,693 kilograms), and 62% of its rubber extraction (187,460 kilograms) (Guerra 1954, 312).

15. The remaining 212,119 hectares of expropriated land are located in inaccessible sections of the upper Maracá Basin and have not been given a specific public interest function.

16. According to the law, the government has two years from the date of creation to apply for expropriation of the lands contained in the extractive reserve, a requirement that was fulfilled by IBAMA on the last day of the deadline.

Chapter Four: Disputing Territorial Claims

1. The incompatibility between this short, two-year time frame and the long-drawn-out process of expropriation means that many existing protected areas in Brazil are technically illegal, at least according to this particular article of the law. Other legal dispositions allow the protected areas to continue to exist despite this technical illegality.

2. The western portion of the Cajari Reserve was the principal area of conflict not only with the Jari Complex but also with squatters, provoking the mayor of the Laranjal do Jari municipality (Cruz) to call for the elimination of buffer zones, since, in his words, "buffer zones create nothing but conflicts." The northern edge of the Cajari Reserve is contiguous with the Maracá Extractive Settlement Projects and does not have a buffer zone, while the eastern border of the reserve is formed by the North Canal of the Amazon River, where the buffer zone concept is not applicable.

3. Under Brazilian law, squatters can gain title to occupied lands under state control (*posse de terras devolutas*) through three means: (1) legalization of their occupation, (2) regularization of their occupation, and (3) special concessions.

4. The time of travel varies according to whether one travels upstream or downstream, how heavily the boat is loaded with passengers and freight, and the size of the boat.

5. The environmentalist side of the debate was led by IEA, the Brazilian NGO that had played an active role in establishing the Cajari Extractive Reserve and

the Maracá Settlement Projects, but also included an international letter-writing campaign organized by the United States–based National Wildlife Federation (Ricardo 1996, 301).

6. The management of the Jari Complex took a low profile at this meeting and expressed its opposition in other forums.

7. The kaolin (Caulim da Amazônia) and bauxite (Mineração Santa Lucrécia) mining and processing operations, which are a part of the CAEMI consortium, are both highly profitable.

8. Companies producing wood pulp on lands that were once covered by Brazil's Atlantic Forest (Mata Atlântica), such as Aracruz, the world's largest wood pulp producer, have been spared most critiques of rain-forest destruction, since they are not located in Amazonia, in spite of the fact that the Atlantic Forest has extremely high rates of biodiversity and is one of the most endangered ecosystems in all of South America.

9. The continued presence of all three factors has long made Amapá, in its incarnations as both a federal territory and a state, a preferred site for large-scale projects.

10. Presidential decree 552, signed the same day, established the entire southern portion of the Yasuni National Park as an untouchable zone, thereby eliminating an entire petroleum block from subsequent bidding processes.

11. Later that year Azuero would be elected prefect of the Sucumbíos province.

12. This reduced the total area of the Cuyabeno Reserve to 603,781 hectares.

13. By multiplying the 78-kilometer length of the disputed border by its approximate 6-kilometer width, one can determine that the specific geographical area under dispute totals 468 square kilometers.

14. A national survey taken at the time revealed that 94% of Ecuadorians believed that the Shuar troops were an essential element in the success of the Ecuadorian troops.

15. In yet another irony, the same armed forces that just a year and a half earlier had refused to negotiate with Borman for being a gringo now placed him in charge of a small contingent of Ecuadorian soldiers.

16. The first formally established Indian territory in Ecuadorian Amazonia was the Huaorani Territory, with an area of 612,560 hectares, given out by President Rodrigo Borja in May 1990. Subsurface rights were not granted, and oil development has already begun in the new Huaorani territory (Kane 1993; Kimerling 1996).

Field Interviews

The interviewee's position held at the time of the interview and the date and place of the interview are given.

Acosta, Alberto. Coordinator of Amazonian Programs, Latin American Institute for Social Studies (ILDIS). January 1995: Quito.

Allegretti, Mary Helena. Secretary, Planning Secretariat, Amapá State Government. July and October 1995: Macapá.

Almeida, José. Director, Department of Anthropology, Pontifical Catholic University of Ecuador (PUCE). February 1995: Quito.

Alvarado, Rocío. Colonist from Tarapoa. October 1991: Tarapoa, Sucumbíos.

Amend, Stephen. Coordinator, Cuyabeno Reserve Project, PROFORS. February and March 1995: Quito.

Borbor, Luis. Superintendent, Cuyabeno Wildlife Production Reserve. February 2000: Tarapoa, Sucumbíos.

Borman, Randy. President, Association of Cofán Indigenous Communities of Cofán Nationality. February 1995: Zábalo, Sucumbíos.

Bragas, Jonas. President, Association of Agroextractivist Workers of the Maracá Settlement Projects I, II, III (ATEX-MA). September 1994: Vila Maracá, Amapá.

Bravo, Elizabeth. Biologist, Acción Ecológica. February 1995: Quito.

Campoverde, Olimpio. Political Administrator (Teniente Político) of Tarapoa. March 1995: Tarapoa, Sucumbíos.

Capiberibe, João. Governor, State of Amapá, Brazil. July 1995: Macapá; September 1995: Brasilia.

Carvalho, José Carlos. Agency Chief, IBAMA, Monte Dourado. July and September 1994: Monte Dourado, Pará.

Castello, Sebastian Paraujo (Brás). Member, Extractivist Cooperative of Producers of the Iratapuru River (COMARU). September 1994: Rio Iratapuru, Amapá.

Castro, Luis Claudio. Director, Environmental Department, Companhia Florestal Monte Dourado. July and October 1994: Monte Dourado, Pará.

Chagas, Marco Antônio. Department of Natural Resources, State Coordinating Agency for the Environment (CEMA), Amapá State Government. July 1994: Macapá.

Chavez, Fabiola. Resident of Playas de Cuyabeno community. February 1995: Playas de Cuyabeno, Sucumbíos.

Coello H., Flavio. Biologist, Metropolitan Touring. October 1991: Lago Agrio, Sucumbíos.

Cruz, José. Prefect, Laranjal do Jari Municipality. July 1995: Serra do Navio, Amapá.

Delgado, José. Superintendent, Cuyabeno Wildlife Production Reserve. October 1991: Tarapoa, Sucumbíos.

Donoso, Patricio. Park Ranger, Cuyabeno Wildlife Production Reserve. February 1995: Playas de Cuyabeno, Sucumbíos.

Dubois, Jean. Director, Brazilian Agroforestry Network (REBRAF), Rio de Janeiro. July 1994: Vila Maracá, Amapá.

Farias, Antônio Carlos. Director, State Coordinating Agency for the Environment (CEMA), Amapá State Government. July 1994: Macapá.

Gallois, Dominique. Professor, Anthropology Department, University of São Paulo. October 1994: Macapá.

Gonzales, Fausto. Forestry Specialist, Cuyabeno Wildlife Production Reserve. March 1995: Tarapoa, Sucumbíos.

Jucá, Maria Benigna Nacimento. Director, Amapá Land Institute (TERRAP), Amapá State Government. July 1995: Macapá.

Lopez, Susana. Consultant, Fundación Natura. November 1991: Quito.

Marchán, José. Head of Perforation, Petroproduction. March 1995: Lago Agrio, Sucumbíos.

Martinez, Esperanza. Biologist, Acción Ecológica. February and March 1995: Quito.

Mattoso, Maria Raquel. Executive Secretary, Institute of Amazonian and Environmental Studies (IEA). December 1994: Brasilia.

Moran, Emilio. Professor, Department of Anthropology, Indiana University. January 1995: Bloomington, Indiana.

Muñoz, Oswaldo. President, Ecuadorian Ecotourism Association. September 1991: Laguna Grande, Sucumbíos.

Naranjo, Marcelo. Professor, Department of Anthropology, Pontifical Catholic University of Ecuador (PUCE). February 1995: Quito.

Norteño, Hector. President, Commune of Playas de Cuyabeno. February 1995: Playas de Cuyabeno, Sucumbíos.

Prado, Julio. Subdirector, Pacayacu Petroleum Compound, Petroproduction. March 1995: Pacayacu, Sucumbíos.

Proaño, Pedro. Director, Transturi Inc. February 1995: Quito.

Ramos, Ivonne. Biologist, Acción Ecológica. February 1995: Lago Agrio, Sucumbíos.

Real, Byron. Director, Corporation for the Defense of Life (CORDAVI). February 1995: Quito.

Román, Luis. President, Petroecuador. September 1991: Lago Agrio, Sucumbíos.

Salazar, Manuel. President, Parish Board (Junta Parroquial) of Tarapoa. March 1995: Tarapoa, Sucumbíos.

Schmidt, Wini. Co-director, Environmental Management, Petroleum Exploitation and Sustainable Development in the Ecuadorian Amazon Project (PETRAMAZ). January 2000: Quito.

Schmink, Marianne. Director, Tropical Conservation and Development Program, Center for Latin American Studies, University of Florida. January 1995: Gainesville.

Simonian, Ligia. Professor, Center for Superior Amazonian Studies (NAEA), Federal University of Pará. July 1995: Belém.

Soares, Luzia. Resident of the Maracá Extractive Settlement Project II. September 1994: Pancada, Amapá.

Varea, Ana María. Coordinator, Forests, Trees and People Programme–Ecuador. January 1995: Quito.

Villaverde, Xabier. Director, FEPP-Lago Agrio. March 1995: Lago Agrio, Sucumbíos.

Bibliography

Ab'Saber, Aziz. 1970. "Províncias geológicas e domínios morfoclimáticos no Brasil." *Geomorfologia* 20:1–26.

Aguilar, Juan Pablo. 1992. "Conservación de áreas naturales." Quito: Presidencia de la República.

Aguilar, Juan Pablo, Gerardo Obando, and Pablo Ospino. 1990. "Colonización en el Cuyabeno: Problema ecológico—problema social." Quito: Universidad Central del Ecuador.

Albert, Bruce. 1995. "O ouro canibal e a queda do céu: Uma crítica xamânica da economia política da natureza." In *Série Antropologia*, no. 174. Brasilia: Departamento de Antropologia, Universidade de Brasília.

Allegretti, Fernando, and Paul E. Little. 1993. "Relatório sócio-econômico do Projeto de Assentamento Extrativista Maracá II, Amapá." Brasilia: IEA; WWF.

Allegretti, Mary Helena. 1991. "Reservas extrativistas: Parámetros para uma política de desenvolvimento sustentável na Amazônia." *Revista Brasileira de Geografia* 54 (1): 5–23.

Allen, T. F. H., and Thomas W. Hoekstra. 1992. *Toward a unified ecology.* New York: Columbia University Press.

Almeida, Alfredo W. B. 1994. *Carajás: A guerra dos mapas.* Belém: Falangola.

———. 1989. "Terras de preto, terras de santo, terras de índio." In *Na trilha dos grandes projetos,* compiled by E. Castro and J. Hebbete, 163–96. Belém: NAEA, Universidade Federal do Pará.

———. 1984. "O GEBAM, as empresas agropecuárias e a expansão camponesa." In *Os donos da terra e a luta pela reforma agrária.* Rio de Janeiro: Instituto Brasileiro de Analises Sociais e Econômicas; Editora Codecri.

Almeida, Rita Heloísa de. 1997. *O Diretório dos Índios: Um projeto de "civilização" no Brasil do século XVIII.* Brasilia: Editora Universidade de Brasília.

Altvater, Elmar. 1993. "Ilhas de sintropia e exportação de entropia: Custos globais do fordismo fossílico." *Cadernos do NAEA* 11:3–54.

Alvarez R., Augusto. 1998. "The economic effects of the peace agreement." *Peru El Dorado,* Special Edition, October–December, pp. 76–80.

Amazonía ¡por la vida! 1994. *Una guia ambiental para la defensa del territorio amazónico amenazado por las petroleras.* Quito: Acción Ecológica.

———. 1993. *Debate ecológico sobre el problema petrolero en el Ecuador.* Quito: Acción Ecológica.

Amend, Stephen, and Thora Amend. 1992. "Habitantes en los parques nacionales: ¿Una contradicción insoluble?" In *¿Espacios sin habitantes? Parques nacionales de América del Sur,* edited by S. Amend and T. Amend, 457–72. Caracas: Editora Nueva Sociedad.

Ardrey, Robert. 1966. *The territorial imperative: A personal inquiry into the animal origins of property and nations.* New York: Atheneum.

Århem, Kaj. 1981. *Makuna social organization: A study in descent, alliance, and the formation of corporate groups in the North-Western Amazon.* Uppsala: Acta Universitatis Upsaliensis.

Aristazábal G., Silvio. 1993. "Los Kofán: Un grupo condenado a desaparecer." In *Pasado y presente del Amazonas: Su historia económica y social,* edited by R. Pineda and B. Alzate, 143–50. Bogotá: Universidad de los Andes.

Arruda, Marcos. 1978. "Daniel Ludwig e a exploração da Amazônia." *Cadernos do CEAS* 55:9–25.

ASPLAN (Assessoria de Planejamento e Coordenação Geral). 1977. *Programa de desenvolvimento de polos urbanos-Perfis: Município de Mazagão.* Macapá: Governo do Território do Amapá.

Bachelard, Gaston. 1989. *A poética do espaço.* Translated by A. P. Danesi. São Paulo: Martins Fontes.

———. 1988. *A dialética da duração.* Translated by M. Coelho. São Paulo: Editora Ática.

Baines, Stephen Grant. 1994. "A usina hidroelética de Balbina e o deslocamento compulsório dos Waimiri-Atroari." In *Série Antropologia,* no. 166. Brasilia: Departamento de Antropologia, Universidade de Brasília.

Barabas, Alicia. 1996. "El movimiento zapatista en México." Paper presented at the Department of Anthropology, University of Brasilia, May 15.

Barretto Filho, Henyo. 1997. "Da nação ao planeta através da natureza." In *Série Antropologia,* no. 222. Brasilia: Departamento de Antropologia, Universidade de Brasília.

Bartolomé, Leopoldo J. 1992. "Fighting Leviathan: The articulation and spread of local opposition to hydrodevelopment in Brazil." Brasilia: Faculdade Latino-Americana de Ciências Sociais-Brasil.

Becker, Berta K. 1989. "Grandes projetos e produção de espaço transnacional: Uma nova estratégia do estado na Amazônia." *Revista Brasileira de Geografia* 51 (4): 7–20.

———. 1988. "Significância contemporânea da fronteira: Uma interpretação geopolítica a partir da Amazônia." In *Fronteiras,* compiled by C. Aubertin, 60–89. Brasilia: Editora Universidade de Brasília.

Beckerman, Stephen. 1991. "A Amazônia estava repleta de gente in 1492?" In *Origens, adaptações e diversidade biológica do homen nativo da Amazônia,* compiled by W. A. Neves, 143–60. Belém: Museu Paraense Emílio Goeldi; Secretaria da Ciência e Tecnologia; Conselho Nacional de Desenvolvimento Científico e Tecnológico; Presidência da República.

Belaúnde Terry, Fernando. 1965. *Peru's own conquest*. Lima: American Studies Press.

Belo, Eduardo. 1996. "Jari investe para se tornar realidade: Empresa gasta US$133 milhões em quatro anos e amplia cortes nos custos para ter lucro e apagar imagem de aventura na selva." *Folha de São Paulo*, January 28, sect. 2, pp. 2, 7–8.

Bennett, John W. 1969. *Northern plainsmen: Adaptive strategy and agrarian life*. Chicago: Aldine.

BID (Banco Interamericano de Desarrollo). 1991. *Amazonia sin mitos*. Washington, D.C.: BID.

Boas, Franz. 1940. "The study of geography." In *Race, language, and culture*, 639–47. New York: Free Press.

Borges, Jorge Luis. 1962. *Ficciones*. Translated by H. Temple and R. Todd. New York: Grove Press.

Borman, M. B. 1982. "Cambios semánticos en la terminología del parentesco Cofán y costumbres matrimoniales de los Cofanes." Quito: Ediciones Instituto Lingüístico de Verano, Ministerio de Educación y Cultura.

Bourdieu, Pierre. 1998. *Practical reason: On the theory of action*. Palo Alto: Stanford University Press.

——. 1977. *Outline of a theory of practice*. Translated by R. Nice. Cambridge: Cambridge University Press.

Brack Egg, Antonio, and Gunter Reck. 1991. "Identificación de las posibilidades de protección sostenida de áreas protegidas y reservas forestales en la provincia de Sucumbíos (Ecuador) con énfasis en la Reserva de Producción Faunística de Cuyabeno." Quito: PROFORS.

Briggs, John. 1992. *Fractals: The patterns of chaos*. New York: Simon and Schuster.

Briggs, John, and F. David Peat. 1989. *Turbulent mirror: An illustrated guide to chaos theory and the science of wholeness*. New York: Harper and Row.

Bromley, Ray. 1980. "The role of tropical colonization in twentieth century economic development of Ecuador." In *Land, people, and planning in contemporary Amazonia*, edited by G. Barbira-Scazzocchio, 174–84. Cambridge: Cambridge University Press.

Browder, John O., and Brian J. Godfrey. 1997. *Rainforest cities: Urbanization, development, and globalization of the Brazilian Amazon*. New York: Columbia University Press.

Brown, Lawrence A., Rodrigo Sierra, and Douglas Southgate. 1991. "Complementary perspectives as a means of understanding regional change: Frontier settlement in the Ecuador Amazon." Columbus: Ohio State University.

Bruck, Eugênio Camargo, et al. 1983. "Unidades de conservação." *Revista de Serviço Público* 111 (4): 21–27.

Bryant, Raymond L., and Sinéad Bailey. 1997. *Third World political ecology*. London: Routledge.

Bunker, Stephen G. 1985. *Underdeveloping the Amazon: Extraction, unequal exchange, and the failure of the modern state.* Urbana: University of Illinois Press.

Calderón, Fernando. 1995. "Latin American identity and mixed temporalities." In *The postmodernism debate in Latin America,* edited by J. Beverley, J. Oviedo, and M. Aronna, 55–64. Durham: Duke University Press.

Canaday, Christopher. 1994a. "Estudio para una zonificación del territorio de la comunidad quichua de Playas de Cuyabeno en la R.P.F. Cuyabeno." Quito: PROFORS.

———. 1994b. "Estudio para una zonificación del territorio de la comunidad quichua de Zancudo en la R.P.F. Cuyabeno." Quito: PROFORS.

Carneiro, Edson. 1956. *A conquista da Amazônia.* Rio de Janeiro: Ministério da Viação e Obras Públicas.

Carpentier, Alejo. 1967. *The lost steps.* Translated by H. de Onis. New York: Knopf.

Casagrande, Joseph, Stephen Thompson, and Phillip Young. 1964. "Colonization as a research frontier: The Ecuadorian case." In *Process and pattern in culture,* edited by R. A. Manners, 281–325. Chicago: Aldine.

Casimir, Michael J. 1992. "The dimensions of territoriality: An introduction." In *Mobility and territoriality,* edited by M. J. Casimir and A. Rao, 1–26. New York: Berg.

Castro, Edna Maria Ramos de. 1989. "Resistência dos atingidos pela barragem de Tucuri e construção de identidade." In *Na trilha dos grandes projetos,* compiled by E. Castro and J. Hebbete, 41–70. Belém: NAEA, Universidade Federal do Pará.

Castro, Eduardo Viveiros de, and Lúcia M. M. de Andrade. 1988. "Hidroelétricas do Xingú: O estado contra as sociedades indígenas." In *As hidroelétricas do Xingu e os povos indígenas,* compiled by L. Santos and L. Andrade, 7–23. São Paulo: Comissão Pro-Índio.

Castro, Manoel Borges de, and William Elias. 1981. "Viagem de reconhecimento da área a ser instalada a sede da Estação Ecológica do Jari e demarcação das vias de acesso que a ligará a Monte Dourado-PA." Brasilia: SEMA, Ministério do Interior.

Caufield, Catherine. 1991. *In the rainforest: Report from a strange, beautiful, imperiled world.* Chicago: University of Chicago Press.

CEDI (Centro Ecumênico de Documentação e Informação). 1983. *Povos indígenas no Brasil.* Vol. 3: *Amapá/Norte do Pará.* Coordinated by C. A. Ricardo. São Paulo: CEDI.

Chaloult, Yves. 1978. *Estado, acumulação e colonialismo interno.* Petrópolis, Brazil: Editora Vozes.

Chirif, Alberto. 1980. "Internal colonization in a colonized country: The Peruvian Amazon in historical perspective." In *Land, people, and planning in contemporary Amazonia,* edited by F. Barbira-Scazzocchio, 185–92. Cambridge: Cambridge University Press.

Cleary, David. 1990. *Anatomy of the Amazon gold rush.* Iowa City: University of Iowa Press.

Coello H., Flavio. 1991. "Área de ampliación propuesta para la R.P.F. Cuyabeno en el noreste de la amazonía ecuatoriana." Quito: Ministerio de Agricultura y Ganadería.

Coello H., Flavio, and James Nations. 1987. *Plan de manejo de la Reserva de Producción Faunística Cuyabeno.* Quito: Ministerio de Agricultura y Ganadería.

COICA (Coordinadora de Organizaciones Indígenas de la Cuenca Amazónica). n.d. "Amazonian reality and anti-Amazonian policies." Lima: COICA.

Colchester, Marcus, and Larry Lohmann, editors. 1993. *The struggle for land and the fate of the forests.* Penang: World Rainforest Movement.

Comissão Especial de Investigação-Projeto Chamflora. 1997. "Relatório final (Decreto 3457/96)." Macapá: Governo do Estado do Amapá.

———. 1995. "Relatório final (Decreto 3229/95)." Macapá: Governo do Estado do Amapá.

Companhia Florestal Monte Dourado. 1994. *Jari: Sustainable development model in the Amazon.* Rio de Janeiro: Companhia Florestal Monte Dourado.

CONAIE (Confederación de Nacionalidades Indígenas del Ecuador). 1989. *Las nacionalidades indígenas en el Ecuador.* Quito: Ediciones Tinkui-CONAIE.

Conferencia Episcopal Ecuatoriana. 1977. "Declaración de la Conferencia Episcopal sobre la promocción de la justicia social." Quito: Conferencia Episcopal Ecuatoriana.

Conklin, Beth A., and Laura R. Graham. 1995. "The shifting middle ground: Amazonian Indians and eco-politics." *American Anthropologist* 97 (4): 695–710.

CPRM (Companhia de Pesquisa de Recursos Minerais). 1978. "Planejamento da utilização de recursos hídricos: Jari." Brasilia: Ministério das Minas e Energia.

C.R. Almeida. 1991. "Relatório de impacto ambiental da BR 156 no trecho que liga Rio Preto a Laranjal do Jari." Curitiba: C.R. Almeida.

Cronon, William. 1983. *Changes in the land: Indians, colonists, and the ecology of New England.* New York: Norton.

Crosby, Alfred W., Jr. 1986. *Ecological imperialism: The biological expansion of Europe, 900–1900.* New York: Cambridge University Press.

Cruz, Ernesto. 1960. *Temas da história do Pará.* Belém: Superintendência do Plano de Valorização Econômica da Amazônia.

da Cunha, Euclides. 1909. *A margem da história.* Porto, Portugal: Chardron.

Darnton, Robert. 1995. "As grossas camadas do tempo." *Folha de São Paulo,* August 20, sect. 5, p. 7.

Dasmann, Raymond. 1988. "National parks, nature conservation, and 'Future Primitive.'" In *Tribal people and development issues: A global overview,* edited by J. H. Bodley, 301–10. Mountain View, Calif.: Mayfield.

Davis, Shelton, and Katrinka Ebbe. 1995. *Traditional knowledge and sustainable development* (Environmentally Sustainable Development Proceedings Series, no. 4). Washington: World Bank.

Dean, Warren. 1995. *With broadax and firebrand: The destruction of the Brazilian Atlantic Forest*. Berkeley and Los Angeles: University of California Press.

———. 1987. *Brazil and the struggle for rubber: A study in environmental history*. Cambridge: Cambridge University Press.

Denevan, William M. 1976. "The aboriginal population of Amazonia." In *The native population of the Americas in 1492*, edited by W. M. Denevan, 205–34. Madison: University of Wisconsin Press.

Descola, Phillipe. 1994. *In the society of nature: A native ecology in Amazonia*, translated by N. Scott. Cambridge: Cambridge University Press.

Diegues, Antonio Carlos Sant'Ana. 1994. *O mito moderno da natureza intocada*. São Paulo: Núcleo de Apoio à Pesquisa sobre Populações Humanas e Áreas Úmidas Brasileiras, Universidade de São Paulo.

Dimenstein, Gilberto. 1992. *Meninas da noite: A prostituição de meninas-escravas no Brasil*. São Paulo: Editora Ática.

Di Paolo, Pasquale. 1990. *Cabanagem: A revolução popular da Amazônia*. Belém: Edições Cejup.

Dogan, Mattei, and Dominque Pelassy. 1984. "El análisis político comparado: Cinco estrategias para la selección de países." *Contribuciones* 4:37–56.

Dubois, Jean, coordinator. 1989. "Relatório do trabalho de campo realizado no Maracá I e II: Período 25/05 a 02/06/89." Macapá: CNS; IEA; ASTER-AP.

Dubois, Jean, Virgilio M. Viana, and Anthony B. Anderson. 1996. *Manual agroflorestal para a Amazônia*, Vol. 1. Rio de Janeiro: REBRAF.

Dyson-Hudson, Rada, and Eric Alden Smith. 1978. "Human territoriality: An ecological reassessment." *American Anthropologist* 80 (1): 21–41.

Ecuanet. 1993. "Boletín 1 de noviembre." Quito: Ec-noticias-l@Ecnet.ec.

"Elecciones contra ecología." 1992. *Hoy* (Quito), February 28, p. 4.

Espin Z., Gerardo, and Jose Guerrero. 1992. "Informe da la comisión de inspección de la colonización dentro de la Reserva Faunística Cuyabeno." Quito: CEDMA/IERAC.

Evans, Clifford, Jr. 1950. "The archeology of the Territory of Amapá, Brazil." Ph.D. diss., Columbia University, New York.

Evans, Peter. 1979. *Dependent development: The alliance of multinational, state, and local capital in Brazil*. Princeton: Princeton University Press.

Evans, Peter, and John D. Stephens. 1988. "Studying development since the sixties: The emergence of a new comparative political economy." *Theory and Society* 17:713–45.

Fearnside, Phillip M. 1988. "Jari at age 19: Lessons for Brazil's silvicultural plans at Cajarás." *Interciência* 13 (1): 12–24.

Fearnside, Phillip M., and Judy M. Rankin. 1985. "Jari revisited: Changes and the outlook for sustainability in Amazonia's largest silvicultural estate." *Interciência* 10 (3): 121–29.

———. 1983. "O novo Jari: Riscos e perspectivas de um desenvolvimento maciço amazônico." *Ciência e cultura* 36 (7): 1140–56.

———. 1982. "Jari e Carajás: O futuro incerto das grandes plantações de silvicultura na Amazônia." *Interciência* 7 (6): 328.

———. 1979. "Avaliação da Jari Florestal e Agropecuaria Ltda. como modelo para o desenvolvimento da Amazônia." *Acta Amazônica* 9 (3): 609–15.

Foresta, Ronald A. 1991. *Amazon conservation in the age of development: The limits of providence.* Gainesville: University of Florida Press.

Fundación Natura. 1992. "Manejo del territorio Cofán de Zábalo dentro de la Reserva de Producción Faunística Cuyabeno." Quito: Fundación Natura.

Galarza, Jaime. 1983. *Petróleo de nuestra muerte.* Quito: CEDIS.

Gallois, Dominique Tilkin. 1994. *Mairi revisitada: A reintegração da Fortaleza de Macapá na tradição oral dos Waiãpi.* São Paulo: Fundação para o Amparo à Pesquisa do Estado de São Paulo.

———. 1986. *Migração, guerra e comércio: Os Waiapi na Guiana.* São Paulo: Faculdade de Filosofia, Letras e Ciências Humanas, Universidade de São Paulo.

———. 1981. "Populações indígenas da várzea do Baixo Amazonas nos séculos XVII a XIX." São Paulo: Universidade de São Paulo.

Galvão, Eduardo. 1976. *Santos e visagens: Um estudo da vida religiosa de Itá, Baixo Amazonas.* São Paulo: Companhia Editora Nacional.

———. 1960. "Áreas culturais indígenas do Brasil, 1900–1959." *Boletim do Museu Paraense Emílio Goeldi* (Série Antrop. 8). Belém: Museu Paraense Emílio Goeldi.

Gama e Silva, Roberto. 1991. *Olho grande na Amazônia brasileira.* Rio de Janeiro: Rio Fundo Editora.

———. 1987. "O setor mineral precisa ser purificado." *Brasil Mineral* 5 (41): 198–200.

Garcés D., Alicia. 1994. "Estudio de caso: Conflicto entre colonos y el Estado por el acceso legal a la tierra en la Reserva Faunística Cuyabeno." Quito: FTP; Unión International para la Conservación de la Natureza; ILDIS.

García Canclini, Nestor. 1989. *Culturas híbridas: Estrategias para entrar y salir de la modernidad.* Mexico City: Grijalbo.

Garrido Filha, Irene. 1980. *O Projeto Jari e os capitais estrangeiros na Amazônia.* Petrópolis, Brazil: Vozes.

GEA (Governo do Estado do Amapá). 1995. "Ecoturismo no Amapá: Implantação de modelos." Macapá: Secretaria Estadual do Meio Ambiente.

Giddens, Anthony. 1990. *The consequences of modernity.* Stanford: Stanford University Press.

———. 1984. *The constitution of society: Outline of the theory of structuration.* Berkeley and Los Angeles: University of California Press.

Godelier, Maurice. 1986. *The mental and the material.* Translated by M. Thom. London: Verso.

Golob, Ann. 1982. "The Upper Amazon in historical perspective." Ph.D. diss., City University of New York.

Gomes, Manoel Eduardo, and Luiz Daniel Felippe. 1994. "Tutela jurídica sobre as reservas extrativistas." In *O destino da floresta: RESEX e desenvolvimento sustentável na Amazônia*, edited by R. Arnt, 73–90. Rio de Janeiro: Relume-Dumará.

Gonçalves, Marco Antônio. 1995. "Fábrica de papel desencadeia crise no Amapá." *Parabólicas* 12:4–5.

Gondim, Neide. 1994. *A invenção da Amazônia*. São Paulo: Marco Zero.

Goodland, Robert J. A. 1980. "Environmental ranking of Amazonian development." In *Land, people, and planning in contemporary Amazonia*, edited by F. Barbira-Scazzocchio, 1–20. Cambridge: Cambridge University Press.

Goodland, Robert J. A., and S. Irwin Howard. 1975. *Do inferno verde ao deserto vermelho*. Belo Horizonte, Brazil: Editora Itataia.

Guerra, Antonio Teixeira. 1954. *Estudo geográfico do Território do Amapá*. Rio de Janeiro: Instituto Brasileiro de Geografia e Estadística.

Guzmán, Marco Antonio. 2000. "Quito: Referente de la nacionalidad." *Cuidad para Todos* 1 (4): 12.

Hall, Anthony. 1989. *Developing Amazonia: Deforestation and social conflict in Brazil's Carajás programme*. Manchester: Manchester University Press.

Hanson, Earl Parker. 1944. *The Amazon: A new frontier?* Headline Series. New York: Foreign Policy Association.

Harner, Michael J. 1972. *The Jívaro: People of the sacred waterfalls*. London: Robert Hale.

Haubert, Maxime. 1990. *Índios e jesuitas no tempo das missões: Séculos XVII–XVIII*. Translated by M. Appenzeller. São Paulo: Companhia das Letras.

Hecht, Susanna. 1993. "The logic of livestock and deforestation in Amazonia." *Bioscience* 43 (10): 687–95.

———. 1985. "Environment, development and politics: Capital accumulation and the livestock sector in Eastern Amazonia." *World Development* 13 (6): 663–84.

Hecht, Susana, and Alexander Cockburn. 1989. *The fate of the forest: Developers, destroyers, and defenders of the Amazon*. New York: Verso.

Hemming, John. 1987. *Amazon frontier: The defeat of the Brazilian Indians*. Cambridge: Harvard University Press.

———. 1978. *Red gold: The conquest of the Brazilian Indians*. Cambridge: Harvard University Press.

Hennessy, Alistair. 1978. *The frontier in Latin American history*. Bristol, England: Edward Arnold.

Hudelson, John Edwin. 1981. "The expansion and development of Quichua transitional culture in the Upper Amazon Basin." Ph.D. diss., Columbia University, New York.

Hudson, W. H. 1904. *Green mansions: A romance of the tropical forest*. London: Duckworth.

Hurtado, Osvaldo. 1969. *Dos mundos superpuestos: Ensayo de diagnóstico de la realidad ecuatoriana*. Quito: INDES; Ed. Offsetec.

IBGE (Instituto Brasileiro de Geografia e Estadística). 1994. "Grande regiões, unidades da federação, superifície terrestre e população." In *República federativa do Brasil.* Rio de Janeiro: IBGE.

IEA (Instituto de Estudos Amazônicos e Ambientais). 1993. "Projeto 'Políticas Públicas para o Meio Ambiente'—Relatório Narrativo Final." Brasilia: IEA; Ford Foundation–Brazil.

IEA and INCRA (Instituto Nacional de Colonização e Reforma Agrária). 1995. "Plano de Utilização: Projetos de Assentamento Extrativista Maracá I, II, e III." Brasilia: IEA; INCRA.

Irvine, Dominique. 1987. "Resource management by the Runa Indians of the Ecuadorian Amazon." Ph.D. diss., Stanford University.

Isaacs, Anita. 1993. *Military rule and transition in Ecuador, 1972–1992.* Pittsburgh: University of Pittsburgh Press.

Jacome H., Luis Ignacio. 1992. "External shocks and the real exchange rate in the Ecuadorean economy, 1972–1990." Ph.D. diss., Boston University.

Jari Energética S.A. 1996. "Atualização dos estudos ambientais da UHE Santo Antônio." Monte Dourado, Pará.

Jarrín A., Gustavo. 1994. "Ingreso y salida del Ecuador de la OPEP." *Petróleo y Sociedad* 2:85–100.

Kandell, Jonathan. 1984. *Passage through El Dorado: Travelling the world's last great wilderness.* New York: Avon.

Kane, Joe. 1993. "Letter from the Amazon: With spears from all sides." *New Yorker,* September 27, pp. 54–79.

Kimerling, Judith. 1996. *El derecho del tambor: Derechos humanos y ambientales en los campos petroleros de la Amazonía Ecuatoriana.* Quito: Abya-Yala.

——. 1991. *Amazon crude.* New York: Natural Resources Defense Council.

Kinkead, Gwen. 1981. "Trouble in D. K. Ludwig's jungle." *Fortune,* April 20, pp. 102–17.

Klein, Thilo. 1998. "Measuring the peace dividend." *Peru El Dorado,* Special Edition, October–December, pp. 88–89.

Kupfer, José Paulo. 1981. "A agonia do Jari." *Isto É,* May 13, pp. 24–31.

Lathrap, Donald W. 1970. *The Upper Amazon.* London: Thames and Hudson.

Lefebvre, Henri. 1991. *The production of space.* Translated by D. Nicholson-Smith. Oxford: Blackwell.

Leite, S. I. Serafim. 1943. *História da Companhia de Jesus no Brasil. Tomo IV, Norte 1: Século XVI, a obra.* Rio de Janeiro: Instituto Nacional do Livro.

——. 1938. *História da Companhia de Jesus no Brasil. Tomo II, Século XVI, a obra.* Rio de Janeiro: Instituto Nacional do Livro.

Lewis, Martin W. 1991. "Elusive societies: A regional-cartographic approach to the study of human relatedness." *Annals of the Association of American Geographers* 81 (4): 605–26.

Lima, Guimarães. 1970. *Na linha do equador.* Brasilia.

Lima, Rubens Rodrigues. 1973. *A conquista da Amazonia: Reflexos na segurança nacional* (Boletím no. 6). Belém: Faculdade de Ciências Agrárias do Pará.

Lins, Cristovão. 1991. *Jari: 70 anos de história*. Almeirim, Pará: Dataforma.

Lisansky, Judith. 1990. *Migrants to Amazonia: Spontaneous colonization in the Brazilian frontier.* Boulder, Colo.: Westview Press.

Little, Paul E. 1999. "Environments and environmentalisms in anthropological research: Facing a new millennium." *Annual Review of Anthropology* 28:253–84.

——. 1995. "Ritual, power and ethnography at the Rio Earth Summit." *Critique of Anthropology* 15 (3): 265–88.

——. 1992. *Ecología política del Cuyabeno: El desarrollo no sostenible de la Amazonia.* Quito: ILDIS; Abya-Yala.

Little, Paul E., and Antonio Sérgio Filocreão. 1994. *Relatório sócio-econômico: Projetos de Assentamento Extrativista Maracá I, II, III—Amapá, Brasil.* Macapá: IEA.

Loureiro, Violeta Refkalefsky. 1992. *Amazônia: Estado, homem, natureza.* Belém: Edições Cejup.

Macdonald, Theodore, Jr. 1967. "Processes of change in Amazonian Ecuador: Quijos Quichua Indians become cattlemen." Ph.D. diss., University of Illinois, Urbana.

MAG (Ministerio de Agricultura y Ganadería). 1993. *Plan de manejo de la Reserva de Producción Faunítstica Cuyabeno.* Quito: MAG.

Maldonado, Simone Carneiro. 1993. *Mestres e mares: Espaço e indivisão na pesca marítima.* São Paulo: Anna Blume.

Malkki, Liisa. 1992. "National Geographic: The rooting of peoples and the territorialization of national identity among scholars and refugees." *Cultural Anthropology* 7 (1): 24–44.

Malmberg, Torsten. 1980. *Human territoriality: Survey of behavioral territories in man with preliminary analysis and discussion of meaning.* The Hague: Mouton.

Mandelbrot, Benoit B. 1977. *The fractal geometry of nature.* New York: W. H. Freeman.

Marcus, George E. 1995. "Ethnography in/of the world system: The emergence of multi-sited ethnography." *Annual Review of Anthropology* 24:95–117.

Martínez, Patricio. n.d. *Las raíces del conflicto: Síntesis del proceso histórico ecuatoriano.* Guayaquil, Ecuador: Publicaciones de la Universidad Católica de Santiago de Guayaquil.

Martins, Edilson. 1981. *Amazônia: A última fronteira. A saga dos oprimidos, as multinacionais, a iminência de um deserto.* Rio de Janeiro: Editora Codecri.

Martins, Elson. 1996. "Megaprojeto da Champion assusta ambientalistas." *Folha do Amapá,* August 25, pp. 8–9.

Martins, José de Souza. 1990. "The political impasses of rural social movements in Amazonia." In *The future of Amazonia: Destruction or sustainable development,* edited by D. Goodman and A. Hall, 245–63. New York: St. Martin's Press.

Mattoso, Maria Raquel, and Vanessa Fleischfresser. 1994. "Amapá-Reserva Extrativista do Rio Cajari." In *O destino da floresta: RESEX e desenvolvimento sus-*

tentável na Amazônia, edited by R. Arnt, 91–149. Rio de Janeiro: Relume-Dumará.

McIntyre, Loren. 1980. "Jari: A billion dollar gamble." *National Geographic* 157 (5): 686–711.

McNeely, Jeffery A., Jeremy Harrison, and Paul Dingwall. 1994. "Introduction: Protected areas in the modern world." In *Protecting nature: Regional reviews of protected areas,* edited by J. A. McNeely, J. Harrison, and P. Dingwall, 1–28. Gland, Switzerland: International Union for the Conservation of Nature.

Meggers, Betty. 1979. *América pré-histórica.* Translated by E. T. de Carvalho. Rio de Janeiro: Editora Paz e Terra.

———. 1971. *Amazonia: Man and culture in a counterfeit paradise.* Chicago: Aldine Atherton.

———. 1967. "The archeological sequence on the Rio Napo, Ecuador, and its implications." In *Atas do simpósio sobre a biota amazônica.* Vol. 2: *Antropologia,* edited by H. Lent, 145–52. Rio de Janeiro: Conselho National de Pesquisas.

Meggers, Betty, and Clifford Evans. 1957. *Archeological investigations at the mouth of the Amazon.* Washington: Smithsonian Institution.

Meira, Sílvio. 1989. *Fronteiras septentrionais: Três séculos de luta no Amapá.* Belo Horizonte, Brazil: Itataia.

Melamid, Alexander. 1968. "Enclaves and exclaves." In *International encyclopedia of the social sciences,* Vol. 5, edited by D. Sills, 60–62. New York: Macmillan Company and Free Press.

Melatti, Júlio César. 1995. "Áreas ethnográficas da América do Sul." Paper presented at the Seminar "Arqueologia-Tendências Atuais," University of Brasilia.

Mendes, Chico. 1989. *Fight for the forest: Chico Mendes in his own words.* London: Latin American Bureau.

Merchant, Carolyn. 1989. *Ecological revolutions: Nature, gender, and science in New England.* Chapel Hill: University of North Carolina Press.

Millikan, Brent H. 1992. "Tropical deforestation, land degradation, and society: Lessons from Rondônia, Brazil." *Latin American Perspectives* 19 (1): 45–72.

Mintz, Sidney. 1998. "The localization of anthropological practice." *Critique of Anthropology* 18 (2): 117–33.

Moran, Emilio F. 1990. *A ecologia humana das populações da Amazônia.* Petrópolis, Brazil: Vozes.

———. 1981. *Developing the Amazon.* Bloomington: Indiana University Press.

———. 1974. "The adaptive system of the Amazonian caboclo." In *Man in the Amazon,* edited by C. Wagley, 136–59. Gainesville: University Presses of Florida.

Moreira Neto, Carlos de Araujo. 1988. *Índios da Amazônia, de maioria a minoria, 1750–1850.* Petrópolis, Brazil: Vozes.

Moya, Ruth. 1992. *Requiem por los espejos y los tigres: Una aproximación a la literatura y lengua secoyas.* Quito: Abya-Yala.

Muratorio, Blanca. 1991. *The life and times of Grandfather Alonso: Culture and history in the Upper Amazon.* New Brunswick, N.J.: Rutgers University Press.

Murphy, Alexander B. 1990. "Historical justifications for territorial claims." *Annals of the Association of American Geographers* 80 (4): 531–48.

Myers, Norman. 1984. *The primary source: Tropical forests and our future.* New York: W. W. Norton.

Naranjo, Marcelo F. 1977. "Zonas de refugio y adaptación étnica en el Oriente: Siglos XVI, XVII, XVIII." In *Temas sobre la continuidad y adaptación cultural ecuatoriana,* edited by M. Naranjo, J. L. Pereira, and N. E. Whitten, 105–68. Quito: Ediciones de la Universidad Católica.

Narvaez H., Julian. 1982. *Colombia indígena.* Bogotá: Litografía Arco.

Nash, Roy. 1926. *The conquest of Brazil.* New York: Harcourt Brace.

Nations, James D., and Flavio Coello H. 1989. "Cuyabeno Wildlife Production Reserve." In *Fragile lands of Latin América,* edited by J. O. Browder, 139–49. Boulder, Colo.: Westview Press.

Neves, Walter. 1992. "Biodiversidade e sociodiversidade: Dois lados de uma mesma equação." In *Desenvolvimento sustentável nos trópicos úmidos,* edited by L. E. Aragón, 365–97. Belém: Associação de Universidades Amazônicas.

Nogueira-Neto, Paulo. 1991. *Estações ecológicas: Uma saga de ecologia e de política ambiental.* São Paulo: Banespa.

Nugent, Stephen. 1993. *Amazonian caboclo society: An essay on invisibility and peasant economy.* Providence: Berg.

Oelschlaeger, Max. 1991. *The idea of wilderness: From prehistory to the age of ecology.* New Haven: Yale University Press.

Oliveira, Francisco de. 1994. "A reconquista da Amazônia." In *A Amazônia e a crise da modernização,* compiled by M. A. D'Incao and I. M. da Silveira, 85–96. Belém: Museu Paraense Emílio Goeldi.

Oliveira Filho, João Pacheco de. 1983. "Terras indígenas no Brasil: Uma tentativa de abordagem sociológica." *Boletim do Museu Nacional* 44:1–28.

Onis, Juan de. 1992. *The green cathedral: Sustainable development of Amazonia.* New York: Oxford University Press.

Paine, Robert. 1996. "Aboriginality and authenticity—a confoundment." Paper presented at the Department of Anthropology, University of Brasilia, April 22.

Paiva, Glycon de. 1979. "Declarada a guerra ecológica na Amazônia." *Carta Mensal* 25 (295): 1–12.

Parajuli, Pramod. 1998. "Beyond capitalized nature: Ecological ethnicity as an arena of conflict in the regime of globalization." *Ecumene* 5 (2): 186–217.

Parker, Eugene. 1985a. "The Amazon caboclo: An introduction and overview." In *The Amazon caboclo: Historical and contemporary perspectives,* edited by E. Parker, xvii–li. Williamsburg: College of William and Mary.

——. 1985b. "Caboclization: The transformation of the Amerindian in Amazonia, 1615–1800." In *The Amazon caboclo: Historical and contemporary perspectives,* edited by E. Parker, 1–50. Williamsburg: College of William and Mary.

Peet, Richard, and Michael Watts, editors. 1996. *Liberation ecologies: Environment, development, social movements.* London: Routledge.

Petroproducción. 1992. "Evaluación del proyecto Pañacocha, Paujil, Sábalo, Tiputini, Ishpingo, Tambococha, Imuya." Quito: Petroecuador.
——. 1991. "Proyecto Pañacocha Tiputini." Quito: Petroecuador.
Pineda C., Roberto. 1993. "La vida cotidiana en los barracones de la Casa Arana." In *Pasado y presente del Amazonas: Su historia económica y social,* edited by R. Pineda and B. Alzate, 55–66. Bogotá: Universidad de los Andes.
Pinto, Lúcio Flavio. 1986. *Jari: Toda a verdade sobre o projeto de Ludwig.* São Paulo: Editora Marco Zero.
Porto, Hannibal. 1917. "Castanhas: Producção, commércio e exportação." *Jornal do Commércio,* Rio de Janeiro.
Posey, Darrell, and William Balée, editors. 1990. "Resource management in Amazonia." *Advances in Economic Botany* 7:1–287.
Prance, Ghillean T. 1976. *The phytogeographic subdivisions of Amazonia and their consequences on the selection of biological reserves.* Bronx: New York Botanical Garden.
PROFORS (Programa Forestal-Sucumbíos), editor. 1993. *La Reserva de Producción Faunística Cuyabeno: Un área protegida con potenciales y problemas.* Quito: MAG.
Prous, Andre. 1991. *Arqueologia brasileira.* Brasilia: Editora Universidade de Brasília.
Rabelo, Genival. 1968. *Ocupação da Amazônia.* Rio de Janeiro: Stúdio Alfa.
Radding, Cynthia. 1997. *Wandering peoples: Colonialism, ethnic spaces, and ecological frontiers in northwestern Mexico, 1700–1850.* Durham: Duke University Press.
Raffestin, Claude. 1993. *Por uma geografia do poder.* São Paulo: Editora Ática.
Raiol, Domingos Antônio. 1970. *Motins políticos ou históricos dos principais acontecimentos políticos da Província do Pará, 1822–1835.* Belém: Universidade Federal do Pará.
Raiol, Osvaldinho. 1992. *A utopia da terra na fronteira da Amazônia.* Macapá: Editora Gráfica O Dia.
Ramos, Alcida. 1995. "Seduced and abandoned: The taming of Brazilian Indians." In *Questioning otherness: An interdisciplinary exchange,* edited by V. R. Domínguez and C. M. Lewis, 1–23. Iowa City: University of Iowa Libraries.
——. 1994. "The hyperreal Indian." *Critique of Anthropology* 14 (2): 153–71.
——. 1986. *Sociedades indígenas.* São Paulo: Editora Ática.
Redford, Kent H. 1990. "The ecologically noble savage." *Orion Nature Quarterly* 9 (3): 24–29.
Registro Oficial. 1991. "No. 0328: El Ministerio de Agricultura y Ganaderia," July 12, pp. 2–4. Quito: Gobierno del Ecuador.
Reichel-Dolmatoff, Gerardo. 1973. "The agricultural basis of the sub-Andean chiefdoms of Colombia." In *Peoples and cultures of native South America,* edited by D. R. Gross, 28–38. Garden City, N.Y.: Doubleday.
Reis, Arthur Cezar Ferreira. 1949. *Território do Amapá: Perfil histórico.* Rio de Janeiro: Departamento de Imprensa Nacional.

Restrepo G., Marco. 1991. "El proceso de acumulación en la Amazonia ecuatoriana: Una breve visión histórica." In *Amazonía nuestra: Una visión alternativa*, compiled by L. Ruiz, 125–48. Quito: Centro de Documentación e Información de los Movimientos Sociales del Ecuador; Abya-Yala; ILDIS.

Ribeiro, Benjamin Adiron. 1992. *Vila Serra do Navio: Comunidade urbana na selva amazônica*. São Paulo: Pini.

Ribeiro, Darcy. 1970. *Os índios e a civilização: A integração das populações indígenas no Brasil moderno*. Rio de Janeiro: Civilização Brasileira.

Ribeiro, Gustavo Lins. 1994. *Transnational capitalism: Hydropolitics in Argentina*. Gainesville: University Press of Florida.

———. 1987. "¿Cuánto más grande mejor? Proyectos de gran escala: Uma forma de producción vinculado a la expansión de sistemas económicos." *Desarrollo Económico* 27 (105): 3–27.

Ribeiro, Gustavo Lins, and Paul E. Little. 1998. "Neo-liberal recipes, environmental cooks: The transformation of Amazonian agency." In *The costs of modernization in Latin America*, edited by L. Phillips, 175–91. Wilmington, Del.: SR Books.

Ricardo, Carlos Alberto, editor. 1996. *Povos indígenas no Brasil, 1991–1995*. São Paulo: Instituto Socioambiental.

Rivera, José Eustasio. 1935. *The Vortex*. Translated by E. K. James. New York: Putnam.

Rivera, Rigoberto, and Paul E. Little. 1996. "Bipolaridad étnico-regional y la constitución de la nación y el estado en Bolívia y Ecuador." In *Etnia y nación en América Latina*, edited by G. Zarur, 133–50. Washington: Organization of American States.

Rojas R., Carlos. 1995. "Mundos simbólicos y subjetividad." *Revista de Investigaciones* 8:1–144.

Rojas U., Martha, and Carlos Castaño U. 1991. *Áreas protegidas de la cuenca del Amazonas*. Bogotá: Tratado de Cooperación Amazónica.

Román, Luis. 1991. "El futuro del petróleo y sus implicaciones para el desarrollo del Ecuador." Quito: Petroecuador.

Roosevelt, Anna C. 1991. *Moundbuilders of the Amazon: Geophysical archeology on Marajó Island, Brazil*. San Diego: Academic.

———. 1987. "Chiefdoms in the Amazon and Orinoco." In *Chiefdoms in the Americas*, edited by R. D. Drennan and C. Uribe, 153–85. Lanham, Md.: University Press of America.

Roth, Walter Edmund. 1974. "Trade and barter among the Guiana Indians." In *Native South Americans: Ethnology of the least known continent*, edited by P. J. Lyon, 159–67. Boston: Little, Brown.

Rowe, William, and Vivian Schelling. 1991. *Memory and modernity: Popular culture in Latin America*. London: Verso.

Ruiz M., Julio, and Rafael Pinzón R., editors. 1995. *Reservas extrativistas*. Gland, Switzerland: Unión Internacional para la Conservación de la Naturaleza.

Ruiz M., Lucy. 1991a. "Fuentes para la historia de la Amazonia: Periódicos ofici-
ales." In *Amazonía nuestra: Una visión alternativa,* compiled by L. Ruiz, 295–
308. Quito: Centro de Documentación e Información de los Movimientos
Sociales del Ecuador; Abya-Yala; ILDIS.

——. 1991b. "Pueblos indígenas y etnicidad en la Amazonia." In *Indios,* edited by
I. Almeida et al., 449–97. Quito: Logos.

Sack, Robert David. 1986. *Human territoriality: Its theory and history.* Cambridge:
Cambridge University Press.

Saenz A., Edgar. 1994. "La torre ecológica." *Petrolitos,* September, pp. 18–9.

Sale, Kirkpatrick. 1985. *Dwellers in the land: The bioregional vision.* San Francisco:
Sierra Club.

Salomão, Elmer Prata. 1984. "O ofício e a condição de garimpar." In *Em busca do
ouro: Garimpos e garimpeiros no Brasil,* compiled by G. A. Rocha, 35–86. Rio de
Janeiro: Editora Marco Zero.

Salzano, Francisco M., and Sidia M. Callegari-Jacques. 1988. *South American Indians: A case study in evolution.* Oxford: Clarendon Press.

Sampedro V., Francisco. 1992. *El espacio territorial ecuatoriano de 1830 a 1992.*
Quito: DIMAXI.

Santos, Fernando Rodrigues dos. 1993. *História do Amapá.* Macapá: Imprensa
Oficial.

Santos, Roberto. 1980. *História econômica da Amazônia, 1800–1920.* São Paulo:
T. A. Queiroz.

Sautchuk, Jaime, Horácio M. Carvalho, and Sérgio B. de Gusmao. 1979. *Projeto
Jari: A invasão americana.* São Paulo: Ed. Brasil Debates.

Sawyer, Donald. 1993. "População e meio ambiente na Amazônia brasileira." In
População, meio ambiente e desenvolvimento: Verdades e contradições, compiled by
G. Martine, 149–70. Campinas: Editora da Unicamp.

——. 1984. "Frontier expansion and retraction in Brazil." In *Frontier expansion in
Amazonia,* edited by M. Schmink and C. Wood, 180–203. Gainesville: University of Florida Press.

Schmink, Marianne, and Charles H. Wood. 1992. *Contested frontiers in Amazonia.*
New York: Columbia University Press.

——. 1987. "The 'political ecology' of Amazonia." In *Lands at risk in the Third
World: Local-level perspectives,* edited by P. D. Little and M. Horowitz, 38–57.
Boulder: Westview Press.

Schuurman, Frans J. 1980. "Colonization policy and peasant economy in the
Amazon basin." In *Land, people, and planning in contemporary Amazonia,* edited
by F. Barbira-Scazzocchio, 106–13. Cambridge: Cambridge University Press.

Schwoch, James. 1995. "Manaus: Television from the borderless." *Public Culture* 7
(2): 455–64.

Scofield, Gilberto, Jr. 1996. "Caemi quer sócio estrangeiro no Jari: Clã Azevedo
Antunes-Frering contrata banco para captar parceria no exterior." *Jornal do
Brasil,* March 16, p. 13.

SEMA (Secretaria Especial do Meio Ambiente). 1979. "Programa integrado de pesquisas nas Estações Ecológicas." Brasilia: Ministério do Interior.

——. 1976. "Programa de Estações Ecológicas." Brasilia: Ministério do Interior.

Serres, Michel. 1995. *The natural contract.* Translated by E. MacArthur and W. Paulson. Ann Arbor: University of Michigan Press.

Sheridan, Thomas E. 1988. *Where the dove calls: The political ecology of a peasant corporate community in northwestern Mexico.* Tucson: University of Arizona Press.

Siguad, Lygia. 1988. "Implicações sociais da política do setor elétrico." In *As hidroelétricas do Xingu e os povos indígenas,* compiled by L. Santos and L. Andrade, 103–10. São Paulo: Comissão Pro-Índio.

Silva, Lígia Osorio. 1996. *Terras devolutas e latifúndio: Efeitos da lei de 1850.* Campinas: Editora da Unicamp.

Silveira, Modesto da. 1980. *Ludwig, Imperador do Jari.* Rio de Janeiro: Civilização Brasileira.

Siqueira, Joésio Deoclécio Pierin, coordinator. 1992. "RIMA—Relatório de impacto ambiental do projeto de reflorestamento da área Felipe II no Município de Laranjal do Jari-AP." Curitiba: C.R. Almeida.

Smith, Carol A., editor. 1976. *Regional analysis.* 2 volumes. New York: Academic Press.

Smith, Sheldon, and Ed Reeves. 1989. "Introduction." In *Human systems ecology: Studies in the integration of political economy, adaptation, and socionatural regions,* edited by S. Smith and E. Reeves, 1–18. Boulder, Colo.: Westview Press.

Steward, Julian H. 1948. "Culture areas of the tropical forest." In *Handbook of South American Indians.* Vol. 3: *The tropical forest tribes,* edited by J. H. Steward, 883–99. Washington: Smithsonian Institution.

Stocks, Anthony W. 1978. "The invisible Indians: A history and analysis of the relations of the Cocamilla Indians of Loreto, Peru, to the state." Ph.D. diss., University of Florida.

Stonich, Susan. 1993. *"I am destroying the land!" The political ecology of poverty and environmental destruction in Honduras.* Boulder, Colo.: Westview Press.

Sweet, David Graham. 1974. "A rich realm of nature destroyed: The Middle Amazon Valley, 1640–1750." Ph.D. diss., University of Wisconsin, Madison.

Tambs, Lewis A. 1974. "Geopolitics of the Amazon." In *Man in the Amazon,* edited by C. Wagley, 45–87. Gainesville: University Presses of Florida.

Taussig, Michael. 1987. *Shamanism, colonialism, and the wild man.* Chicago: University of Chicago Press.

Taylor, Anne Christine. 1994. "El Oriente ecuatoriano en el siglo XIX: 'El otro litoral.'" In *Historia y región en el Ecuador, 1830–1930,* edited by J. Maiguashca, 17–68. Quito: Corporación Editora Nacional.

Telban, B. 1988. *Grupos étnicos de Colombia: Etnografía y bibliografía.* Cayambe, Ecuador: Abya-Yala.

Toro, Blasio. 1991. "Estudio de recursos naturales basado en información satelitaria." Quito: CLIRSEN.

Torres, Haroldo da Gama. 1991. "Migração e o migrante de origem urbana na Amazônia." In *Amazônia: A frontiera agrícola 20 anos despois*, compiled by P. Lena and A. E. de Oliveira, 291–304. Belém: Museu Paraense Emílio Goeldi; Orstom.

Transturi. 1992. "La Amazonía Ecuatoriana: Un paraíso para el intrépido aventurero." Quito: Metropolitan Touring.

Trujillo, Jorge, coordinator. 1986. "Diagnóstico socio-económico de los assentamientos de colonos e indígenas en la Reserva Faunística del Rio Cuyabeno." Quito: Instituto de Estudios Ecuatorianos.

Trujillo, Jorge, and Lucy Ruiz. 1982. *Políticas e procesos de colonización*. Quito: ILDIS; CIESE; Consejo Nacional de Desarrollo.

Tuan, Yi-fu. 1977. *Space and place: The perspective of experience*. Minneapolis: University of Minnesota Press.

——. 1974. *Topophilia: A study of environmental perception, attitudes, and values*. Englewood Cliffs, N.J.: Prentice-Hall.

Turner, Frederick Jackson. 1920. "Significance of the frontier in American history." In *The frontier in American history*, 1–38. New York: Holt, Rinehart and Winston.

Uquillas, Jorge, editor. 1982. *Informe para la delimitación de territorios nativos Siona-Secoya, Cofán y Huaorani* (publication no. 39). Quito: Ediciones INCRAE.

Vargas, Getúlio. 1943. *Ideário político de Getúlio Vargas*. Compiled by R. Guastini. São Paulo.

Vega M., Nestor. 1980. *La economia ecuatoriana en la década de los años 70 y perspectivas futuras*. Quito.

Velasco, Fernando. 1979. *Reforma agraria y movimento campesino indígena de la Sierra*. Quito: Editorial Conejo.

Vespucio, Américo. 1985. "Carta del 18 de julio de 1500 dirigida desde sevilla a Lorenzo Peir Francesco de Médici en Florencia." In *El nuevo mundo: Viajes y documentos completos*, translated by A. M. R. de Aznar, 11–27. Madrid: Ediciones Akal.

Vickers, William T. 1994. "Siona-Secoya." In *Encyclopedia of world cultures*. Vol. 7: *South America*, edited by J. Wilbert, 306–9. Boston: G. K. Hall.

——. 1983. "The territorial dimensions of Siona-Secoya and Encabellado adaptation." In *Adaptive responses of native Amazonians*, edited by R. Hames and W. T. Vickers, 451–78. New York: Academic Press.

Villacrés M., Jorge W. 1963. *Geopolítica del mundo tropical sudamericano*. Guayaquil, Ecuador: Universidad de Guayaquil.

Villarejo, Avencio. 1959. *La selva y el hombre: Estudio anthropo-cosmológico del aborigen amazónico*. Lima: Editorial Ausonia.

Vogt, Kristina, Miguel Pinedo-Vásquez, Mary Allegretti, and Fernando Allegretti.

1993. "Castanhal forests: Management perspectives in the Maracá I, II, and III Extractive Reserves." Curitiba: IEA.

Vovelle, M. 1987. *Ideologias e mentalidades*. São Paulo: Editoria Brasiliense.

Wagley, Charles. 1985. "The Amazon caboclo." In *The Amazon caboclo: Historical and contemporary perspectives*, edited by E. Parker, vii–xvi. Williamsburg: College of William and Mary.

——. 1967. "O estudo das comunidades amazônicas." In *Atas do simpósio sobre a biota amazônica*. Vol. 2: *Antropologia*, edited by H. Lent, 41–57. Rio de Janeiro: Conselho Nacional de Pesquisas.

——. 1964. *Amazon town: A study of man in the tropics*. New York: Alfred A. Knopf.

Watts, Michael J. 1992. "Space for everything (a commentary)." *Cultural Anthropology* 7 (1): 115–29.

Weiss, Gerald. 1969. "The cosmology of the Campa Indians of Eastern Peru." Ph.D. diss., University of Michigan.

Westerman, Olaf. 1995. "The impact of Vila Maracá on Projetos de Assentamento Extrativista Maracá I, II, III." Macapá: IEA.

Whitehead, N. L. 1993. "Ethnic transformation and historical discontinuity in Native Amazonia and Guyana." *L'Homme* 126–28:285–305.

Whitten, Norman E., Jr. 1994. "Canelos Quichua." In *Encyclopedia of world cultures*. Vol. 7: *South America*, edited by J. Wilbert, 98–102. Boston: G. K. Hall.

——. 1976. *Sacha Runa: Ethnicity and adaptation of Ecuadorian jungle Quichua*. Urbana: University of Illinois Press.

Wilbert, Johannes. 1994. "Introduction." In *Encyclopedia of world cultures*. Vol. 7: *South America*, edited by J. Wilbert, xxiii–l. Boston: G. K. Hall.

——. 1979. "Geography and telluric lore of the Orinoco delta." *Journal of Latin American Lore* 5 (1): 129–50.

Wolf, Eric. 1982. *Europe and the people without history*. Berkeley and Los Angeles: University of California Press.

Wood, Charles, and John Wilson. 1984. "The magnitude of migration to the Brazilian frontier." In *Frontier expansion in Amazonia*, edited by M. Schmink and C. Wood, 142–52. Gainesville: University Press of Florida.

Wood, Denis. 1992. *The power of maps*. New York: Guilford Press.

Worster, Donald. 1979. *Dust Bowl: The southern plains in the 1930s*. New York: Oxford University Press.

——. 1993. *The wealth of nature: Environmental history and the ecological imagination*. New York: Oxford University Press.

Index

pine trees, 79, 201
Pizarro, Gonzalo, 42
Planalto, 84
Plateau of Maracanaquara, 140
Playas de Cuyabeno, 57, 149–50, 154,
    163, 166–67, 170, 172, 212–13, 225;
    map, 100, 160, 206; *photo,* 168
Plaza Lasso, Galo, 52, 70
Pleistocene Refuge Theory, 254–55n
policy, public: in Amazonia, 237–39.
    See also Brazil, Amazonian policies
    of; Ecuador, Amazonian policies of
Pombal, Marquis of, 21
Pontifical Catholic University of Quito,
    149; biological research station of,
    150
Porto Seguro, 248n
Portugal, 15, 18; settlers from, 17–20,
    22, 64, 248n
Portuguese Crown, 17, 19, 21, 24, 62–
    63, 248n
Portuguese language, 26, 66
Prado, Julio, 205
Preto River, 248n
Proaño, Pedro, 208
PROFORS, 164, 166–67, 217
Programa Forestal-Sucumbíos. *See*
    PROFORS
property, private, 68, 85–86, 91, 108–9,
    192, 234
prostitution, 117, 122, 124, 130, 254n
protected areas, 12, 134–36, 148, 231–
    32, 237; delimitation of, 217; man-
    agement of, 155, 157–58; and man-
    agement plans, 164–67, 172, 179,
    218; as "paper parks," 139, 148, 152;
    and petroleum industry, 209–10;
    size of, 255n; and traditional peo-
    ples, 154–58
Protestant sects, evangelism of, 47
Protocol, Mosquera-Pedemonte (1830),
    47
Protocol, Rio de Janeiro (1942), 51–52,
    93, 223

Puerto Bolívar, 54, 57, 97, 149–50, 152,
    154, 166–67, 170–74, 249n; *map,*
    100, 160, 206
Puerto El Carmen, 59–60, 255n; *map,*
    100, 160, 206
Putumayo River, 39, 48, 50, 53, 55, 60,
    69; *map,* 6, 56, 100, 160, 206
Putumayo River basin, 49, 250n
Puyo, 44, 110

quartz, 228
Quichua indigenous people, 49–50, 55–
    58, 62, 72, 152–54, 162–64, 229–30;
    Canelos subgroup, 44; ethnogenesis
    of, 44–45, 65; homelands ca. 1950,
    map, 56; and petroleum industry,
    96–97, 212–13; population of,
    255n; Quijos subgroup, 44, 45; and
    rubber trade, 249n; as soldiers, 52,
    213, 225
Quichua (Quechua) language, 249n; as
    lingua franca, 44, 49; spread of, 45
Quichuaization process, 45, 50, 57
quilombolas, x
quilombos, 3; in Amapá, 34, 72, 130
quinine, 234
Quito, 17, 42, 46, 62, 101–3, 106, 111,
    118, 149, 162, 165, 210, 222, 248n;
    map, 6

racial categories: and Cabanagem rebel-
    lion, 25; and *caboclos,* 26
RADAMBRASIL, 138
railroads: in Jari Project, 84, 190; —,
    photo, 85; proposal for Ecuadorian
    Amazonia, 47
rain forest, tropical, ix, 131–33, 144,
    158, 200, 213, 219, 227, 254–55n,
    257n; as tourist commodity, 159–
    61, 234. *See also* Amazon River
    Basin
ranching, 237; in Aguarico Region, 114;
    cattle, x, 132, 136, 175; in Jari Proj-
    ect, 79, 80; in Jari Region, 36, 175; in

About the Author

Paul E. Little was born in Indianapolis, Indiana, in 1953. He gained his B.A. in anthropology at Kalamazoo College in Michigan, his M.S. in education at Black Hills State College in Spearfish, South Dakota, and his Ph.D. in anthropology and Latin American studies at the University of Brasilia. His scholarly articles and essays have appeared in *Annual Review of Anthropology, Critique of Anthropology, Development,* and *Textos de História,* among other journals, and his books include *River of People: A Multicultural History of the Cheyenne River Reservation Area* (1983), *Estados Unidos Postmoderno* (1991), and *Ecología Política del Cuyabeno: El Desarrollo No Sostenible de la Amazonía* (1993). In 1994, Dr. Little received First Prize from the Brazilian Anthropological Association/Ford Foundation scholarship fund for research in ecology and society. He has taught in the Department of Anthropology at the University of Brasilia since 1997 and has worked as a consultant in the development of new public policies in Brazil in the fields of the environment and indigenous affairs. During the fall semester of 2000, he occupied the position of Elena Amos Eminent Visiting Scholar for Latin American Studies at Columbus State University in Georgia.